# The Politics of People

SUNY series in Global Modernity
———————
Ravi Arvind Palat and Roxann Prazniak, editors

# The Politics of People

## Protest Cultures in China

SHIH-DIING LIU

Published by State University of New York Press, Albany

© 2019 State University of New York

All rights reserved

No part of this book may be used or reproduced in any manner whatsoever without written permission. No part of this book may be stored in a retrieval system or transmitted in any form or by any means including electronic, electrostatic, magnetic tape, mechanical, photocopying, recording, or otherwise without the prior permission in writing of the publisher.

For information, contact State University of New York Press, Albany, NY
www.sunypress.edu

### Library of Congress Cataloging-in-Publication Data

Names: Liu, Shih-Diing, author.
Title: The politics of people : protest cultures in China / Shih-Diing Liu.
Description: Albany : State University of New York Press, [2019] | Series: SUNY series in global modernity | Includes bibliographical references and index.
Identifiers: LCCN 2018052661 | ISBN 9781438476216 (hardcover) | ISBN 9781438476209 (pbk.) | ISBN 9781438476223 (ebook)
Subjects: LCSH: Political participation—China. | Protest movements—China. | China—Politics and government—2002–
Classification: LCC JQ1516 .L5827 2019 | DDC 322.4/40951—dc23
LC record available at https://lccn.loc.gov/2018052661

10 9 8 7 6 5 4 3 2 1

*To my family, Wei and Walter*

# Contents

List of Illustrations　　　　　　　　　　　　　　　　ix

Acknowledgments　　　　　　　　　　　　　　　　xiii

Introduction　　　　　　　　　　　　　　　　　　　1

## Part I
## Body and State

1. Embodied Practices of Citizenship　　　　　　　　29

2. Migrant Workers' Right to Appear　　　　　　　　55

## Part II
## Politics of Articulation

3. Engagement with the State　　　　　　　　　　　87

4. The Two Occupy Movements in Hong Kong　　　113

## Part III
## Cultural Resistance

5. Political Protest as Artistic Practice　　　　　　　143

6. Macau's Cyberpolitics　　　　　　　　　　　　　163

| | |
|---|---|
| Conclusion: For the Appearance of a Subject | 179 |
| Notes | 191 |
| Bibliography | 199 |
| Index | 213 |

# Illustrations

| | | |
|---|---|---|
| Figure I.1 | Map of China. | 2 |
| Figure 2.1 | The Artigas Factory. | 56 |
| Figure 3.1 | Map of Guangdong Province. | 99 |
| Figure 3.2 | The Villagers in Wukan Held Banners Bearing Their Signatures. | 102 |
| Figure 3.3 | The Honda Worker Protest. | 107 |
| Figure 4.1 | Map of the Hong Kong Special Administrative Region. | 114 |
| Figure 4.2 | The Slogans Read: "Anti-MPF & Capitalism," "Down with Real Estate Hegemony, Strive for Worker's Rights." | 119 |
| Figure 4.3 | The Propaganda Department Area Set Up by the Occupiers. | 120 |
| Figure 4.4 | The Students Attempted to Occupy the Civic Square. | 125 |
| Figure 4.5 | A Slogan Poster Writes: "I Boycott Classes, Because I Love Hong Kong." | 127 |

| | | |
|---|---|---|
| Figure 4.6 | A Poster Reads: "Recovering Mong Kok, Umbrella Revolution." | 129 |
| Figure 4.7 | An Occupied Zone in Causeway Bay. | 130 |
| Figure 4.8 | The Pro-China Group Held Their Rallies in Mong Kok. | 135 |
| Figure 5.1 | Some Improvised Artworks in the Occupied Zone. | 144 |
| Figure 5.2 | A Spoofed Image of the Hong Kong Chief Executive Leung Chun-ying. | 153 |
| Figure 5.3 | A Comic Storytelling Drawn by the Protesters to Describe the Clash with Police. | 154 |
| Figure 5.4 | The Political Use of Daily Objects (Yellow Umbrella). | 154 |
| Figure 5.5 | Artists Attempted to Portray the Participants in the Occupied Zone. | 159 |
| Figure 6.1 | A Flash Mob Event Was Staged to Protest Against the Monopoly of CTM. | 170 |
| Figure 6.2 | Macau's Local Artists Used Facebook to Disseminate Protest Spectacles. | 171 |
| Figure 6.3 | Macau's Internet Users Launched a Campaign during the National Security Legislation, Known as Article 23, in November 2008. | 172 |
| Figure 6.4 | The Dissident Publication *Concealing Daily*. | 174 |
| Figures 6.5 and 6.6 | Hong Kong Films Referencing Corruption Scandals. | 175 |
| Figure 6.7 | Critiquing Corruption. | 176 |

| | | |
|---|---|---|
| Figure 6.8 | Macau's Netizens turn on the Policeman Firing Gunshots on the May Day Protest in 2007, Resulting in Many Spoofs. | 176 |
| Figures 6.9 and 6.10 | Heroic Figures Used to Spoof Police Involvement. | 177 |
| Figure 6.11 | *Egao* Allows the Two Previously Different Worlds—Popular Culture and Politics—to Converge into One Another. | 178 |

# Acknowledgments

I thank the friends and colleagues who provided various kinds of help and assistance during the writing of this book: Baik Young-Seo, John Erni, Chu Yuan-Horng, Christopher Connery, Laurence Simmons, Feng Chien-San, Pun Ngai, Chien Sechin, Hao Yufan, Tony Schirato, and Chen Kuan-Hsing. I am especially grateful to Wang Hui and Ralph Litzinger, who read the first draft of this manuscript and from whose comments I benefited. Wang Hui has helped me stay motivated since 2004; Ralph provided really helpful feedback on the manuscript.

Some chapters emerge from exchanges with scholars working on questions of China, Hong Kong postcolonial, and global modernity. Chapter 3, "Engagement with the State," began as a conference paper that I gave at the 2014 Global Studies Conference, Shanghai University. I thank my interlocutors at the Hong Kong Betwixt and Between Conference held by the Institute of Ethnology, Academia Sinica, who responded helpfully to an early version of Chapter 4, "The Two Occupy Movements in Hong Kong." I thank the organizers of the two panels/conferences, Daniel Vukovich and Allen Chun, for their invitations and input.

I thank Andrew Kenyon for his excellent editorial advice throughout, and his patience in waiting for the final version of this book. Thanks also to Chelsea Miller, Diane Ganeles, and Hugo Lok for their help during the pre-production process. My appreciation to the Faculty of Social Sciences and RDAO at the University of Macau, for their long-term support of my research project. I also thank my graduate students at the University of Macau for their invaluable assistance, both intellectual and material: Lin Zhongxuan, Kong Mengxun, Su Chang, Geng Li, Zheng Qi, Zhao Zhilong and Xu Min. They have been a stimulating presence during the years that this book was taking shape. Thanks to their participation in the working meetings from which I have greatly benefited.

Finally, I would like to express my deep appreciation and memory to Arif Dirlik, who had enthusiastically supported this book project. I still remember when I was a student in Taipei and London during the late 1990s and early 2000s, I came across Arif's work and was extremely inspired by his critical spirit. In April 2013, when he came to visit the University of Macau and we met in person for the first time, he encouraged me to develop this project. He read my papers, provided suggestions, and invited me to publish in the SUNY series in Global Modernity. Unfortunately he cannot see the final version anymore. I still remember the conversation with him, his mental strength, voice and laughter—all these moments will never be forgotten. Thank you, Arif.

∼

Earlier versions of some chapters have appeared as follows, and I thank Taylor and Francis for permission to reprint here:

Chapter 3, "Engagement with the State," has been significantly rewritten for this volume from a paper published in 2015, titled "The New Contentious Sequence since Tiananmen," *Third World Quarterly* 36 (11): 2148–2166.

Chapter 4, "The Two Occupy Movements in Hong Kong," was first published in slightly different form as "The End of Occupation," *Interventions: International Journal of Postcolonial Studies* 19 (4): 507–531, in 2017.

Chapter 6, "Macau's Cyberpolitics," is a revised adaptation of an essay titled "The Cyberpolitics of the Governed," *Inter-Asia Cultural Studies* 14 (2): 252–271, originally published in 2013.

# Introduction

> People do revolt; that is a fact. And that is how subjectivity (not that of great men, but that of anyone) is brought into history, breathing life into it.
>
> —Michel Foucault, "Useless to revolt?"

## Occupy!

On September 28, 2014, a student protest against the restrictive suffrage for the Hong Kong chief executive election, which opposition groups criticized as depriving Hong Kong people of their democratic rights to elect their own leader, quickly took on a wider and more serious significance. After the police arrested student leaders and activists who attempted to seize hold of Civic Square, thousands of people swarmed onto the streets downtown, chanting "Release the students" and "We want true democracy." The protestors resisted the police's pepper spray with umbrellas, in the process creating a global media spectacle. Failing to disperse the recalcitrant crowd, the police fired teargas bombs at protestors. Incensed at the police response, protesters blocked the traffic arteries of the business districts of Hong Kong and Kowloon Islands. The occupied streets were transformed into a space of gathering resistance against state power and its apparatuses. This militant action created both partial anarchy and multiple points of resistance around the occupied zones. Some 200,000 participants turned out at the peak of the protest movement, and the confrontation lasted for an unexpectedly long period (79 days). The movement's explosive intensity and magnitude surprised many, generating arguably the Chinese government's most serious political crisis since the 1989 Tiananmen occupation.

2 / The Politics of People

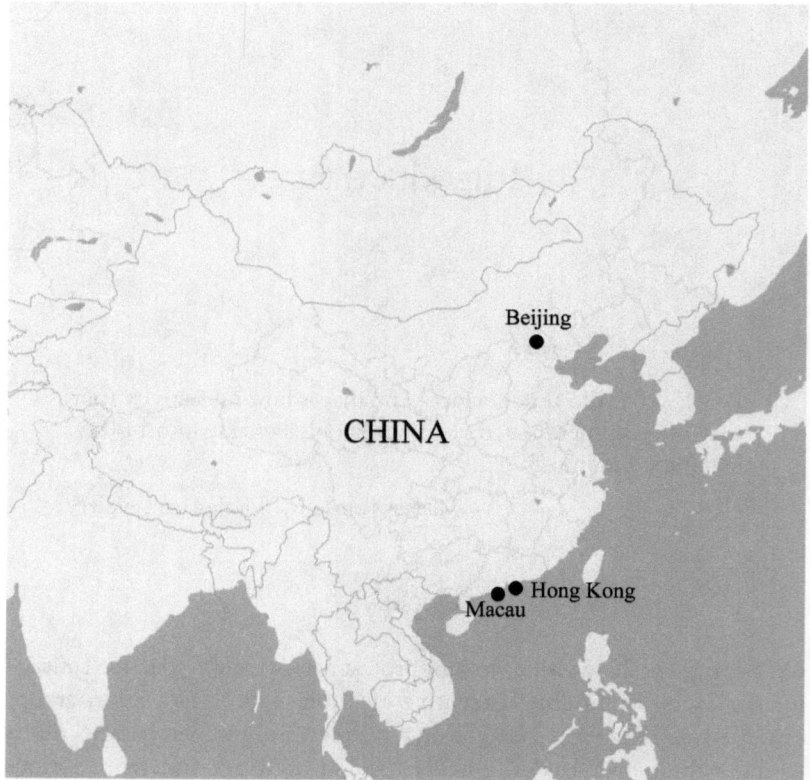

Figure I.1. Map of China. The map was created by the author via the software Mapbox.V4.3.0, www.mapbox.com.

In a context where political action is becoming more risky and tightly controlled, the physical occupation of public spaces, which has been characterized as an "easily replicable tactic" (Gould-Wartofsky 2015, 44), has come to be seen as a defiant political act. In light of the political sequence that followed, physically occupying Hong Kong public spaces served to both undermine the political authority of the government, and to disrupt routine business and bureaucratic activity. The act of occupation, different in a myriad of ways from conventional protest tactics, demonstrated the resolve of protestors to force the state to respond to their demands. The unfolding of the "occupy" protest provides an example of how popular politics can be expressed in a variety of unpredictable ways. If the ultimate aim of the occupation was to produce a response, the bodily, discursive, and creative dimensions of the political practices enacted during the process were successful.

It can be argued that this spectacular event opened up a new space for popular political activity. Yet what exactly are the deeper political and theoretical implications of these practices, the relations of power in which they are enacted, and the creative capacities and energies that were manifested? What, broadly speaking, was the meaning of occupation? I want to suggest that what happened in Hong Kong needs to be considered and understood beyond its local and spatial connotations, and should to be situated within the context of regimes of popular political activity broadly characteristic of China (a term that I will use to designate the political entities of mainland China, Hong Kong, and Macau). Contentious episodes of this kind are not uncommon in China. Today, with its rise to the status of a global economic power, China has been facing continuous political unrest since the crackdown on the Tiananmen protest movement in 1989. Demonstrations, rallies, strikes, and disturbances occur across the country on a daily basis, most of which are concerned with issues of local governance. The Hong Kong disturbance and the popular political activity in Macau are part of this dynamic. Despite their obvious differences in constituencies and demands, these actions imply a strong disaffection with various forms of political governance.

The recent protest movements and activities in China offer an opportunity for rethinking contemporary popular politics in that region. This wave of activism has drawn attention to what Judith Butler refers to as the performativity of political practices (Butler 2015), whereby people express their dissent by and through performances of collective discontent; and in consequence have raised a number of important questions about the possibility of popular democracy and sociopolitical change in China. Apart from occupation, what are the main forms of popular political activity? How are they performed? What are their conditions of constraint and possibility? How and to what extent do their practices challenge or reconfigure existing structures of power? More specifically, how do resource-poor people articulate what Chatterjee refers to as the "politics of the governed" (Chatterjee 2004)? These questions constitute the primary interests of this book, articulated in the form of an analysis of expressive forms of activism through the analytical prism of "performative politics," with the aim of developing an understanding of popular politics in the post-1989 era. It engages in a dialogue with Postcolonial Studies, the emerging field of Occupy movement studies, and China protest movement studies.

*Postcolonial*

The discipline of Postcolonial Studies is facing a peculiar impasse of a twofold nature. This has to do, first, with the field's continued focus on "old" colonialism, leaving new forms of domination—for instance, as they operate under the guise of "globalization"—largely unquestioned and unexamined. What is missing from Postcolonial Studies is an appreciation of the historical continuity between past and present, in particular in terms of how the present conjuncture has been shaped by state-sponsored neoliberalism. If we want to adequately understand the political modernity of postcolonialism and the way it legitimizes power, it is necessary to pay attention to the actions of the people in negotiating political and discursive regimes. What are the forms of fundamental contradictions today? Why do people take to the streets to make contentious claims? What forms of dispossession do they resist? These questions are barely examined by postcolonial theorists. The absence of the problematization of the present has led to the failure to engage critically with the neocolonial structure of power and its antithesis. I share Dirlik's (2007, 99) view that the postcolonial is important because of the relevance of colonialism to understanding the present. This book seeks to address this failure by shifting the analytical focus to the postcolonial present, and in situating its politics in the wider context of the demise of state socialism and the rise of neoliberalism.

The second problem lies in the field's inability to analyze the concrete political practices that are directed against neoliberalism. Partly due to postcolonial theory's emergence from the intellectual vacuum left empty by the decline of radical politics (Hallward 2001, xiv), the field has been characterized by a neglect of popular practices as an analytic category: while there has been a widespread emphasis on advancing the theoretical understanding of cultural difference, this has been at the expense of explaining "the real politics of the people" (Sethi 2011, 27). As Hallward (2001, xv) points out, there has been a privileging of "cultural, linguistic and rhetorical issues over social, historical and economic concerns" in Postcolonial Studies. As a result, the people as a political category have never been taken as a unit of analysis, and the subaltern masses remain a voiceless object within postcolonial discourses. Although culture is occasionally viewed as site of anti-imperialist resistance (Ahmad 1992), questions of how such resistance is made possible, by whom and under what circumstances, remain largely unexplored. Ahmad's (1992) treatment of Third World discourse, for instance, fails to problematize the role of the state. Even though some scholars are concerned with oppressed groups (Dirlik 1997) and highlight the enunciations of the subaltern (Spivak 1988), there has been no concern as to how perpetuations of hegemonic constructions can be contested.

To follow from previous points, it can be argued that postcolonialism has also become "a statement of identity alone" (Chun 2012, 679), while the role of the state is mostly neglected. Under what circumstances, and in what ways, do voiceless subalterns act out and address the state? What are the possibilities for popular political activity and how do political actors push the boundaries of state tolerance? How do they come up with different strategies in order to exercise their rights and turn themselves into political subjects? Although some studies have paid attention to political practices, their analyses are largely focused on national-liberation movements, which are mainly expressed through the building of a new state (San Juan 1999), leaving other forms of activism unexamined. Although Subaltern Studies has provided insights into the notion of popular politics, the field has almost exclusively focused on the context of India and privileged traditional forms of practices. This book seeks to reconnect the postcolonial to politics by investigating the ways that the different kinds of struggle that "postcolonial" stands for (Young 2001) contribute to the development of popular politics in different postcolonial settings.

*Occupy*

If Postcolonial Studies neglects popular politics, the emerging field of Occupy Studies has left China largely unexamined. The field is filled with valuable empirical descriptions of the new tendencies manifested in recent protest movements across Europe, America, and North Africa, which are marked by the rejection of formal leadership structures and organizations.[1] With its strong interest in the collective capacity of popular power in forging new democratic cultures, the field presents a range of creative practices and considers their implications for radical democracy. It should be noted, however, that most cases deal with entities that have multi-party structures and enjoy some freedom to organize and forge strategic alliances, and political practices tend to be read as autonomous from and opposed to the state, which is very different from what happens in the Chinese context. If there is any reference to China (for example, Mason 2013), it tends to be uniformly portrayed as an economic powerhouse that drives the global economy and nothing more than an outright repressive regime where any dissent is crushed, without any substantive analysis of its political forms. Moreover, the field's analytic efficacy is weakened by an uncritical enthusiasm for the potential of the movements to oppose the state, and of universalist presumptions about what popular politics looks like and could be.

Manuel Castells (2012), for example, makes the point that occupations—charged with the symbolic power of invading sites of official power—usually occur as an alternative expression of the will of citizens when "avenues of representation" are closed. However, this leaves unanswered the question of how local specificities of popular protest fit into the supposedly "global" approach of network society. According to Castells, the agency of social change is driven by the ways people appropriate global communication networks and create new spaces of autonomy. However, this juxtaposition of state power and network counter-power obscures the more complex interaction between regime trajectories and protestors. Although he briefly mentions Hong Kong's 2014 Umbrella Movement to illustrate the notion of networked activism, an analysis of its performative power is absent from his study.

Three issues are worth noting. First, although scholarship has presented an informative account of the multifarious practices of political activism, there has been a lack of adequate elaboration of the body and its performative force in concrete contexts. If public assembly and occupation is a highly embodied event drawing on an array of physical practices and performances, questions surrounding what the protesting body can do and its capacity to minimize precariousness remain unanswered. What is the political function of the body in creating and sustaining political action? How does the body enable protestors to reconfigure the notion of publicness and visibility? In a regime that maintains its rule by tightly controlling the political use of bodies, it is theoretically and politically important to examine how the body shapes popular politics. Most existing studies have focused on urban contexts, without paying attention to the various ways migrant workers and landless villagers formulate distinctively different strategies of occupation in the face of a repressive and paternalistic state, which must be understood on their own terms.

In the past few years, some scholars have started to pay more attention to the performative dimension of embodied protest, and seek to explore the political significance of protesting bodies. In a pioneer study that addresses this issue, Abby Peterson (2002) argues that massive bodily presence constitutes the tangible sources of power during protests. Barbara Sutton's (2010) research on Argentinian gendered resistance shows that protest action demands intense bodily commitment and sacrifice. Judith Butler, whose recent work focuses on embodied resistance to the condition of precarity, argues that the persistence of the body may pose a challenge to the state, and addresses the hegemonic struggle over both the body and its "appearance" in public spaces (Butler 2011, 2015). These studies can offer insights into the embodied aspect of Occupy movements.

The explanatory power of the field of Occupy Studies is also weakened by a one-dimension characterization of political practices. The field's celebration of decentralized, "leaderless" movements, horizontal structures, and the refusal to engage with official politics runs the risk of romanticizing these tendencies and detaching them from actual contexts and constraints. Some studies have addressed the influence of anarchism and the rejection of representation as the core principle around which these movements are organized (Bray 2014). Yet every protest movement consists of different components and internal tensions, and how to accommodate them is always a political question. What are the conflicts that emerge from processes of occupation? How do occupiers negotiate differences? The field has generally avoided the central question of political representation and failed to explain why they succeed (or fail) to sustain the momentum. To take one example: Simon Tormey's (2015) study, with its enthusiastic celebration of "a politics without representatives," is unable to explain why some occupational protests cannot be sustained.

Another concern is more contextual: although public assembly and occupation have become global protest tactics that can be easily adopted to diverse contexts, the dynamic in China thus far seems to have followed its own logic. By way of example, against the presumption that occupation is inherently antagonistic to the state, its manifestations in China have their own codes and logics that are locally grounded in its political tradition in which the state's political mediation remains crucial. And it has a distinctively different trajectory in which popular politics operates mainly within the boundaries of the established political system. In mainland China's limited political opportunity structure, where any organized mass protest is prohibited and frequently repressed, it is extremely difficult to forge broad-based coalitions and sustain political pressure. As a result, mass gathering tends to be transient and much less hostile to the state. The language Chinese people use and the social "experiments" they conduct are not so much expressions of "anti-representational" and "anti-party" politics; rather, most practices aim at engagement with the state in the hope of producing a positive response.

*Protest in China*

The third research area which this book deals with is the field of Chinese Protest Studies. Although the field has documented various kinds of collective political activities, the notion of action tends to be reified and objectified as a product of social or political structures, without acknowledging the autonomy and contingency of practices. Sociological theories and normative political perspectives have dominated this field, which is characterized by a tendency to reduce culturally infected practices to instrumental, self-interested, rationally motivated purposes and structural patterns, or side effects of the shift in institutional arrangements. Despite some treatments of cultural themes such as political beliefs (Chen 2008), rhetorical strategies (Lee 2007b), and political traditions (Wasserstrom and Perry 1994), the cultural dimensions remain obscured by an overly instrumentalist tendency. Too much emphasis is placed on causal explanations of protest outcomes and efficacies (Cai 2010), without appreciating the cultural construction and influence of protest. The lack of an appropriate appreciation of culture has led to an overly structuralist, and consistently one-sided, account of popular politics.

Studies drawing on social movement concepts such as political opportunity, farming, and mobilizing structures (for example, O'Brien 2008) have suffered from similar limitations: by focusing exclusively on practices determined by preexisting structures, organizational patterns, and economic resources, they lose sight of a wide range of cultural activities, processes, and spaces that enable resource-poor people to create possibilities of agency. Many studies (Chen 2012; Perry and Goldman 2007) fail to pay attention to the creative forms of political expression that fall outside mainstream analytical frameworks. There is also insufficient consideration of people's creative capacities, in particular in terms of how existing norms, traditional cultures, and moral economies are reinvented. Goldman's (2005) study, which documents how the struggle for rights in mainland China has broadened out to include the disenfranchised masses of peasants and workers, is an example of this tendency. Its preoccupation with "rights consciousness," which is presumed to precede action (as Goldman claims, "this rights consciousness gradually *spread to* the population in general," p. 2; my emphasis), has led to an inability to analyze the diversity and performativity of rights practices through which people *become* rights-bearing subjects in ways that might deviate from state norms and articulate different politics.

This book addresses "the agency of the masses as creative and transformative force" (San Juan 1999, 228), which is not predetermined or presupposed but produced through expressive actions. People's actions can release a robust creativity through which to constitute themselves as political subjects and produce unpredictable outcomes. A cultural lens, I suggest, is crucial to understanding this political process. In recent years, with more studies incorporating a cultural perspective to study protest movement, there has been "a recognition of more fluid, situational, or transient forms of social movement resistance" (Buechler 2000, 179). If the aim of a protest is to craft messages, alter public perceptions, and prompt desired responses, the cultural dimension of meaning construction and identity performance cannot be taken for granted.[2] Rather than upholding the view that culture is a set of given, unchanged, and deeply held beliefs, a more nuanced understanding of Chinese protest movements needs to pay more attention to how culture is played out through practices (Reed 2005). A performative perspective conceptualizes protest as a site of cultural performances that address a variety of audiences who also produce meanings (Johnston 2009; Johnston and Klandermans 1995).

Cultural analysis has increasingly called attention to how various kinds of cultural forms—ranging from costume, object, art, and built environment to narrative, jokes, visual image, and music (Jasper

2014)—are improvised to construct the meaning of protest in creative ways (Johnston 2009). Protest movements are viewed as discursive constructions, which produce new meanings, symbols, identities, and relations (Edwards 2014; Buechler 2000; Johnston and Klandermans 1995). With protestors becoming cultural producers, their practices have constituted a distinctive terrain of popular politics as protest culture diffuses into society (Reed 2005). Reed argues that dramatic events can generate profound emotional and moral power beyond the control of protesters, and "offer some degree of symbolic challenge to the dominant order just by their existence outside normalized political activity" (Ibid. 307). Occupying public spaces, for instance, is a symbolic action that can contest normative meanings, evoke moral support, construct political identities, and produce various kinds of creative practices that challenge existing cultural codes. Traditional symbols and rituals can also be turned into radical acts of protest (Jasper 2014). In arguing that action is where contestation of meaning takes place, the book investigates how people create political codes, discourses and logics that need to be understood on their own terms.

## A Narrative of Argument

In the past several years, there has been a dramatic rise of popular protests on a world scale, and China, as a rising economic power characterized by remarkable social inequalities and contradictions as a result of neoliberal policies, is no exception. Ever since the crackdown on the Tiananmen Square protest in 1989, people have continued to protest. And there has unfolded a distinctive political formation in which the state has sought to regain its legitimacy by channeling and neutralizing widespread popular discontents through a new legal regime. This dramatic turn to legality as a source of legitimacy has, probably beyond the Communist Party of China's (hereafter CPC) anticipation, spawned widespread rights-based politics from below. Meanwhile, the central government has also tried to curb the revival of popular politics through selectively tolerating protest actions as a means to monitor local states. The proliferation of welfare and security provisions has given rise to new forms of governmentality without substantive democracy. Corrupt practices of local governments—as crystallized in the predatory activities of development, the absence of accountability for vital decisions concerning people's lives, and the general non-responsiveness to their grievances—have triggered widespread protests. Numerous precarious subjects—who experience massive privatization of natural resources, environmental pollution, lack of proper social security, and exploitative working conditions—act out and deploy various practices to demand favorable responses from upper-level authorities. Under the circumstances, where law enforcement remains ineffective in terms of protecting people, some rights need to be obtained through radical struggles to create opportunities for public appearance and contestation.

These practices, which mostly target the unacceptability of existing social or political arrangements, have created the spaces of popular political activity in China. Yet the conventional state vs. society framework is unable to explain the complex forms and spaces of these political struggles. Although popular protest has become familiar in the post-Tiananmen political landscape, the meaning of these practices and spaces is yet to be fully explored. Since the state has been seeking some degree of legitimacy from its populations to resolve the crisis caused by neoliberalism, methods of how to grab public attention and elicit upper-level intervention have become a central focus of popular democracy. Rather than viewing these practices as merely an instrumental means of carrying pre-constituted messages to the public, it is necessary to explore how they facilitate popular political activity and have "the potential to be an active source of agency" (Sethi 2011, 72). Significantly, people often make contentious claims in dramatic actions that others cannot ignore, or invent new forms of practices in the face of new opportunities. What are these forms, what is the politics they articulate, and how do they enable resource-poor people to constitute themselves as political subject? This book explores these questions by way of the analysis and evaluation of a series of empirical case studies in China. Contrary to traditional notions that reduce these practices to instrumental tools for achieving a goal, it will be argued that they constitute a form of "performative politics" characteristic of "the will not being governed like that" (Foucault 2007). In the face of censorship and repression, performative politics is usually precarious and transient, yet increasingly crucial to the development of popular democracy.

This book also argues that the idea of performative politics provides an alternative way to understand popular politics in China. The emphasis is on the practices, rather than an idea, of popular politics. Performative politics encompasses a constellation of expressive practices, spaces, and situations created by the people to contest governmentality. As this book illustrates, performative politics, which can be expressed through different forms of performativity (Butler 2015), mainly operates in the domain of visibility and intervenes in what Jacques Rancière (2004) calls the "realm of perception, visibility and audibility" in response to the non-acknowledgment of the voices of people. Simply put, performative politics reconfigures the conditions of what is to be seen, when, and by whom (Fabricant 2009), and thus reallocates the mode of appearance of grievances. Performative politics aims to elicit state intervention. By reconfiguring the visibility of grievances, performative politics has the potential to alter public perceptions and subvert the ways people are governed. A march demonstration intended to influence the public, the media, and government decisions is an instance of performative politics. A "spoofed image" that critiques official rhetoric and entails unpredictable responses can also be seen as fragments of performative politics. Such politics is performative in the sense that it aims to draw the attention of the state by creating a temporary space of *appearance* from which to make claims.

If the social order is founded on the distinctions of who can speak in the public sphere and who cannot, of who is visible and who is not (Rancière 2004), performative politics is about disturbing the distinctions and reshaping what should be recognized, what Rancière calls the "distribution of the sensible," which "produces a system of self-evident facts of perception based on the set horizons and modalities of what is visible and audible as well as what can be said, thought, made, or done . . . 'distribution' . . . refers both to forms of inclusion and to forms of exclusion." The sensible "does not refer to what shows good sense or judgement but to what is . . . capable of being apprehended by the senses" (Rockhill 2004b, 85). Within such a reconfiguration: "Politics is a matter of subjects or, rather, modes of subjectification. By *subjectification* I mean the production through a series of actions of a body and a capacity for enunciation not previously identifiable within a given field of experience" (Racniere 2004, 35). As Karen Zivi summarizes it:

> A performative perspective on rights moves us from an almost exclusive focus on questions about what rights *are* to a more careful consideration of what it is rights *do*; from a tendency to treat rights as things or instruments we use to bring about a particular end to a recognition that rights claiming is a complex linguistic activity, the outcomes of which are quite often beyond our complete control. A performative perspective on rights . . . moves us beyond concerns about the formal definitions of rights and allows us to take seriously rights claiming as a social and political practice. (Zivi 2012, 9; original italics)

Since performative politics always responds to specific modes of governmentality and entails differing outcomes, its manifestations are necessarily contextual and historically specific. How these occasions are acted out, what forms they take, what resources they use and what effects they generate depend entirely on how they take advantage of the specific condition of possibilities available to them. With China it is necessary to consider the role of the state and its enduring legacies. In China, control over the sensible—as clearly manifested in the prohibition of street protest and media censorship of public events—is the primary strategy for constructing a loyal and obedient subject. The state, which presupposes a division between the sayable and the unsayable, actively filters, classifies, and denies the sensory data considered politically threatening.

For this reason, methods of how to redistribute the sensible (such as increasing the possibility of public attention) have become a focus of struggle and crucial to the emergence of political subject (Rancière 2004; Davis 2010, 86). Although the Chinese state has continued to impose severe restrictions on self-organized politics of the people, the practices and rhetoric of socialism, traditional rituals and cultural values, official buildings, state norms and directives, as well as state-authorized media cultures, have all facilitated the development of Chinese performative politics in different ways. Paradoxically, people's agency is derived from the power regime that constitutes their subjectivity, and can sometimes bring about sweeping political turbulences. Since the reform era, the most spectacular expression of performative politics is probably the protest movement of 1989, which offered a highly visible and emotionally charged arena for displaying a variety of counter-hegemonic practices and forced a process of political negotiation with the state (Zhao 2001). The rise of performative politics has prompted the state to develop new forms of governmentality, which in turn create a heterogeneous social space for nurturing new forms of performative politics.

Yet very few forms of performative politics, especially in the face of the tightening up after 1989, can produce the same level of affective intensity and influence as the Tiananmen protest did. In fact, there has been a dramatic shift in the concrete actors and demands over the last two decades. Like many instances in the postcolonial world, popular struggles in the post-Tiananmen era have tended to have a less overtly political agenda, and do not seek to hegemonize civil society or contest state power. Instead, most are aimed at socioeconomic rights, which inevitably involves a critique of governmentality. The political figure of democratic struggles has also shifted since 1989. The performative subjects identified by this book are no longer limited to the restricted segments of urban college students, intellectuals, and state-firm workers, as present during the mass protest in 1989, but encompass a wide variety of people who are living under increasingly precarious conditions and whose lives are increasingly subject to the intense processes of exploitation induced by neoliberalism. These vulnerable people—who are nominally designated as "citizens" entitled to a set of newly instituted legal rights—are de facto excluded from the state's decision-making processes, and thus seek to claim their rights to subsistence, land, housing, political participation, education, and social security at multiple points of dissent. Most of these struggles are transitory and fragmented, and are marked by a lack of horizontal articulation among and across different groups.

Their locally grounded and culturally informed practices are the central focus of this book. The existing literature is predominantly limited to the verbal form of interaction with the state and other social sectors. Partha Chatterjee's (2004) analysis of subaltern politics in India demonstrates that subaltern people are not merely the object of governmentality to be mobilized by the state, but are capable, resilient and strategic in organizing their politics. The outcome of their actions depends on their innovative practices of political mobilization. In China, since most struggles are concerned with citizenship rights granted by the state, there is a need to create a space from which to make contentious claims about these rights. The formulation of such spaces, which is crucial to the development of popular democracy, is associated with nonverbal practices. Some scholars have suggested that practices of claim-making are crucial to democratic politics (Zivi 2012); however, there is a need to attest to a variety of expressive forms improvised from within the state-controlled space. This expressive aspect is ignored by Chatterjee's categorization of the politics of the governed. The practices presented in his study mainly center on the work of organization, mobilization, and negotiation with political parties, NGOs, and state authorities, which are specific to the context of India. In China and the mainland in particular, where any horizontal form of self-organization and popular mobilization is strictly monitored and forbidden by the state, people need to constitute themselves in other ways to attract the attention of government. Given that the Chinese state remains the only de facto source of political representation, people stage different kinds of expressive actions to generate immediate pressure on governmental authorities, after failing to make their voices heard via official channels of petitioning.

But the ways these actions create a space of politics are very different from the operation of political society in India. The regime's deep concern for legitimacy has encouraged the proliferation of performative politics that demands that the state live up to its political promises. In mainland China, the most common practice is to gather the masses and create disorderly scenes on the streets, which contributes to the formulation of spaces of appearance where people gather and interact (Butler 2015; Matynia 2009). The deployment of the body, which has been previously assumed to be insignificant in the study of Chinese politics, can provide a crucial source of agency, even though its performative condition is highly risky and temporary. Political actors take on a variety of expressive forms of contained, peaceful, or institutionalized actions to appear in public spaces, including mass petitioning,[3] rallies, sit-ins, strikes, demonstrations, boycotts, and spectacular banners. These practices can produce eye-catching scenes.[4] Occasionally, they disrupt existing patterns of bureaucratic and institutional activity, such as building "human walls" to paralyze public transportation, surrounding and breaking into government offices, erecting barricades, smashing police cars, occupying symbolic spaces, and lying down on rail tracks, in an attempt to generate more pressure on governmental authorities. Disruption of this kind can spread uncertainty and potentially facilitate the condition for desired intervention. Most of these practices are characterized by actions carried out in concert in public spaces as a performative force to surprise, shock, and frighten, rather than to "rationally persuade" the state and the wider public. In response, the state seeking popular legitimation will be motivated to selectively compromise.

Although some of these direct actions can create dramatic tensions, they are usually swiftly crushed by local authorities. Therefore, the masses have to employ some other creative yet non-regime-threatening tactics that carry smaller risks. This requires a reinvention of strategies and spaces, and explains why there are so many creative and theatrical forms of practices that are diffused out into the wider space of public culture and address broader audiences. Some of these political forms have become central to the formulation of a culture of solidarity, while others nurture new norms of behavior in imaginative ways. Such a trajectory, however, requires an understanding of political practice as a distinct, locally grounded cultural phenomenon, as well as the enormous potentials and resources available in the heterogeneous social realm. What needs to be further emphasized is that the existing scholarship on China popular politics has privileged expressions through words or vocalization, focusing almost exclusively on words and narratives as carriers of popular voices, instead of the deployment of nonverbal, expressive forms, for consciousness-raising and mobilization. Failing to capture the complex cultural dynamics in a global new media setting, culture tends to be viewed as a monolithic, homogeneous, and unchanging system of belief embedded in an arguably reified notion of "tradition" (for example, Perry 2008a), rather than produced and circulated through the concrete practices of protestors, the media, and the broad spectrum of Internet users.

Studies of performative politics have pointed out the key cultural dimensions that are crucial to a performative analysis of popular political activity. Fabricant's (2009) research identifies various forms of performative actions enacted by right-wing groups, including seizing government buildings and erecting roadblocks, as well as staging rituals and other spectacular events. She argues that these expressive practices, some of which are deeply embedded in local traditions, have powerful signifying functions that create a symbolic struggle over identity. Ziv's (2010) study of an Israeli queer group demonstrates the way political activism is performed through a cluster of subversive practices to foster visibility, in particular via the use of stereotypes and provocative bodily strategies to transgress hegemonic norms. In addition to these theatrical practices, the group attempts to make connections between different struggles as a means to repoliticize the political discourse of the public sphere. Some other studies have looked at the "carnivalistic" mode of political engagement in Poland (Matynia 2009), the creation of Arendtian spaces of appearance in Pakistan (Mustafa et al. 2013), as well as the theoretical implications of bodily practices and production of political spaces (Rose-Redwood and Glass 2014). All of these treatments are valuable in their illustration of the ways cultural practices can produce agency.

The cultural inventiveness and novelty of the performative practices in China is remarkable. The social realm of the everyday lifeworld offers rich strategic sources of cultural innovation embedded in local and global geographies: mundane objects, symbols, traditions, speeches, rituals, media products, or images layered with cultural meanings of communal identities can be used to make claims. Here, the symbolic restructuring of the meaning and subversive use of cultural artifacts plays out as a crucial means to perform popular politics. Some subcultural formations, even expressed in seemingly nonpolitical or overtly playful style, constitute performative transgression of official rhetoric and symbols by opening them up for subversive interpretations. Figurative forms of performativity such as satire, parody, or jokes, which perform oppositional identities as a mild form of dissent (Jasper 2014), can produce subversive forces through symbolic repetition, citation, and modification of dominant cultural codes. Performative conceptions of popular democracy can also be illustrated through various kinds of aesthetic practices, which often take on political valence and constitute a temporary site of intervention. Rather than being uniformly passive and powerless victims of dictatorship, the people are capable of constituting themselves as political subjects through performative practices. They can engage in struggles and contest political boundaries.

It is worth stressing that the nature and outcome of political struggles cannot be presupposed and predetermined. They are brought into being by contexts and their practices. Rather than merely being shaped by the sedimentation of daily conventions and repetition of rituals, creative practices can produce unpredictable outcomes and thus create forms of sociocultural and political agency. If practices of claim-making enable people to contest forms of their political subjectivity (Golder 2015, 137), the scholarship of Chinese politics has failed to appreciate this process of subject-formation. Esherick and Wasserstrom's (1994) seminal study, which stands out as a path-breaking work on Chinese performative politics, situates the 1989 Tiananmen demonstration within the long tradition of what they call "political theater" in China, and examines the continuities from the imperial time to 1989. Despite their attention to various dramatic expressions, the focus is somewhat restricted to a limited range of institutionalized actors (such as the state, the party, students, and civil society organizations) and respective theatrical "stages," leaving little room for other kinds of engagement undertaken by disenfranchised groups such as workers and peasants. The cases explored by the authors seem more centralized, organized, and sustained in terms of their sites, leadership, and endurance, as well as more directed against the central authorities, than the contemporary dispersive form of popular democracy since 1989.

What needs to be emphasized is that popular political activity always needs to create a space to appear and perform. The space of popular politics does not preexist but needs to brought into being through performative practices (Rose-Redwood and Glass 2014). Where, then, are the spatial locuses that enable people to appear? The rebalancing of center-local relations since the 1990s has reshaped the condition of appearance. As the spatiality of state power has become more decentralized, dispersed, and localized, popular struggle has scattered out, shifting toward specific localities, targets, and issues. Such a tendency is clearly manifested in the spreading of democratic struggles over such everyday spaces as urban streets, factories, schools, government buildings, and villages. There is no doubt that the Internet—in particular social media platforms—has now been employed as an indispensable means through which to perform popular democracy. As many cases demonstrate in the chapters that follow, the Internet has facilitated the fluidity and distribution of such performative power. The circulation of officially forbidden information, utterances, and visual images that convey moral judgments across social media plays a pivotal role in expanding the spatial boundaries of popular democracy and formulating oppositional identities. For example, the live streaming of a series of striking images of a protest scene can easily evoke powerful emotions among the crowds and gather mobilizing power from a broader base via social media networks.

Physical space remains crucial to the performances of popular politics, which are carried out through the spatial practice of assembling the politicized bodies in public spaces where people can make claims (Zivi 2012). In a political context where the right to appear in public is extremely restricted, the carving up of such a space is absolutely necessary. But such a space does not preexist the performative practices of the body that is vulnerable against state violence. As Butler makes clear, politics requires the appearance of the body, which lays claim to legal rights and the preservation of life through collective physical presence, and constitutes a performative action that enables the enactment of an embodied agency. "When people take to the streets together," she writes, "they form something of a body politic" (Butler and Athanasiou 2013, 196). The protesting body also needs a space to perform, which is not pre-given but must be *transformed* and produced by action. Butler suggests that an action staged by collective bodies produces the "space of appearance," which in turn offers a material condition for political engagement. Rather than a pre-given and fixed spatial location, the space of appearance is something that is always in process of becoming and taking place (p. 194).

In China generally but also in the mainland in particular, the body carries complex moral implications, so any unusual presence or performance of the body in public can evoke broad responses. To urge the government to uphold the stated rules and professed commitment to justice, protestors do not necessarily confront the authorities, but stage a variety of embodied acts to present their demands in legal and moral terms, in the hope of forcing conditions of intervention. It is often through scenes performed by vulnerable bodies that the public starts to pay attention. The outcome of these embodied actions depends mostly on the ability of protestors to mobilize moral support and elicit state intervention in their favor.

Paying attention to the performative potential of the body may help reorient the research field of Chinese politics and protest movements, which has been dominated by an emphasis on "consciousness" and the cognitive capacity to engage in contentious mobilization and interaction, instead of bodily possibilities. As Butler (2015) has argued, the performative body possesses political potentials and enacts a message when it lays claims to a certain space as public space. In China the performative body can do many different things and turn any built environment into powerful political message. Petitioning governments, or disrupting ceremonies attended by government officials, signifies utterly different challenges to political authorities. Transient gatherings in villages prove the strength of people. Occupying a commercial district poses a symbolic questioning of the public character of urban space. Silent gatherings such as funerals signify an implicit sense of protest. A dramatic action staged by workers can shift the way their situations are seen and perceived, and open up the possibility of alternative interpretations.

The performativity of the body and space has never been taken seriously by the scholarship of Chinese politics. Although Esherick and Wasserstrom (1994), for instance, observe the ways official rituals and ceremonies are turned into what they call political theaters, their study does not explain how political agency can be made possible through performative bodily actions and spatial practices, and how the media transposes the body and widens the visibility. What is missing is a consideration of how the body "invents" its own stage on which to perform resistance. To take one example, in a context where mass assemblies are severely prohibited, the practice of occupation, an "easily replicable tactic" in the liberal context of the United States (Gould-Wartofsky 2015, 44), can hardly be sustained. Rather than forming a movement-type of extended occupation, protestors usually take the form of transitory gathering, through which people turn government buildings, roads, corporate properties, and factories into temporary political theaters, which may last a few hours (such as mass meetings held to publicize central directives in the town center) or a few weeks (such as workers' factory sieges), depending on not only bodily endurance but also on the opportunities available to them.

As the occupation of Tiananmen Square demonstrates, public space occupation can offer a site not only for displays of autonomy and defiance against the political class, but also for improvisational forms of self-organization and collective creation (Zhao 2001). As the recent manifestations of civil unrest in Hong Kong have illustrated, concerted bodily actions and encounters can create free, decentralized, ad hoc, and loosely connected spaces of encounter where like-minded individuals and affinity groups interact, build a sense of community, and conduct social experiments with prefigurative politics. The actions of occupation, some of which tend to focus on the organizational culture of internal processes along participatory lines, have the potential of realizing some utopian forms of popular politics, such as egalitarian social relationships, respect for different opinions, and collective decision-making by consensus. In some cases of protracted struggles, the spaces of encounter created by participants are governed by temporary, informal rules, or evolve into a more organized political theater for a variety of performative practices that can reconfigure the wider political discourse, cultural values, and relations with the state.

Yet the creation of a space of bodily encounter does not automatically lead to mutual solidarity, especially for those broad-based movements with distinctive constituencies and conflicting subject positions. In addition to the coordination of collective actions, what is needed to sustain a democratic force is the performative articulation of imaginaries and identities among different subjects. As Laclau argues (2005), there needs to be an articulatory subject who can, through the creation of a symbolic surface of inscription, offer a common language to build broad-based alliances; and such practices are performative in the sense that hegemonic articulation that is historically specific and contingent. Therefore, how to articulate a counter-hegemonic bloc through various acts of identification (Ziv 2010), how political subjects converge as a collective force to defend and sustain their spaces of appearance, and how to grapple with various strategic dilemmas that arise from the process, become a central theoretical and political issue.

Contrary to the notion that the state is the obvious adversary of radical politics (Hardt and Negri 2000; Badiou 2012), the state remains the central focus of performative politics. Performative politics in mainland China aims to create the condition for a strategic engagement with the state, rather than seek direct political confrontation (as the last resort). With the intensification of neoliberalism, the state, with its claim to a monopoly of legitimate authority, has become more than ever indispensable to the issue of how to address popular needs. As a result, political struggles are largely directed at state promises and responsibilities, using politically normative language as their means of articulation. In this sense, performative politics depends on the state's claim on legitimacy to thrive. The state, on the other hand, has selectively tolerated and co-opted some versions of popular politics, so long as its hegemony is not threatened. Broadly speaking, protesters do not attempt to delegitimize or challenge the state, but expect its sovereign power to more effectively address their grievances. They remain highly dependent on the state's authorizing conditions and legitimate authority through which to seek redress performatively. Moreover, since performative politics is highly risky, its condition of possibility remains restrictive and uncertain, and there has always been a strategic combination of obedience and disobedience in negotiation with the state. Its outcome is necessarily temporary and conditional—unless actions are large scale, receive widespread coverage, and involve casualties, upper-level authorities usually do not intervene.

Mainland China's popular politics has its specific mode of engagement with the state, where exerting pressure on different layers of bureaucracies is most crucial. Thus, the strategic condition of dealing with a disenfranchisement of access to power in mainland China is very different, for instance, to the Indian experience depicted by Chatterjee, who argues that the actual practice of democratic politics tends to be connected less to the logic of popular sovereignty than to that of governmentality predicated on differentiated citizenship:

> In short, the classical idea of popular sovereignty, expressed in the legal-political facts of equal citizenship, produced the homogenous construct of the nation, whereas the activities of governmentality required multiple, cross-cutting and shifting classifications of the population as the targets of multiple policies, producing a necessarily heterogeneous construct of the social. Here, then, we have the antimony between the lofty political imaginary of popular sovereignty and the mundane administrative reality of governmentality: it is the antimony between the homogeneous national and the heterogeneous social. (Chatterjee 2004, 36)

But his distinction of the two categories is too rigid. In mainland China, where the CPC's legitimacy remains based on the historical claim to represent the people, popular sovereignty remains the key legitimate source of popular politics. It does not foreclose the possibility of political agency, but enables the people to reenact its legitimate claims to pursue their agenda. This is illustrated through the performative use of state-approved populist rhetoric and state laws. Chatterjee is too quick to dismiss the function of the universal notion of equal citizenship, while ignoring the continued importance of the dispositions of popular sovereignty in facilitating democratic struggles. Although the populations are governed differentially in the absence of genuine equality (compare, for example, the traditional *hukou* system of the peasants, and the "special administrative regions" of Hong Kong and Macau), the normative claims of exercising equal citizenship and political representation (as often expressed in the official language of "lawful rights of citizens," "rule on behalf of the people" and "care for the welfare of the masses") can and do provide crucial legitimate sources for questioning and protesting governmentality. Popular sovereignty and governmentality are not necessarily in binary opposition. Although some forms of questioning often involve transgressions of the law, it is exactly the deviance from state laws and claims that offers the grounds for performative politics. The perceived "deviance" of local practices represents the possibility of opening up a crucial, however precarious and unstable, space for democratic intervention that mediates between the state and people. As the CPC continues to shift its boundary of tolerance, Chinese protestors have formed a tacit, strategic alliance with the state in constraining local authorities. It is secure so long as the alliance remains supported by the people.

These protestors often draw inspiration from the symbolic resources embedded in Chinese political tradition where legitimate rule requires constant renewal through popular support. They demand that the state treats them as "citizens," and they use the official language of rights to advance their goals. This means that the political spaces and processes they create locate not entirely outside of state norms, but are located somewhere within the realms constituted by the shifting rupture between (universal, normative) notions of popular sovereignty and (localized, contingent) practices of governmentality, and mediated by the terrain of established law. At issue here is not really whether popular sovereignty becomes obsolete or is replaced by governmentality, but how the latter is deployed and rearticulated through invoking the former performatively by the people. The state, which has monopolized political representation, actually offers the opportunities and resources for protestors to contest governmentality on the local level. For this reason, the strategic opportunities and dilemmas for popular intervention should not be taken for granted. These various embodied and expressive dimensions are crucial to an understanding of Chinese political modernity.

## The Chapters

This book is arranged in three parts and six chapters. Each part deals with a major aspect of performative politics, and builds on each one. What is central to this study is the theme of cultural struggle. Part I, "Body and State," deals with the ways that Chinese groups utilize their bodies to negotiate with state authorities, and resist or challenge the practices and consequences of neoliberalism. It focuses on issues of bodily performativity and creative forms of claim making that produce visibility and publicity. Chapter 1, "Embodied Practices of Citizenship," examines the forms of these embodied acts, rituals, and activities deployed by protestors through which they attempt to create or invoke agency. It draws on a multiplicity of embodied practices and analyzes how the body is deployed as a medium of resistance and struggle, and to express dissent and increase visibility. In Chapter 2, "Migrant Workers' Right to Appear," I investigate an instance of a factory occupation involving one of UNIQLO's subcontractors in Shenzhen in order to consider the ways in which Chinese migrant workers utilize their bodies to cope with the shifting condition of exploitation. Drawing upon a fieldwork investigation conducted in 2015, the chapter considers the changing context of labor regime and worker politics, the potentialities and vulnerabilities of the body in countering neoliberalism, and the ways their practices create spaces of appearance. The chapter proposes that although the body is constantly exposed to risk and repression, its potential is unpredictable.

Part II, "Politics of Articulation," concerns the strategic practices for articulating counter-hegemonic politics in mainland China and Hong Kong. The primary focus is on the ways that protestors perform and produce political identities and construct alliances with the institutional and symbolic resources available to them. Chapter 3, "Engagement with the State," presents two case studies to demonstrate how such groups strategically engage with the state. Profound changes in state governance, state-society linkages, and media culture, in addition to the symbolic resource of socialism, have combined to consolidate the strategic alliance with the state, within which the upper-level authorities are the desired audience. It is the perceived cleavage between the center and local power that offers performative possibilities for triggering intervention. Such an alliance, however, is highly unstable and precarious, and its outcome is conditional.

The protests dealt with in this chapter mainly operate within the state construction of what Laclau (1990) calls the "mythical space of representation," which offers different levels and spaces of surface on which social demands can be inscribed. Chapter 4, "The Two Occupy Movements in Hong Kong," examines the political practices and struggles that unfolded during the two Occupy protests in 2011 and 2014. The study draws upon fieldwork investigation and considers the implications of the "leaderless" tendency manifested in both movements. The chapter traces the trajectories of mass organizing during the two movements, specifically considering the question of how "representation" became a site of struggle. Both movements had experimented with forms of participatory democracy. The 2014 Occupy movement was characterized by a cult of spontaneity, an obsession with horizontalism and a desire for self-representation. There were divisions, tensions, and conflicts in this movement, partly as a consequence of its "leaderless" tactics.

Part III, "Cultural Resistance," considers the relationship between the emergence of political subjectivity and cultural forms of dissent. Creative and aesthetic practices, I suggest, provide alternative avenues and resources for constructing counter-hegemonic politics. In Chapter 5, "Political Protest as Artistic Practice," I examine the ways acts of dissent and resistance are aestheticized as a means for social and political struggles. In analyzing the various kinds of critical artistic engagements in mainland China and Hong Kong, I will discuss the features and role of aesthetic forms in performing social activism. In Hong Kong, politicized arts are crucial in sustaining movement visions and values. Chapter 6, "Macau's Cyberpolitics," examines the practices and voices of dissent and resistance enacted in Macau's Internet spaces. This chapter examines how people turn themselves into political subjects by producing satirical images aimed at government officials. In Macau, people do not make explicitly political statements, but instead use the Internet to protest against corruption and a lack of accountability and representation.

Part I

Body and State

# 1

# Embodied Practices of Citizenship

During mid-February 2017, a massive protest in a northeastern Chinese city drew widespread attention at home and abroad. Hundreds of residents swarmed the streets and the car park outside the city government of Daqing, protesting against the construction of a massive aluminum processing plant proposed by China Zhognwang Holdings, a Hong Kong-listed company. The city of Daqing in Heilongjiang province, once home to China's first and largest major oilfield, has been severely depressed as a result of the depletion of the region's petroleum deposits and the global drop in oil and coal prices (*The Standard* 2017). The rustbelt city has seen large population outflows and the local government has desperately sought a new source of economic growth (AlCircle 2017). Like many other Chinese industrial towns, the Daqing municipal authorities have attached greater importance to economic development at the expense of environmental concerns. Usually the investors, despite the heavily polluting activities associated with their production, receive favorable tax treatment and enjoy local government support. In 2011, Zhongwang and the Daqing government agreed to collaborate on the $6.7 billion plant, which would be close to the urban area, amid promises of more than 30,000 jobs (AP 2017).

The protest, which swelled suddenly within a few days, was mainly triggered by growing pollution fears and a keen sense of environmental protection. Despite the Daqing government's announcement that it would temporarily suspend the project due to growing public concerns over health risks, there was little trust in its assurance. "Why would we trust them? They had already told us the project was halted, but then people went and filmed it, and the construction trucks are still heading to the site," said one protester as quoted by a media report (Yang 2017). Despite the promise of employment and prosperity, residents worried about the plant's pollution turned out en masse to claim their right to sustainable development, as promised by the state. The protest was marked by a large crowd gathering outside government offices in the face of a contingent of police, where the protestors chanted and held banners saying "We love China and Daqing," as well as "Protect our homes." Leaflets were circulated detailing all the negative impacts of the plant. Protestors also launched a social media campaign through which images and video footage of the protest quickly spread and increased the publicity of the collective action (AI 2017). To defuse the stern protest before it gains national attention, the city government issued a statement that it would review the environmental impact of the project and a decision would be "based on a broad consensus of citizens." Yet local governments in mainland China often halt controversial projects following protests, and then quietly restart them later after the controversy has passed from public attention. To contain unrest, the Daqing government also warned that any "illegal gatherings, defamation, starting rumors and disturbing social order would be dealt with according to law." Despite the government's attempt to quell the protest, public concerns remain over whether people's voices can truly be heard regarding public health issues.

This dramatic sequence provides some clues to understanding the political meaning of protest cultures in China, where performative politics aims at reclaiming citizenship rights that are promised by the state, but not always implemented. In the literature on Chinese citizenship, citizenship rights tend to be considered as granted by the state (Perry 2008b). But such an assumption seems to have oversimplified the dynamic process in which citizenship rights are enacted in mainland China.[1] With the state putting greater emphasis on legal rights, more and more urban residents, villagers, dissidents, pensioners, and workers can make claims for their citizenship rights through a variety of expressive means and mechanisms. This chapter will consider how "acts of citizenship" (Isin 2008) are performed by the people in order to negotiate state power. As this chapter illustrates, these embodied practices are performed within a legitimation crisis generated by widespread unrest. The state's recent promotion of citizenship rights is founded on the idea that its legitimacy increasingly depends on whether it can provide a decent livelihood and a livable environment for the people. Despite the efforts to consolidate the legal dimension of citizenship and incorporate more social rights into local governance to ameliorate growing inequalities, in actual practice many local bureaucracies do not recognize these rights, and problems of non-compliance and arbitrary treatment remain severe. The state-approved legal channels and institutions through which to lodge complaints are also often blocked. Unprotected by independent judicial review and trade unions, citizenship retains an ambiguous status subject to different local situations. Since the lower levels of the government tend to be strongly pro-capital and are unwilling to enforce people's legal rights, substantive citizenship rights are severely restricted, unavailable, or inaccessible to many groups. Many people have a precarious existence without adequate protection, and their only avenue is to undertake dramatic actions in order to obtain access to rights endorsed by the state.

## Limitations of Traditional Approaches

The academic field has tended to privilege the structure of state provision, institutional arrangement, and legal membership in its analysis and understanding of issues of citizenship in China (Liu 2007; Goldman 2005; Pei 2010); and there remains a strong emphasis on the role of state in producing citizenship classifications and inequalities (Fong and Murphy 2006). These studies tend to view citizenship in terms of a relatively predetermined and unchanging status, position or entitlement, a set of repetitive state-sponsored practices, or as an institutionally accumulated processes. Scholars often presume that Chinese citizenship is exclusively founded on a transcendental, given and unchanged order, in which Chinese authorities—with a deep sense of moral responsibility toward the collective good—could always effectively address the subsistence need of the masses, and thus sustain their legitimacy (Perry 2008b). What is missing here is an understanding of how people make their voices heard and gain access to the rights upheld by the state. Citizenship, in this context, needs to be viewed as something more than a by-product of these statist definitions.

From the performative perspective, citizenship is played out in an arena that requires expressive and dramatic enactment to create new scenes and spaces of struggle (Joseph 1999), and it is when those who are not recognized by the state start to make a claim to be counted that, Isin (2008) argues, a truly political moment is brought into existence. Such moments can only be created by various kinds of politically motivated performances staged by people in order to widen their visibility. In this context, citizenship rights only become effective in practice (Isin 2012). Different forms of acts contribute to "the formation of new subjects, sites and scales of claim making" (Isin 2008, 17).

Isin's approach also emphasizes the contingency and situatedness of citizenship formation. One of the principles of investigating acts of citizenship is to "interpret them through their grounds and consequences, which includes subjects becoming activist citizens through scenes created" (Isin 2008, 38–39). Rather than always following already-written "scripts," "activist citizens"—those subjects who act out and transform themselves into citizens through acts—are creative in writing their new scripts and creating the scene that brings political subjectivity into being. Isin argues (2008, 18) that this process "inevitably involves a break from habitus." To identify what he calls "momentous" acts (2008, 17–18) requires that we "focus on those moments when, regardless of status and substance, subjects constitute themselves as citizens—or, better still, as those to whom the right to have rights is due . . . To investigate acts of citizenship is to draw attention to acts that may not be considered as political."

There has been very little literature conceptualizing citizenship through the body. Attention has tended to focus on people's cognitive capacity to make decisions, instead of their bodily capacity to disturb the distribution of the sensible. The dual emphasis on "consciousness" and non-bodily notions of discourse, for instance, has dominated Chinese citizenship literature. Prokhovnik (2014), on the other hand, argues that the body offers a site of public contestation. In understanding the body as a *situation* involving embodied locations and interactions, she extends Isin's conception by proposing that Citizenship Studies should go beyond the mind-based aspect of citizenship, and investigate how people make use of the body for political ends.

## Political Uses of the Body

Where there is an ineffective implementation of citizenship, resource-poor people rely heavily on their bodies to present their demands in moral terms. Embodied actions such as gatherings, demonstrations, strikes, and blocking traffic and factories are familiar ways to "speak" to authorities: some of which are theatrical, non-regime-threatening tactics that lower the risk of repression. Protestors have sought to operate in the expanding space of this "moral economy" in which the gap between the state's professed commitment and the plight of the people provides a political space for making claims. Some of their embodied practices, whether staged in individual or collective forms, may not seem obviously political at first sight, but they articulate "the active ability to *assert rights* in a public space or, better yet, dialectically, the possibility of *not being excluded from the right to fight for one's rights*" (Balibar 2015, 66).

## The Power of "Walking"

The street demonstration is an obvious political tactic, but in mainland China people demonstrating in public places are at risk of being arrested by the police. Since Chinese authorities frequently suppress mass rallies in the name of maintaining social order, protestors need to come up with alternatives. In mainland China, mass demonstrations require the approval of the public security department; thus, in the 2007 Xiamen anti-PX protest, citizens mobilized en masse, taking to the street to forestall government repression by "walking collectively" rather than by demonstrating, which added a lighthearted tone to a protest event and reduced the sense of fear among participants (Yang 2009). Since then, "collective walking" has gradually become a common act of citizenship in mainland China. Protestors often call on citizens through the Internet or mobile phones to participate in rallies with specific times and routes, as well as in the name of "watching" (*wei guan*) public events.

Walking remaps space and renders space visible (Pile 2013). Michel De Certeau argues that "to walk is to lack a place"; that is, not affixed to a place. Walking has the potential of disrupting the spatial relations of power (Tally 2013, 128).[2] Chinese-style collective walking extends the potential of walking by enabling a crowd to move their bodies as one and thus create their own itineraries and visibility in a context that avoids retaliation directed at people on the streets. In this context, walking serves as an "act of enunciation" (Phadke et al. 2009; Sitrin and Azzellini 2012), which facilitates the process of coming and struggling together to achieve public visibility.

The usual locations for collective walking are public squares, commercial streets, government office areas and business districts where a crowd can concentrate and create their own routes. Generally, the walkers will stage protests in a peaceful and low-key manner: for example, in the 2008 Chengdu anti-PX walking protest, people wore masks, and walked in silence. As the police cannot clearly distinguish demonstrators from "onlookers," it is difficult for them to intervene against such protests. Walking groups are usually characterized by people protesting about environmental pollution, farmers against land acquisition, and dismissed or exploited employees trying to overturn management decisions. These kinds of activities can sometimes lack clear leadership and sustainable organization. For instance, in July 2010 a group of people in Tong'an Town, Suzhou, who were protesting against the demolition of their houses and their relocation, "walked" to the town government compound and occupied it in the name of "enjoying the cool air" for more than ten days. This attracted the support of the surrounding townspeople, with many thousands of walkers taking to the streets in support of the action. As this event occurred only a few dozen kilometers from the Shanghai World Expo venue, in order to defend the international image of Shanghai, the municipal government decided to adopt a two-hand strategy: to suppress the protesters, while removing the party secretary and head of Tong'an Town.

*The Face that Hides Itself to be Seen*

In addition to embodied actions, protestors also use everyday objects, or necessities habitually associated with the participants, to create unusual visual effects. For instance, a group of veterans conducted a sit-in wearing red hats, which easily reminded the people of their loyalty to the country. Most strikes in recent years use the popular practice of wearing masks. In the past, masks were mainly used in the medical field in Chinese society, and wearing a mask conveys the meaning of needing help and protection. With the rush for masks that occurred during the outbreak of SARS in 2003 and the public tendency to wear masks due to the worsening pollution, masks have been increasingly turned into a symbol of insecurity and self-protection. Moreover, dramatic scenes of people wearing masks are increasingly used by the Chinese and foreign media to critique the poor environmental governance in mainland China, as most pollution cases involve the interests of local governments, businesses, and the consequences of economic development.

While the connotation of "self-protection" associated with a mask remains strong in the most general sense, it does not involve or invoke a level of antagonism necessary for political struggle. The political significance of masks and masked forms of resistance are increasingly constructed by protesters as signifying "the people." From May to September 2008, for example, hundreds of people wore masks and protested against the environmental pollution of chemical plants and landfills in Chengdu and Beijing, the news of which had spread on the Internet and was widely covered by foreign media. In January 2010, a group of citizens in Foshan "walked" the streets wearing masks to protest against waste incineration plants. Since these actions clearly targeted businesses and local governments and were crystalized through the image of wearing masks, the tactic began to attract public attention and was invested with greater political potential. Subsequently, this tactic began to spread out and be adopted, as it expressed a collective sense of frustration and dissatisfaction with state governance, and became a symbol of the voices of the people protesting against unfair treatment.[3]

In the following years, a growing number of pictures appeared in domestic and foreign media, where protestors carried banners and wore masks, and stood in the streets or in front of chemical plants and government buildings. Masks are increasingly being used by protestors for a wide range of performative occasions and present a striking visual image for global media. In Kunming, protestors wore masks printed with "Kunming refuses PX." In a village of Zhejiang, some villagers wore masks and carried banners reading "I want to breathe. Return the blue sky to me and resist pollution," and photographed themselves against the backdrop of smoking chimneys. In Shaanxi, Jiangxi, Sichuan, and Guangdong, netizens launched a "mask assembly" in front of provincial government buildings and in public squares to protest against pollution. Wearing masks functions as a kind of visibility tactic with Chinese characteristics to produce "image events" and generate publicity.[4] As masks have become the predominant symbol of struggle, and wearing a mask is seen as a rebellious act, authorities have begun to take measures to criminalize masked protests. The most well-known example was in May 2013 where the local government of Kunming requiring real-name registration of trading masks in order to prevent the spread of anti-PX protests from troubling the China-South Asia Expo. However, this measure failed due to the exposure created by netizens and the media.

Chinese protestors have also reappropriated other objects and symbols to capture public visibility. For instance, they may wear yellow ribbons or collectively make the same gestures,[5] or let a child hold a banner to attract public attention. Through transforming objects and bodies into a form of enunciation, such symbolic expressions function to construct political identities[6] while providing netizens and media with unusual visual experiences. In recent years, some anti-PX protestors have worn t-shirts of the same color (usually white)[7] printed with their demands. When hundreds or thousands of people wear clothes of the same color and gather together, it creates a spectacle. This is also carried out through collective gestures. For instance, in August 2011 the anti-PX protestors in Dalian walked to the square in front of the municipal party committee building and raised their middle fingers to express defiance. This dramatic scene was widely reported by foreign media. Moreover, in October 2012 at the Ningbo anti-PX demonstration, most media did not cover the main demands of the protest. The official *Ningbo Daily*'s negative coverage of the event led the demonstrators to raise their middle fingers when passing the *Ningbo Daily* building to express their anger. Such practices have greatly expanded the public visibility of protests and protesters.

*Kneeling Down*

Kneeling down in a public place is an unusual act in Chinese society and can easily attract public attention. This is why it is often used by Chinese citizens to express demands. In the past, kneeling down was a ritual for paying tribute and expressing gratitude to kings, elders, ancestors, and masters, and it signified obedience. There is an old saying that goes "kneel down before the heaven, the earth, and parents," which means that casual kneeling down before strangers destroys human dignity and brings humiliation. In some cases, kneeling down means begging or expressing an apology and repentance to someone, and kneeling down before the dead is a way of expressing mourning.

In China, collectively kneeling down has historically been a way for the people to express public grievances (Zhao 2007, 247). It has now been widely adopted by protestors, but the kneeling subjects have become more diverse, and the act of kneeling down has produced different meanings in different contexts. For example, fishermen have protested against the privatization of beaches; residents have knelt down to oppose local government-driven demolitions; villagers have knelt down before city hall to protest against the corruption of the village party secretary, and before a chemical plant causing environmental pollution to request the plant be shut down; female villagers have collectively requested the government to release the protestors; teachers have knelt down before the government to demand proper pension benefits; property owners have knelt down to ask the government to intervene with housing disputes or collectively knelt down before the developers to claim compensation. Compared with public assemblies, sit-ins, street demonstrations and other activities, collectively kneeling down can create a more intense and morally driven visual and emotional effects. Expressing frustration, humbleness, sadness, and begging can trigger moral sympathy and compassion. In 2013, thousands of workers in Shaanxi Province knelt down before a public square and held up banners reading "Begging the government to do justice for the people" and "We are afraid of riot police," which captured the attention of the mainstream media. In another case, on a snowy night in 2012, a group of workers attracted public attention by kneeling down to ask for back pay. Also in 2012, dozens of villagers in Yunnan Province knelt down before the Chinese Premier, Wen Jiabao, who was on an inspection tour of the Yiliang earthquake, to draw his attention to land grabs. Moreover, thousands of villagers from a village in Liaoning Province collectively went to the municipal government to report the corruption of village cadres and collectively knelt down after the mayor refused to hear them, which gave rise to public outcry. Under public pressure, the upper-level government required the mayor to resign to pacify the protestors.

The kneelers at such events are usually drawn from lower classes of the population; however, if the kneelers have higher social status, then the act can draw greater public attention. For instance, in 2011 a group of professors knelt down to protest against the environmental pollution caused by factories. In 2014, some teachers knelt down to oppose the relocation of a school. The showing of such scenes in the media have often led to wide public responses.

## The Elderly and Children

In Chinese culture, "the elderly, the disabled, pregnant women, and children" (*lao ruo fu ru*) are considered to be groups in need of care and protection and are generally not associated with radical actions. Therefore, if the elderly or children participate in a rally, it will often attract attention. Generally, what easily arouses public attention is when elderly people are beaten, shown bleeding, or kneel down. Most examples of elderly people kneeling down are related to petitions and staged before the police or media, hoping to win their sympathy. For example, in 2010, when the old people in a village of Guangxi saw several reporters, they knelt down, hoping to draw attention to the state of disrepair of the local roads. This stimulated widespread public discussion.

The participation of children can invest a meaning of innocence and nonviolence and decrease the risk of repression. In some local protests against environmental pollution, demolition of houses, and relocation, the presence of children has played an important role in arousing public sympathy. Following their parents, they block the roads or stage a protest before government buildings, where a scene of children carrying banners can be particularly effective. For example, after a village of the Hui people in Qinghai had been demolished by the government in 2013, a number of homeless children in the village sat before the village committee building and held up banners, and the photo was widely spread online. In August 2012 a group of unpaid workers let their children carry banners in an attempt to attract social attention. These children, ranging from five-year-olds to teenagers, lined up outside the construction site and held up banners reading "I want to drink milk and eat cake. Just pay back my parents' hard-earned money!" and "I want to go to school." They attracted passers-by to take pictures. The mainstream media and official media reported the event, thus triggering lively discussions on the Internet. Under mounting public pressure, the local government finally addressed the problem of back pay.

## Naked Protest

The dramatic use of bodies always can create unusual visual effects and generate pressure on authorities. One uncommon but extremely dramatic tactic is to go naked in public spaces. In Chinese culture, public exposure of the body, especially with regard to women, is seen as shameful and undignified, and people generally do not adopt this method in rights' struggles. However, impoverished workers have also sometimes gone naked to demand the return of wages; the employees of state-owned enterprises removed their clothes in a company headquarters to demand unemployment compensation and pension; and poor families stood naked on the streets to ask for help in order to pay medical expenses.

Nudity is one of the most extreme and controversial ways employed by Chinese petitioners to obtain attention. Most individuals choose to carry out such protests in front of provincial superior courts or national judicial departments. In 2013, a woman in her seventies from Henan and her 90-year-old mother, came to Beijing and voiced a grievance regarding the arrest of her son by local authorities. She launched many petitions to Beijing and was illegally detained by local authorities. The Ministry of Justice promised to solve her problem, but failed to keep that promise. Finally, in great despair, she staged a naked protest in front of the judicial department building.

Another case capturing public attention was the naked protest of a mother, Sun Aiyun, from the Hui ethnic group. Sun, born into an Islamic culture that imposed strict requirements on the dress code for women, carried out petitions for twenty years regarding the killing of her brother and was illegally imprisoned many times by Henan authorities. Finally, she decided to go naked on top of one of Luoyang court's vehicles, which caused traffic congestion and widespread media attention. In 2011, a 77-year-old woman from Shanghai knelt down naked in front of the Pudong New Area People's Court in protest against the justice system. Some naked protestors have chosen politically symbolic places to remove their clothes. In 2014, three old women from Xinyang, Henan Province, went naked in Tiananmen Square to protest against the detention of their children. In order to avoid interception by the local government, they wrote their demands on their bodies. The striking scene of three naked women in the background of Tiananmen Square was soon uploaded to the Internet, capturing the attention of the domestic and foreign media. As a result, the police quickly took the three women away from Tiananmen Square and detained them for seven days for "disturbing social order." After being released, they protested naked in front of the U.S. Embassy in Beijing and were immediately arrested and sent back to Henan in custody.

## Threaten with Death

To attract attention, some citizens will threaten to take their own lives, such as collectively jumping off a building, lying on railroad tracks, and taking poison. Such acts will instantly cause panic and provoke an emergency response from the authorities, because such extreme actions can more easily attract public concern and the intervention of governments at higher levels. Such acts of claim-making usually involve a wide variety of demands, such as those involving forced relocation, land seizures, wages and severance pay, fraud, and bankruptcy of companies. Some of these demands are directly concerned with government interests, while others are intended to attract the government's intervention on behalf of the protestors.

The main reasons that people choose this type of act as a form of protest are usually related to their experiences dealing with officials. Most seek the sympathy of authorities at higher levels after repeated complaints being ignored and government suppression at lower levels. However, when they discover that upper-level governments have also ignored their complaints, they sometimes take a more aggressive approach. Lying on railway tracks or roads can paralyze traffic, forcing the government to make an emergency response. People jumping off a building generally do so in downtown areas and this can quickly attract crowds. Taking poison also places enormous pressure on authorities. Although these acts of claim-making differ in their tactics and visual effects, they are all intended to attract attention.

Since the vast majority of similar actions aim to attract the attention of the state, and the central government in particular, some Chinese petitioners will choose to protest in the capital city or to paralyze major railways. In 2004, a group of laid-off workers from northeast China climbed Yongding Gate in Beijing, attracting thousands of onlookers, and threatened that they would collectively jump off the gate if the Beijing People's Court did not receive their petition. Also in 2004, thousands of workers lodged a mass protest, which lasted for forty days, against the corporate restructuring of a textile mill in Shaanxi Province. It was not until the workers occupied the Longhai Railway Station (an east-west railway artery) that the authorities started to pay attention. Some of the workers even blocked the Beijing-Guangzhou Railway in order to catch the attention of the central government. During the high-profile "two meetings" of the CPC in 2009, several old men from Fujian intended to take the opportunity to file petitions in Beijing due to demolition of their homes, but failed in their attempt and committed suicide by pesticide poisoning near Tiananmen Square.

In order to attract public attention, protestors will also choose to express their demands in crowded public spaces. For instance, in 2008 a group of migrant workers from a town in Zhejiang Province climbed to the roof of a school building and held up banners reading "Return my hard-earned money," attracting the attention of teachers and students. In another example, in 2015 some workers asking for back pay climbed to the roof of a mall and used the mall's large screen to display their slogans. These unexpected and creative acts immediately attracted public attention and the coverage of the overseas media. In 2015, more than thirty taxi drivers from Heilongjiang intended to collectively commit suicide by taking pesticide in Wangfujing Street, one of the famous shopping streets in Beijing, to protest against the collusion of the government and businesses, and attracted large numbers of onlookers. Since the event was widely reported by the media and imposed immense pressure on the authorities, the government charged these petitioners with "the crime of picking quarrels and provoking troubles" and arrested them after they were rescued. In addition, official buildings are often targeted as sites for making claims. Many acts of collective poison-taking occur in front of courts, the public security bureau, the petition offices, the party discipline organs, and party committees. In 2013 several petitioners from Heilongjiang climbed to the roof of a 12-story building opposite the National People's Congress office, and held up banners and scattered leaflets to express their grievances, attracting many onlookers. The offices of the U.S. Embassy in Beijing, the Xinhua News Agency, the *China Youth Daily*, and other official media are also preferred sites for people to make such claims.

## Suicidal Protest as Political Expression of the Dispossessed

Suicidal protest, as an extreme act of citizenship that is supposed to communicate an embodied message, has escalated among the Chinese people in recent years. Compared with more conventional forms of protesting, acts of bodily self-destruction demonstrate an *absolute* commitment to a cause worth dying for (Fierke 2013; Makley 2015). Such an extreme form of protest is mostly driven by an extreme sense of frustration, hopelessness, and determination, and exercises an extraordinarily intense performative power in creating spaces of appearance. Villagers dispossessed of the right to land and natural resources, workers denied the right to work and dignity, or residents without the prospect of a livelihood or housing, often see no other way to express grievances other than *dispossessing oneself* in the most extreme way. In the face of the state-acquiesced power of dispossession that renders certain populations disposable, "[d]ispossessing oneself as a life becomes the way to dispossess the coercive and privative force of that form of power" (Butler and Athanasiou 2013, 146).

Suicidal protest has a long history in China. In Chinese culture, there is a strong belief that where and how one dies is tied to the "value" of one's death, and that such circumstances should be morally justified. Suicidal protest, as a fatal corporeal act expressing discontent, is generally seen as "untimely" and "unworthy" due to its inappropriateness. However, in the Chinese cultural tradition, "to demonstrate one's will with death" (*yi si ming zhi*) has been morally justified, so suicide does have the potential of generating public controversy and calling into question state legitimacy, in particular when the victim constitutes a symbol of injustices endured by the people. In recent years, leaping off buildings and self-immolation are the most frequently used forms of suicide-as-protest.

In contemporary China, suicidal protest can serve as a means of politicizing issues with regard to survival and dignity, and can provoke widespread moral-political (and media) responses. The sequence of young Foxconn worker suicide attempts in 2010, for instance, expressed the most desperate form of protest against a global labor regime and the unbearable working conditions it produced. The "defiant deaths" of the young workers, argue Chan and Pun (2010, 2), "demand that society reflect upon the costs of a state-promoted development model that sacrifices dignity for corporate profit in the name of economic growth." Activists, academics, and NGOs played a central role in reconfiguring the distribution of the sensible and the visible with regard to mainland China's factory system. In Hong Kong and Beijing, labor activists' concerted efforts—through protests, press conferences, and investigative reporting—attracted widespread media attention and shocked the world, creating what Bargu (2014) calls a global "discursive phenomenon" capable of opening up a new dissensual space in which the meaning of worker suicides and the electronics sweatshop became a site of public contestation. One focus of mainstream discussion was about the young workers' inability to "eat bitterness" (Chan and Pun 2010). In contrast to Foxconn's framing of the serial suicides as isolated and predominantly individual cases of psychological problems that supposedly predated the workers' employment, labor activists and academics raised deep concerns about the military-like management imposed by the suppliers, and called into question the inhumane treatment of workers, the sustainability of Chinese development model, and the systematic lack of labor rights in the "workshop of the world." Some pointed to the world's richest electronics company's tolerance of its suppliers' "race to the bottom" production strategy that inevitably resulted in "the long hours, the repetitive tasks on the factory floor, the lack of overtime pay, the crowded dormitory spaces, the alienation from home, and the empty modernity promised through a life of urban factory living" (Litzinger 2013, 172–73).[8] The activists' political exposure and critique of corporate sweatshops, which created new visibilities and forms of sensory experience about the condition of labor in mainland China, would further put Apple and its suppliers under tremendous pressure, prompting an international scrutiny of corporate practices. Sympathetic media commentaries and Internet postings also initiated a rare public debates on corporate responsibility and social injustice. All these responses motivated other labor struggles and dissensual activities across the country.

One of the most dramatic forms of suicidal protest is self-immolation. Among the widespread suicidal protests associated with local governments' land seizures and forced evictions, Tang Fuzhen is perhaps the most well-publicized case. Tang, a female resident in Chengdu, Sichuan province, had refused a government request to demolish her house. A demolition crew with helmets, shields, and steel pipes, backed by police and firefighters, broke into Tang's three-story building in an attempt to force Tang and her family out of the house. Tang and her family climbed to the roof of her house, and threw rocks, bricks, and bottles at the demolition personnel. In her final act of protest, Tang, who remained on the roof of the building after hours of standoff, poured fuel all over her body and set herself on fire.

The shocking scene of the entire self-burning process, in which Tang's body was burned by the flames amid the screams of witnesses, was recorded by a neighbor's mobile phone and spread instantly on social media, attracting widespread news coverage and becoming a national scandal. Tang died sixteen days later. Despite Sichuan authorities' attempt to suppress coverage of the incident, and their denunciation of it as a "violence against the law," the shocking image of Tang's self-immolation, relayed all over the Internet as well as in the mainstream press and national TV outlets, constituted a powerful symbol of injustice. In a rare campaign that called into question the legality of existing land seizure regulations that allowed local governments to evict people from their homes, several professors wrote an open letter to the National People's Congress, arguing that the regulations were unconstitutional and urging the state to revise them. To pacify mounting discontent, the state intervened by imposing tougher rules on local governments and approving new laws to strengthen homeowners' rights.

In some places, suicide has been configured as a mode of radical political protest delegitimizing the state and the myriad forms of violence it produces in the name of stability and security. In such instances, dying and dead bodies can serve as *interlocutors* (Makley 2015, 453) for those advocating an explicitly political cause such as independence. Protest of this kind utilizes death and dying bodies not simply as a means of politicizing the issues at stake, but more crucially as a form of political expression and protest, for instance as manifested by the waves of self-immolation protests in Tibet, a restless ethnic minority region linked to the problem of political instability and national unification.[9] "Tibet has no history of self-immolation as sacrifice, religious offering, or political protest" (McGranahan and Litzinger 2012), where most of the self-immolators are young Buddhist monks and nuns.

Different from other kinds of suicide acts, the singular act of setting the body on fire operates primarily through the affective and moral responses it provokes on the part of the audience. The embodied act of self-burning, "entails an aesthetics of bodily pain specific to flaming skin. The morality and heroism of the act for a wide variety of observers of the Tibetan immolations lay in the supposedly self-evident courage and bodily self-control to communicate while burning; witnesses are supposed to both lean in and recoil in horror by imagining the sensation on their own skin" (Makley 2015, 463). Such form of protest through flames is "simultaneously politically charged, emotionally fraught, visually graphic, individually grounded, collectively felt" (McGranahan and Litzinger 2012), producing powerful images and receiving widespread international media attention via Tibetans spreading the information to the exile community. In this sense, self-immolation can be seen as a performative "act of speech" through which "the suffering body communicates the injustice experienced by a community to a larger audience" (Fierke 2013, 37). In the view of Litzinger (2012), one of the main audiences is the Chinese state, and the self-immolating body creates an alternative way to "speak back" to the state:

> Is the self-immolating subject, where we arguably see the work of the state and its effects most profoundly on the body, turning violence, through hybrid forms of spectacle, devotion, and signification, back against the state? Is it stealing, in a sense, the state's claim on violence? Is the body in flames unmasking, if only for an instant, the state's claim to be the sovereign subject that most effectively, most foundationally, regulates care and punishment, life and death?

Moreover, the symbolic act functions to *deny* the legitimacy of the state, "if only for that singular moment when the body ignites in flame, its sovereign claim to determine how individuals, in this most precarious of times, will be cared for, how they will live, and how they will die" (Ibid.).

The continued self-immolation protests staged by Tibetan monks and nuns are performed through the figure of a burning protestor who suffers *on behalf of* a broader community. Such a form of protest is "embroiled within a logic of sacrifice that is opposed to our conventional notions of instrumental action because it renders difficult, if not altogether impossible, the achievement of political ends through means lesser than death" (Bargu 2014, 6). The act of selfless martyrdom in this context "can be a means to focus attention . . . An image of self-sacrifice evokes emotions that go beyond words, to something more primal. It is not only that the image captures the attention; it also causes a disruption or a rupture, insofar as it is so perplexing, so contrary to ideas of self-preservation, that the audience has to stop and ask questions about what is happening and why" (Fierke 2013, 11–12). Moreover, such acts of self-immolation, usually considered as courageous, have a "sociopolitical life" that can often lead to highly public and ritualized contests over the disposition and display of the dead body (Makley 2015), which pose a symbolic challenge to the state's obsession with stability and harmony, as well as its foundational relationship to violence.

*Funeral Symbols*

Chinese citizens have used some cultural symbols of funeral rituals to attract public attention. For example, some anti-PX protestors displayed a "portrait of the deceased" of local officials, while others used funerary wreaths to block factories, police stations, or government buildings, or burned joss paper or lit firecrackers to express their dissatisfaction. Some used a coffin to grab attention.

In Chinese culture the coffin is both a symbol of respect for the deceased and an inauspicious object, thus, it can often create strong affective responses. Historically, in China placing a coffin at a gate symbolizes inauspiciousness. In the current political climate in mainland China, this ominous symbol has been employed to signify a curse on those in power, in particular local government officials. One of the reasons for choosing a coffin as a symbol is that land seizures and development projects often involve demolishing ancestral graves, which violates a *feng shui* taboo for villagers. Villagers generally carry the coffin to the controversial land to prevent demolition, or block roads or government buildings with a coffin. The scene can often attract public attention.

Another way of arousing public concern is to set up a monument. In Chinese culture, erecting a monument is a common ritual to commemorate the deceased. In recent years, some people have made use of the monument to express their dissatisfaction with corruption and poor governance. In 2011 some dairy farmers in a town of

Henan organized a "Cow Memorial Service," erected a monument for starved cows, and performed funeral rituals to protest against the local government's policy. After the media exposure, this event triggered widespread discussion. In another case in 2015, a villager in Henan set up a "monument of corrupt officials" on the street out of his dissatisfaction with the government's compensation for land acquisition, but the monument was soon smashed. In 2012, the media reported that a 62-year-old countrywoman in Shandong engraved the names of corrupt officials on a stone, placed this stone in the square and streets of the village, and set off firecrackers to catch the attention of local residents. After the event was revealed by the local media, the village party secretary rushed to stop the scene and physically abused the woman. The entire process was recorded by witnesses via mobile phones, and it quickly became the focus of national media attention. Later, the woman was interviewed by several media outlets, and with the help of her son opened a Weibo account to release information about official corruption.

*Unapproved Mourning*

In China, death is often accompanied by public rituals and demonstrable affective engagement. Historically, mourning for the dead through rituals and ceremonies has been an important custom and a means for the expression of emotions. Mourning has been considered inviolable because it is the paramount expression of filial piety (Kutcher 1999, 1), and is "highly charged with moral significance" (Watson 1994a, 13).

In her account of the politics of performative mourning, Butler (2009, 38–39) suggests that governments seek to control who will be publicly grievable and who will not. In contemporary China, such control of who or what is grievable has always been part of its mode of governance, with public funerals and mourning rites playing a crucial role in maintaining the existing order as well as increasing social solidarity and conformity to the state. During the Cultural Revolution, for instance, those labelled as "counter-revolutionaries" could not be publicly mourned and received no memorial services. During the post-Mao era, national mourning was not frequent and citizens were asked to grieve only for a few top leaders recognized as grievable. Since the 2000s however, the state has deliberately used mourning rituals as a means of legitimizing state rule. It has encouraged patriotism by staging state rituals. National mourning has become more frequently used as an instrument for demonstrating that the state respects and cares for the people. For instance, during serious natural disasters, the state suspends public entertainment, holds memorial services and pays silent tribute to the victims on behalf of the nation. The national mourning for victims of the Nanjing Massacre is another attempt to construct a national subject of grief. These events are usually elaborate, resourceful, carefully orchestrated, and dominated by censorship that serves to conceal any sense of the state's responsibility. In some cases, national leaders pay a silent tribute in the central government compound of Zhongnanhai in Beijing, which is covered by the media.

Traditional mourning rites and state commemorations can provide what Watson (1994a) calls a "dramatic medium" for expressing discontent. In China, there is a long tradition of people expressing dissent by subverting state rituals (Watson 1994b, 69). Funeral rituals of powerful leaders have long provided political sites of contestation (Cheater 1991; Brown 2007). The state normally prohibits unauthorized memorial services for those in conflict with the party line or for unacknowledged victims of state violence. Despite the tight control over mourning however, official memorial events—when bound up with public outrage—can be usurped for subversive purposes. Although the state attempts to control the allocation of what Butler (2015) calls public grievability by defining who can mourn and who can be mourned and remembered publicly, mourning gives people some moral power to share private mourning and perform silent protest, and in some cases it serves as occasions for political action. The dramatic memorializations of central leaders Zhou Enlai in 1976 and Hu Yaobang in 1989 are classic examples of this.[10]

In the face of political risks, public rituals provide a relatively "safe" means through which to express grievances. One of the strategic choices is to convert ritual performances and memorial occasions into acts of "political theater" (Esherick and Wasserstrom 1994), forcing a *repoliticizing of mourning* in ways that defy state norms. Traditional Chinese festivals such as Tomb-Sweeping Day (*qing ming jie*) and the Dragon Boat Festival (*duan wu jie*), for instance, offer an opportunity to express dissent. In recent years there are several cases where these occasions have been used as spaces of political theater. One well-known case is that of Ran Jianxin, a popular local party secretary in Hubei province who protested against the higher-level government over land grabs and forced demolitions, and died in police custody in 2011. Over a thousand angry villagers swarmed to the government compound in mourning, threw bottles at the police, and held up a huge banner that read "Secretly killed for protecting the people and offending the leaders." The widespread media coverage of the event generated considerable pressure on the local government. To appease public outrage, the local authorities held a grand commemorative ceremony to mourn Ran and openly praised him a "good comrade." In the spectacular scene of public grief, the funeral parlor where the memorial service was held was attended by tens of thousands of mourners showing obituaries that referred to Chinese moral discourse of justice and fairness (*gong dao*) and called into question the legitimacy of authorities. This case shows the symbols, rituals, and occasions of mourning can be used in ways not originally intended by the state. Through such symbolic acts state commemorations are "hijacked" by the mourners to open up a space in which social injustice and suffering can be made visible and the violence inflicted by the state can be acknowledged (Watson 1994b).

In recent years, the state's treatment of unnatural death has often become a crucial site of public contestation. Although the regime has consistently downplayed deaths for which the state is responsible and cracked down on unauthorized mourning, there always exists an unofficial and hidden sharing of loss and silent protest that unfolds on the Internet or the streets. In the face of strict censorship, Chinese citizens have sought to capitalize on existing resources and have invented new forms of mourning, such as launching unauthorized mourning campaigns on the Internet, placing wreaths at official buildings, or holding silent vigils commemorating the dead in public spaces. The most notable case is the Tiananmen Mothers' series of campaigns for the right to mourn those killed during the suppression of the Tiananmen protest in 1989.

In Chinese culture a dead person can only find peace after being buried in the soil (*ru tu wei an*), so if a victim whose life is not quite grievable is deprived of the right to be buried and mourned properly, the death will become a site of contestation. In particular, if protest is bound up with grief of unnatural, untimely, or violent death, a more defiant form of mourning can take shape in the acts of aggrieved workers and activists who take their grief to the streets and hold unapproved memorials. In mainland China, the loss of worker's life is usually excluded from the state-imposed culture of grief, but people can still find ways to perform grief. The death of Zhou Jianrong, a female factory worker who committed suicide by jumping out of her dormitory after being sacked in retaliation for participating in a strike by a Hong Kong-owned footwear factory in Shenzhen, led to a series of commemorative protests in Hong Kong. On the seventh day (*tou qi*) of Zhou's suicide, which in traditional Chinese mourning practice means the time when the dead "comes back" for last visit, more than 100 representatives of labor groups from around the country and her family gathered in Guangzhou to mourn her death. Activists had also called for July 17, the day of Zhou's death, to be named "Chinese Workers' Sacrifice Day." The act of naming is defiant in the sense that it was not approved by the state, and the participants advocated a cause that would be considered politically sensitive. Another notable case was the staging of mourning protests regarding the Foxconn suicides. Following the spate of people leaping to their death at the Foxconn plants, some families of the victims took framed photographs and wept outside of the factory. Some of the mourners were dressed in white (the traditional color of grieving in China), and knelt down on the spot of suicide to mourn their loved ones. Labor activists and unionists in cities like Hong Kong, Taipei, New York, and San Francisco also staged a series of commemorative demonstrations in support of the victims. In Taipei, for instance, the activists laid flowers and wreaths at the gate of the Foxconn headquarters, demanding that they treat their workers with dignity. In Hong Kong, activists threw joss paper (or "ghost money" that is supposed to be burnt as offerings for the deceased on special occasions) at the figures characterizing the Foxconn victims. Activists also turned up at the Apple stores on the first day of the release of new products and protested. All these acts garnered extensive media attention.

Sometimes citizens hold unapproved memorial activities to grieve those designated as ungrievable, making it difficult to "distinguish the funeral from the demonstration" (Butler 2015, 197). Butler also indicates that the suspicious death of ungrievable lives "will surely cause enormous outrage on the part of those who understand that their lives are not considered to be lives in any full and meaningful sense" (Butler 2009, 43). In mainland China, one high-profile case is Qian Yunhui, a village head who launched a six-year campaign to protect fellow villagers in land dispute with the local government, and died after being crushed by a truck. The local government initially claimed that it was an ordinary traffic accident, but the shocking images from the scene immediately aroused widespread suspicion. A temporary funeral table was placed on the spot of his death which soon became the center of public grief. The ritual attracted widespread media attention, and thousands of villagers gathered in front of Qian's residence and clashed with police. Such unapproved acts of mourning disrupt political authority by turning the spot of death into a temporary site of protest. When the death of those designated as ungrievable is ignored, such acts enable protestors to transform nonevents into events and challenge the norms of visibility and grievability legitimated by the state.

## Mao as Performative Resource

Chinese people sometimes make use of the portraits and words of national leaders to legitimize their protest actions and to attract attention. The most prominent example involves the invocation of Mao Zedong, a highly controversial but widely respected political figure in mainland China, and the creative use of Maoist language and image to justify claims. Politically, Maoism constitutes the CPC's orthodoxy, and his ideas continues to play a "framing" role that shape political culture in China (Cheek 2008). Yet the ideological frame inspired by Mao has been put to use in different ways and invoked by competing interests to obtain legitimate grounds. In order to consolidate the authority and legitimacy of the regime, the state has long dominated the public discourse on Mao while designating him as the preeminent symbol of the nation. During the Cultural Revolution, Mao's status was elevated above that of the CPC and the state. Though the state later covered up the Cultural Revolution and removed some of the statues and monuments of Mao, he is still regarded as the foundation figure of the state and the basis for the rule of the CPC. Mao's influence remains visible in ordinary people's everyday life: his writings and statements are still treated as the guiding ideology of the regime; his portraits and statues are displayed in public spaces; souvenirs, publications, and TV dramas about Mao are ubiquitous nationwide and become a feature of popular culture. While the CPC leadership has at times attempted to downplay the role of Mao, the nostalgic attachment to Mao that fermented from the late 1980s suggests that Mao is more venerated in civil society than within the state.

In contrast to the official uses of Mao as political doctrine, people also creatively appropriate the symbols and quotations of Mao to create visibility and political leverage. While the image of Mao had been used by the CPC to gather public recognition of the regime in the past, this political symbol is now extensively employed in various popular political activities. In these activities, Mao is idealized as a symbol of fairness, justice, and service to the people, and participants often express their desire for new moral order through performing a series of Mao-worshiping symbols and rituals. The most common expressive practice is that the crowds hold high a portrait of Mao, and then put forward a set of demands in the name of Mao. In these protests, Mao's image or slogan "stands as a contrasting example of the current leadership" (Cheek 2008, 20). For example, in September 2014, hundreds of people in Nanyang, Henan Province, walked to the city hall holding banners reading "Only the Mao Zedong Thought can save China" and "Down with corrupt officials." Some attached a poster of Mao to their motorcycles. Unlike the acts of raising flags and singing the national anthem that communicate an unambiguous allegiance to the regime, the meanings and emotions expressed through the performative use of Mao symbols are more complicated, and sometimes contradictory—the protestors use the worshipful portrait of Mao to denounce current policies. Because Mao remains the basis for the legitimacy of the CPC, holding high the portrait of Mao functions to urge the government not to forget Mao's teachings, especially his emphasis on people's interest and egalitarianism. Since Mao is regarded as "the savior of the Chinese people," holding high the portrait of Mao implies the peoples' deep dissatisfaction with the status quo (Leese 2011; Buruma 2001), and serves to "protect protestors from official violence or retribution and to shame those officials" (Cheek 2008, 18–19). Mao's symbolic resources have thus become "weapons of the weak" employed by Chinese peasants and workers in seeking redress from the state.[11]

Some dramatic rituals of public worshiping are also carried out in the name of Mao. On Mao's birthday, people across the country spontaneously hold activities in parks, squares, or places with statues of Mao. The participants encompass cadres or soldiers, workers, farmers, and teachers. They hold high the red flag, and speakers use a microphone or a loudspeaker to praise Mao, denounce the current leadership, recite Mao's quotations or poems, and sing Red Army songs or the national anthem. Some people will sing and dance wearing clothing worn during the Cultural Revolution. The masses will present flower baskets and bow to the statue of Mao. Sometimes organizers will recruit people bearing a resemblance to Mao and ask them to act out Mao Zedong. Most such ceremonies are concluded by singing the *Internationale*. These activities invariably capture the attention of the public and the media, and local governments sometimes send police to disperse the crowds or prevent the media from covering the activities. In January 2016, a village of Henan raised funds to build a golden sculpture of Mao, but it was forcibly removed by the government after it received widespread media coverage. These official reactions indicate that the state remains wary of the activities associated with Mao and popular subversions of Maoist legacies.

## Conclusion

This chapter has provided an account of and contextualized different embodied practices of citizenship, and analyzed how they constitute citizen-subjects in ways that are deeply rooted in Chinese political culture. These practices spring from multiple causes and are manifested in different ways. In a state that largely lacks channels to voice grievances, bodies are a crucial resource that is available to individuals and groups to make themselves and their grievances visible. These expressive practices take advantage of the specific condition where the regime has attempted to improve its image as a benevolent and responsible government. This analysis has critiqued existing scholarly approaches that overstate the verbal, cognitive, and legal characterizations of citizenship. The evidence derived from contemporary Chinese examples suggest that protestors are not merely passive with regard to state authorities, but actively negotiate with authority by and through the use of the body. These Chinese experiences attest to the conditions of and for political expression available in a setting where the state has severely restricted people's claim-making capacity. Chinese protestors have to perform creative and, on occasions, unlawful acts in order to be properly "counted" by the state. This performative politics does not challenge the state, but occasionally succeeds in shifting the terms and forms of public visibility.

This chapter pays much attention to the eye-catching scenes created by embodied practices, but does not consider sufficiently the *process*, *space*, and *vulnerability* through which the performative body produces political agency. If the performative condition in mainland China is highly risky, how is it possible for the body to force a political process of negotiation with contentious actors? What are the forms of expressive actions people take in order to make their grievances visible? Popular political activity needs a space from which to make claims. In a context where political activism is severely prohibited, how do protestors utilize existing material spaces to voice dissent, and how are these spaces transformed into a temporary political theater? Moreover, if the physical body is vulnerable and precarious, what are the conditions of its persistence, and how much can the body endure the physical and political challenges, and evoke broad public responses? These questions turn us to the embodied practices of a group of migrant workers who attempt to shift the way their situations are seen.

2

# Migrant Workers' Right to Appear

> To rethink the space of appearance in order to understand the power and effect of public demonstrations for our time, we will need to consider more closely the bodily dimensions of action, what the body requires, and what the body can do, especially when we must think about bodies together in a historical space that undergoes a historical transformation by virtue of their collective action: What holds them together there, and what are their conditions of persistence and of power in relation to their precarity and exposure?
>
> —Butler (2015, 73–74)

A group of photographs appeared on Facebook in early July 2015. In one of the photographs, several female workers laid on the equipment of a workshop, while others slept on the floor. Several other photographs showed a group of female workers gathered at the factory gate holding huge banners and confronting the police. The media coverage of their protest, which was enhanced by the use of smartphones to capture the scenes, has widened their public visibility: the striking images of female workers' sleeping on the factory's equipment became a public spectacle attesting to their grievances. The vulnerability and persistence of the body demonstrates the extent to which their lives are subject to economic uncertainties, and raises questions about the hegemonic meaning of its "appearances" in productive and public spaces.

Since the intensification of market reforms in the mid-1990s, Chinese workers have sought to claim their rights to livelihood at multiple points of dissent. The main characters of this contentious episode were rural migrant workers in the Artigas Clothing & Leather factory (hereafter referred to as "Artigas"), a contract manufacturer and supplier of the Japanese fashion brand UNIQLO. Founded in 1992, Artigas is located in Shenzhen, and is a subsidiary of Hong Kong-owned Lever Style. Lever Style is a well-known enterprise in mainland China: it owns three factories, employs over 4,000 people, and serves as the supplier for UNIQLO and G2000. When I did the fieldwork, many migrant workers, who were mostly prompted by impoverishment in the countryside to seek jobs in the cities, had worked for the company for more than one or two decades. Their grievances originated from the intense processes of dispossession associated with the country's increasing flexibilization and disposability of migrant

Figure 2.1. The Artigas Factory. The Artigas factory was closed down after the protest. Author photo. July 27, 2015.

labor force, and were connected to a larger story about the diverse modes of precarity experienced by Chinese migrant workers. If politics is about the possibility of creating and reconfiguring visibility, how such politics is articulated and performed by the vulnerable workers and how their actions shift the way their situations are perceived, are the focus of this chapter.

This protest event is part of the general condition of waged labor in mainland China, where subcontracting and wage arrears are endemic and migrant workers are vulnerable to forms of dispossession. The tipping point of the collective action is that at the end of 2014 the factory decided to relocate to another site five kilometers away, but workers were not informed of the decision. They generally feared that the relocation would affect their employment status, which would affect their legal rights and benefits,[1] and decided to occupy the factory in protest. Their collective actions can be seen as a manifestation of what Rancière calls the "polemical verification of equality" that is "necessarily intermittent and precarious," but can challenge the "police order" (Rockhill 2004b, 86) in an exclusionary political system.

Among the workers, there existed a widespread fear of being deprived of a livable future, as "informal employment has become a new normal for the Chinese workforce" (Lee 2016, 319). The migrant workforce, which accounts for about 72 percent of mainland China's urban workforce, has to confront a set of job insecurities produced by the increasingly unstable market conditions, and seeks desperately to be covered and protected by new labor regulations. "The official categorisation of peasant workers—wage laborers with rural household registration," some scholars indicate, "keeps their social status and class identities ambiguous" (Smith and Pun 2018, 7–8). Although they are nominally designated as "citizens" entitled to a set of rights, in actual practice they are denied the status of formal workers and citizens, and, therefore, are left unprotected by state laws. Facing a volatile employment situation, they turn to draw on an array of physical performances to increase the collective capacity to minimize their precariousness. These and other similar copycat actions raise questions such as: What specific forms of precarity and vulnerability are imposed on the workers? Why do they choose to take such action? How can we make sense of the bodies—which are simultaneously disciplined as an obedient labor force, and dominated by a rigidly unequal citizenship regime that excludes rural migrants from many basic social benefits—that occupy factories and other social spaces? How are factories and other built environments turned into performative spaces for voicing dissent? How do they manage to persist with these actions? If the state is generally considered as a political site of mediation among conflicting social forces, what is its role in this process? In the past decade, labor resistances in mainland China have mainly focused on wages and working conditions (Litzinger 2013). As China becomes the "epicenter of global labor struggles" (Friedman 2012), how does this episode tell us something about Chinese migrant workers' deteriorating conditions of employment, and their defense of collective persistence amid endemic rights violations?

In an attempt to address these questions, a series of field observations and interviews were carried out, and information was obtained from the workers participating in the protests from mid-July of 2015. The data sources of this research includes extensive relevant literature and accounts of similar case studies reported by the media. This chapter will contextualize the Artigas protest and describe how the transient migrant workers' various forms of embodied practices opened up the political process involving employers and governments. I will elucidate the dynamics behind the embodied acts of resistance taken to counteract the destruction of livability. The embodied resistance, in my view, can be seen as a desperate attempt to *expose* and counter the unequal distribution of the value of life and the growing precarity in all spheres of life.

## The Institutional Context of Worker Struggle

The Chinese state's increasing withdrawal from the everyday social space, and its declining surveillance capacity, has reshaped the dynamics of labor struggle since the 1990s. During the pre-reform period, the "work unit" system and production teams played a central role in sustaining citizen-government relations and coordinating conflicts. These grassroots organizations helped the state to monitor, sanction, and represent the interests of the masses (Chen 2012, 62). In the old system, workers were generally loyal to their units or designated affiliations and depended on these organizations for benefits and communication with the state. The decline of these mechanisms since the

1990s, which used to offer an indispensable point of contact between the state and the people, has reconfigured government-citizen linkage that was crucial to the state's social control. Without the mediation of the unit system, ordinary people have started lodging their complaints directly to government agencies at different levels (Chen 2012, 20).

China's rise as the workshop of the world has been accompanied by a reconfiguration of state institutions. Since the 1990s, the increasing devolution of political and economic authority from the center to localities and the bureaucratic differentiation of its governance structure have created divergent conflicts of interest among various government departments and regions, and between the center and localities (Zheng 1997). The functions of governmental departments and agencies have become more complex and differentiated at both vertical and horizontal levels, giving rise to the geographic dispersion and fragmentation of popular struggle across the country. Under these new circumstances, the state's decision-making power has been increasingly transferred to governments at lower levels, although it still retains the power to appoint local party cadres at upper levels. Divergent interests among government agencies have caused more tensions within the political hierarchy, while also providing new political opportunities for Chinese protestors to enact performative articulation. In such a decentralized yet still hierarchical system, the center has relaxed its grip on local economic development; however, it has also found it more difficult to coordinate and monitor the behavior of its local agents. Under pressure to promote rapid economic growth, which is characterized by state-led urban export-oriented development, short-term and speculative behavior has been encouraged at local levels. Local governments have sought to expand revenue relentlessly through various means, often at the expense of workers, including non-signing of long-term contracts, wage arrears, and non-provision of social security (Smith and Pun 2018, 3). More specifically, the global labor regime is founded on the dispossession of Chinese migrant workers' labor and citizenship rights, and the sacrifice of their dignity for profit in the name of economic growth (Chan and Pun 2010).

The loosening of party control of localities and the rise of local interests have combined to create a chain reaction in the past few decades. Above all, the system has created more opportunities for abuses of power at local levels. Since local governments have increasingly depended on local economic activities for income, and are evaluated primarily on their ability to develop the economy, many local cadres are complicit with enterprise management and have abused power to achieve their goals (Fewsmith 2013). Local officials "systematically neglect workers' rights, resulting in widespread misery and deepened social inequalities" (Chan and Pun 2010, 2). Forms of corruption have also evolved, with some local cadres involved in illegal activities. During labor conflicts, for example, it is often the local government that calls in police to suppress the strike and orders unions to side with the management (Friedman 2014).

Under these circumstances, migrant labor protests tend to be cellular and short-lived, and concentrate primarily on economic demands. They are de facto excluded from the state's and enterprises' decision-making processes. They tend to be depoliticized partly because the right to strike was removed from the Constitution in 1982 for fear of encouraging a politically oriented labor movement, and protesting workers have been only allowed to express demands related to purely economic and livelihood issues, which are viewed as much less threatening. The state has systematically suppressed any organized dissent. Freedom of association remains highly constrained; independent unionism and organized resistance have been vigorously repressed amid an escalation of labor unrest triggered by neoliberal reforms facilitated by the state. To break through these constraints, Chinese workers have taken various kinds of action to pursue their rights, including leafleting, lawsuits, collective appeals, demonstrations, traffic blockades, and attacks on official targets (Cai 2006). Migrant labor struggles have been largely uncoordinated and confined to workers at a single factory. "Wages and lawful compensations," according to Lee (2016, 328), "not political representation or institutional empowerment, remain the cardinal concerns among workers."

With China's integration into global capitalism, the state has sought to maintain an obedient labor force in the service of capital and to implement policies to prevent local social upheavals from turning into a general crisis. Since the Hu Jintao and Wen Jiabao administration, a sustained attempt, manifested in a series of labor policy and institutional reforms, has been made to defuse the mounting protests driven by unbridled development, with frequent references being made to "putting people first," as well as the "broadening the legitimate rights and interests" of citizens. The rule of law is claimed to be carried out. Various legal and institutional channels—such as letters-and-visit departments, people's congresses and courts—have been strengthened to "enable citizens to pursue grievances without creating the potential to threaten the regime as a whole" (Perry 2007, 7). The state has also responded to widespread worker unrest with more emergency measures. More crucially, since the 1990s, the state has passed legislation and enacted many laws and regulations that inadvertently allow protestors to frame their grievances in legal terms (Bernstein 1999; Lee 2007b). A series of new labor laws were enacted between 2007 and 2008, for instance, in an attempt to channel growing contention into legal forms of conflict resolution. Government propaganda on labor laws and policies has also produced a growing legal knowledge and rights consciousness among workers. Meanwhile, the establishment of institutions for appeal has offered wider access to legal and administrative procedures, and encouraged migrant workers to frame demands as a matter of "rights protection" (*weiquan*) and to reject illegitimate measures. These institutional efforts of standardizing employment relations through legislation have paradoxically provided legitimate grounds for more labor protests (Smith and Pun 2018, 7).[2] The official claim for maintaining a "harmonious society" has also opened up a space for hegemonic struggle. However, poor implementation of central policies remains the key source of discontent at lower levels.[3] As a result, the majority of transient migrant workers have lived a precarious existence without sufficient legal protection. As Lee (2016, 321) indicates, the ineffectiveness of the state-initiated labor code in protecting workers is

> fundamentally due to the extreme imbalance of class power . . . both the state and the employer have a common interest in preempting workers from developing a capacity for sustainable organization. Without the legal power to independently engage in collective organizing and bargaining, and subject to the state's wavering commitment to implement labor laws, workers' legal mobilization is too atomized to counter the alliance between the local state and capital.

This is why the pro-capital mode of local governance remains an impetus for migrant worker struggle, which is embodied in a set of performative activities that create what Arendt conceptualizes as "spaces of appearance" where hegemonic contestation occurs. With the neoliberal erosion of labor rights, the state's interference and responsibility of recovering workers' egalitarian rights has become ever more crucial.

## Intensification of Precarity

Global capital can "create and harness a highly precarious, substantially unprotected and easily exploited global labour force" (Phillips and Mieres 2015, 246). In the past several decades, the global commodity supply chain has relied heavily on the perpetuation of multiple forms of deprivation of the vast majority of Chinese rural migrant workers, who frequently lack employment security and social insurance coverage, and live a precarious existence without political standing (Li 2012). In the spectacular rural-urban migration flow:

> many women take the opportunities migration offers to escape patriarchal control and oppression in the villages, only to end up in a new industrial world of exploitation under a different patriarchal regime. In combination with the commodification and rising costs of domestic labor, health care, and education, this has produced enormous social misery and deepened existential fears. (16 Beaver Group 2013)

In recent years, the term "precariat" has gained wide currency among scholarly debates on the precarity of Chinese migrant workers (Lee 2016). Guy Standing, in his theorizing of the rise of precarious labor, advocates the "precariat" as a new class of insecurely employed workers, and claims that it emerges as a new working-class subject that challenges the "privileges" of the traditional proletariat. Different from those regular workers with relatively standard, long-term employment status and a stable source of income, members of the disadvantaged precariat, according to his thesis, are largely excluded from the wage-labor market and lack secure employment contracts. They have neither employment nor job security.[4] Those in the precariat can only do irregular, casual work, and are constantly faced with employment informalization. "Their sources of income," writes Standing (2017,

169), "are inherently insecure and volatile. They are faced by chronic economic uncertainty." The employment status thus defines the internal divisions of the working class; the rise of the precariat marks the beginning of a new historical condition.

Indeed, the situation of Chinese migrant workers follows some of the generic trends of precarization, though it has distinctive features. Hundreds of millions of rural migrants flock into cities to find jobs and make a living, but are excluded from many social benefits due to the *hukou* (household registration) system, which is "used by employers to segment workers by different contracts, even though they generally perform similar types of work" (Smith and Pun 2018, 3). They are dispositioned as a highly disposable workforce in service of the export-oriented production. Lacking a sense of labor-based security,[5] their employment status is extremely uncertain and volatile, and their lives are displaced by a double rupture from rural and urban communities. Yet Standing's conceptual distinction is too restrictive to properly explain the situation in mainland China, where precariousness is widespread and ubiquitous to all forms of labor status—"a more or less important attribute of being a worker," rather than evidence of a separate class (Smith and Pun 2018, 8). With the proliferation of precarity, as manifested in the ubiquitous "non-signing of long-term labour contracts, irregular payments of wages, and non-provision of social security" (Ibid. 3), the distinction between regular and non-regular work is often blurred to the extent that all kinds of workers are facing the challenge of precarization, "oscillating between exploitation and exclusion by capital" (Lee 2016, 317). With the neoliberal erosion of rights, even "formal workers" with regular forms of employment are equally subject to an existential insecurity.[6]

Another issue revolves around the sources of precarity, namely who and what participates in the production of the objective condition of instability and insecurity. For Standing, the precariat has a "distinctive relations to the state," referring to "a person's status and a lack of rights within the state. Someone in the precariat is, above all else, a supplicant, dependent on others doing them favors, in response to requests" (Standing 2017, 166). In his theorizing, Chinese migrant workers are part of the emerging precariat, "not the proletariat as conventionally defined . . . they are] workers without rights, put in supplicant positions" (Ibid.). They "lack civil rights because they cannot, in practice, obtain equal access to the law. They lack social rights, because they do not qualify for the range of benefits developed by the state. They lack political rights, because they cannot obtain representation in the political institutions" (Ibid. 168). As a disenfranchised workforce, Chinese rural migrants "have been deliberately denied the urban *hukou* . . . granted discretionarily a more limited range of rights than the citizens of the town. In that status, they have remained almost like beggars, relying on the discretionary benevolence of officials and other authority figures embedded in the state" (Ibid. 167). He goes further to stress that the state has actively promoted that trend, resulting in the widespread deprivation of migrant workers' citizenship rights and entitlements.

There are indeed multiple institutional factors perpetuating Chinese labor precarization. Pun's (2016) study, for example, demonstrates how state policies actively facilitate the exploitative labor regime by partially loosening the *hukou* system and reducing more regular employment. What is missing from Standing's view, however, is the complicit role of global capital and its suppliers in perpetuating the form of dispossession:

> Chinese migrant labor conditions as articulated by the state, are shaped by these intertwined forces: First, leading international brands have adopted unethical purchasing practices, resulting in substandard conditions in their global electronics supply chains. Second, management has used abusive and illegal methods to raise worker efficiency, generating widespread grievances and resistance at the workplace level. Third, local Chinese officials in collusion with enterprise management, systematically neglect workers' rights. (Chan and Pun 2010, 2)

There also exists, as Smith and Pun (2018, 3) observe acutely, a "contradictory movement" with regard to Chinese labor precariousness that is ignored by Standing's thesis:

> On the one hand, legislation has increased security for regular workers in mass production and mass service industries, where more regular forms of employment have been recognised and protected by law . . . Increasingly, urbanised

migrant workers continue to be denied equal citizenship and welfare rights, and hold rural hukou in perpetuity.

These debates around precarity offer a useful conceptual ground for the analysis of this case. What I want to add is that the direct consequence of growing precarity is not only the proliferation of insecure work, but also an insecure *future*. In light of the recent economic distress, the Artigas workers' precarious situations should be situated against the deteriorating conditions of their precarious employment, and the increased insecurity felt by Chinese contract manufacturers in general. For a long time, fierce competition between manufacturing countries has resulted in widespread casualization, informalization, and abuse of labor.[7] The economic crisis in Europe and America since 2008 led Chinese manufacturing production, which had been reliant on export markets, to gradually relocate its factories to inland China and Southeast Asia where costs were lower (Young 2015; Lin 2015). The clothing industry tends to rely less on a stable regular workforce (which is predominantly female), and its production is more vulnerable to market volatility (Parry 2018, 9). As global brands squeeze their suppliers in developing countries to compete against each other on price, the suppliers in turn transfer the cost-cutting pressure to frontline workers (Chan and Pun 2010, 23). These buyers often fail to enforce ethical codes of conduct in their suppliers, but foster their "race to the bottom" production strategy (Litzinger 2013, 176) creating downward pressures on wages and conditions. Moreover, the Chinese government's control of the value of the currency (the Renminbi) has made it difficult for manufacturers to compete with countries with currency devaluation (Bradsher 2015). Against the background of economic downturn, order outflows, and increasing labor costs, the manufacturing sectors in coastal areas have tended to reduce their size, transfer places of production, informalize the workforce, lay off workers, or close down temporarily and sometimes permanently. It is increasingly harder to find a stable job; and when employed, the contracts and incomes are not secure. Workers are increasingly left unprotected when thrown into the labor market. Frequent shutouts and relocations adversely affect workers' lives, leading to the loss of their sense of employment and job security. All these trends have created the condition for more radical labor politics.[8] Rage and fear about not being able to satisfy the basic bodily needs for the future provides the impetus for their struggles.

UNIQLO is one of the multinational enterprises transferring their capital outside China (Shi 2015). At the time of my fieldwork, roughly 85 percent of the products of the largest clothing retail company in the world were manufactured in mainland China; however, in recent years it has started to increase the proportion of its production in Bangladeshi and Indonesian factories that operate at lower costs. Artigas used to be a relatively large-scale supplier; however, between 2011 and 2013, the number of its employees in mainland China dropped by one-third, as they transferred the OEM business to Vietnam, where worker's salaries were only half of those at the Shenzhen factory (Gong 2015). Due to massive order outflows, workers at Artigas had not worked full time for several months before the protest, which threatened their livelihood. They had experienced a marked deterioration of their working conditions, with wages being cut and benefits curtailed. Even if there were written labor contracts, the workers generally lacked the coverage of social insurance that is legally required.[9] Their sense of escalating precarity is part of a more general condition of labor in mainland China.

This precarious employment situation has triggered waves of migrant labor protests in the Pearl River Delta region—in particular, the protests regarding social insurance staged by to-be-dismissed workers grew more frequent (Becker 2014, 39). Their sense of precarity was reinforced by the worry about the future after returning to hometowns (because many workers were separated from their families). In 2014, a spectacular strike action staged by workers of mainland China's largest footwear manufacturer, Taiwanese-owned Yue Yuen, in which about 30,000 workers participated and which lasted for 12 days, drew attention to the issue of pension contributions.[10] Since the Yue Yuen protest, strikes and demonstrations about lawful compensations have been on the rise (Haoxiana 2014). These protests are concerned with the rights conferred by the Social Insurance Law, which took effect on July 1, 2011, and provides basic social security for the majority of the labor population. However the state-initiated law has often failed—there are huge loopholes in the legislation, and problems with implementation at local levels. In the first years after the law came into effect, most Chinese workers still did not understand the rights conferred by this law, and had no idea of how, or if, their companies were complying with or implementing it.[11] According to the law, workers are only eligible to receive a pension after retirement if they and their employers pay at least 15 years of social security. However, many local governments have frequently acquiesced in the enterprises' illegal evasion behaviors in order to attract investment.[12] Like the vast majority of Chinese manufacturers, Artigas did not legally pay full social security funds for its employees. While the regulations of Guangdong Province do not specify limits on the length of paying social insurance in arrears, Shenzhen's regulations provide that "municipal social security institutions shall not accept complaints and reports made over two years ago" (Huang 2014).[13] This regulation has limited migrant workers' rights-seeking options and activities in Shenzhen.[14]

This is the specific context in which the struggle of the Artigas workers unfolded. Before the protest, there were reports exposing the poor working condition of the factories of UNIQLO, such as long working hours, low wages, unsafe working conditions, a harsh punishment system, and a lack of representation in the workers' union (Chan 2015). There was an accumulation of deep-seated grievances, only to erupt when the workers felt that they were on the verge of losing control of their livable future. Only when faced with the choice of leaving or staying did Artigas workers realized that their employer had not been paying full social security funds since their recruitment, nor did they pay the housing provident fund that was required of them. This provided the impetus for the workers to take expressive actions.

## Embodied Struggle against Precarization

What Chinese migrant workers—also known as *dagongzai* (working boys) or *dadongmei* (working girls) in daily Chinese slangs—are facing is a regime that arbitrarily disposes of their labor and their bodies.[15] That regime also renders them silenced and invisible—they are divested of the means to speak up. There is no functioning union that can make their voices heard, so they can only resort to collective actions to draw attention to their precarity. Through a series of performative embodied actions, they declare that social protection is not a *private* matter, or something that can be determined by the employer. The entire struggle over pension contributions necessarily involves the body:

> Hunger, poverty, joblessness, lack of access to health care, and housing insecurity maybe described as macro processes, but they are also deeply embodied events, experienced by living human beings in the flesh. Responses to these conditions, including collective political resistance, should also be understood as involving the body. (Sutton 2010, 2596–597)

The embodied actions of migrant workers, whose political subjectivity is denied, share a number of characteristics and patterns in terms of tactics: they frequently resort to peaceful *and* disruptive actions, including petitions, strikes, rallies, sit-ins, demonstrations, blockades, and occupation. There is, as Pun indicates, political potential in migrant workers' laboring bodies:

> As a worker-subject dagongmei is a subject over which the process of subjectivation fights with the process of subject making and the struggle for a return to the actor. The political techniques of control over rural bodies meet with the tremendous desire of Chinese peasants to liberate themselves from their long-segregated lives, and hence act as agents in changing their lives. Dagongmei, as a specifically Chinese subaltern, embodies the dual process of domination and resistance and is marked by various forms of collaboration, transgression, and defiance that together come to make up its complex, dissident, and heterogeneous subjects . . . Dagongmei is formed of complex, dissenting, and tactical subjects who are up against a system of inherently incomplete domination . . . Before the disciplinary regime, no matter how powerless they are, dagongmei are more than simply docile bodies. Rather, they are also tactical and resistant bodies, confronting domination, sometimes covertly, sometimes overtly, and sometimes successfully subverting or breaking down disciplinary power. (Pun 2005, 15–16)

Under the tightly controlled political circumstances, public spaces where workers can freely express their concerns are extremely restricted. This is why workers often *act together as a collective* to reclaim sites and spaces such as the street, government buildings, and the factory, and turn them into temporary spaces of appearance. Despite the tendency of compliance with state norms, the gatherings of crowds often create "peaceful chaos for local governments" (Cai 2006, 117), which makes possible what Butler calls "a performativity of embodied agency" (Butler and Athanasiou 2013, 178). These actions require putting the body into action, and in most episodes, collective bodily presence plays a crucial role. Their physical presence outside of normalized political activity can pose some degree of challenge to the precarious state:

> [M]any of the public demonstrations we are seeing now are militating against induced conditions of precarity. And I think they pose the question of how performativity operates as an enacted politics. Sometimes a performative politics seeks to bring a new situation into being, or to mobilize a certain set of effects, and this can happen through language or through other forms of media. But when bodies assemble without a clear set of demands, then we might conclude that the bodies are performing the demand to end conditions of induced precarity that are not livable. (Butler and Anathasiou 2013, 102)

When petition fails, workers will choose more disruptive and direct actions to create visibility. This means a radicalization in action. For those resource-poor protestors, disruption may offer new political opportunities by drawing attention. Different from peaceful petitioning, disruptive practices allow workers to create their own political realms where the previously *invisible* is intensely questioned and contested. Under the strict law against assembly however, disruptive actions are necessarily unauthorized and forbidden, and considered as a threat to stability. Disruptive actions can be seen as political activities that always "involve forms of innovation that tear bodies from their assigned places and free speech and expression from all reduction to functionality" (Corcoran 2010, 1). Assemblies without official permits make audible and visible their anger and bodies, and assert the dignity of workers. When these actions momentarily pause time and space, new opportunities of visibility arise. In this political process, the body serves as a site of radical self-expression and a resource for protracted struggle, with workers reclaiming and deploying their bodily potentialities, capacities, and endurance in spectacular ways in order to achieve their goals. The bodies assemble and act in concert to exert a force so that their demands are made *visible*. In the Chinese context, such embodied practices are frequently deployed to widen visibility: the workers' bodies are turned into visible, active, and publicly enacted bodies in order to allow their grievances to be heard and seen more widely.

The function of gathering, a common form of resistance in mainland China, is to seize upon and *resignify* existing spaces, obtain wider public appearance, and open a political process that renders their grievances visible. It can also exert pressure on the state to respond. Through collectively gathering in spaces, such embodied practices disrupt the normative role assigned to bodies, as well as the norms of bodily visibility and the spatial organization of power. This sequence involves a reshaping of what Jacques Rancière (2014) calls "the landscape of the visible," or the creation of a theatrical stage on which political action plays out.

Since the bodily forms manifested in the UNIQLO protest event are diverse, this case study will help shed light on the major forms and features of Chinese migrant labor politics of our time. What follows is a narrative account of the ways in which political agency arose from and in response to Artigas's corporate actions, as the workers took a decision to participate in an embodied struggle and invented their own performative spaces.

## Expressions of Worker Militancy

The Artigas's workers expressed their demands in what was a highly risky setting. The protesting workers articulated their protest through a series of embodied actions, including gatherings, sit-ins, strikes, hanging banners, holding slogans, blocking access to the factory, going on hunger strikes, signing petitions, besieging the local police station, and guarding the factory. These actions created highly charged "contentious events" that placed considerable pressure on the employer and governments. Contention, according to Tilly and Tarrow (2007, xi), "comes in clusters." In what follows I will give an account of the two contentious sequences triggered by the workers' militant actions. Emotional protest events "almost always come in sequences and clusters . . . [and] may transform the dynamics of collective action. They do so by dramatizing the relationships among movement activists, publics, and opponents" (Yang 2005, 80).

*The First Contentious Process (December 2014–January 2015)*

The protest was triggered by rumors about factory relocation, which prompted some veteran workers—who were asked by factory management to retire early—to check their social insurance accounts and discover the problem. The workers' actions escalated in late 2014. Initially, they did not intend to complain to the government or take aggressive actions, but required the employer to respond to their demands before December 8, otherwise they would report to the government. Although the management made a verbal commitment, it ultimately punished the ringleaders because the workers allegedly "damaged the company's image" via social media. In addition, the workers were not notified of a clear timetable for negotiations. After the deadline had passed, they decided to take actions around the factory and put pressure on the employer by interrupting production.

The disgruntled workers launched the first strike and blocked the factory gates on December 10, 2014. The representatives of the local social security department and staff from the public security and housing provident fund department came to the factory trying to help with negotiations; however, the workers did not accept the official statement that "social security repayment only has two years of a valid retroactive term." Since the employer started to shift production lines to a nearby factory, the workers hoped to recover their social security and housing provident funds before the New Year, otherwise it would be difficult for them to do so (some would quit their jobs after the holiday). The workers began to block the access to the factory on both day and night shifts in order to prevent the employer from emptying the factory. The workers said, "If the employer refuses repayment, we must not allow goods to be removed out of the factory. If the employer adopts psychological tactics, we will brave it." Two workers threatened to commit suicide on December 12. On the fourth day of the strike, the employer started to cut off water and electricity to the workers' dormitories. During this period, government officials sometimes visited the scene, while the employer alternated threats and inducements to workers and required them to return to work.

On December 16, some workers went to the Shenzhen Federation of Trade Unions and the Shenzhen Municipal Letters and Visits Office to express their grievances, but they did not receive any positive response. Then, on the morning of the ninth day (December 18), the company owner appeared at the factory surrounded by 400 police officers. The workers originally thought that negotiations would be held, but unexpectedly the police officers forced their way into the factory and arrested some workers, while the employer removed his own goods. In the afternoon the workers refused to return to work and conducted sit-ins. The arrested workers also refused to sign a document depriving them of their legal rights. The workers arrested by the police were released after 12 hours. Under intense pressure from the police the workers reluctantly went back to work. The police appeared in the workshop and worked with company security to monitor the workers.

During the strike, the workers had forced the employer to pay back their housing provident fund that had accrued from December 2010.[16] They used smartphones to spread scenes of the protests, capturing the attention of some local media and activist groups in Hong Kong.[17] But the pressure on the employer and the local government was insufficient to bring about any significant changes. The employer dismissed uncooperative workers in the name of absenteeism. The workers decided to place pressure on the local trade union. They sent representatives to petition the Guangdong Province Federation of Trade Unions, but they only received a reply in the form of note without any follow-up measures. During this period, the local union and police officers attempted to prevent the workers' petition from going ahead.

*The Second Contentious Process (June 2015–July 2015)*

In the next six months, the employer started to relocate equipment, and the workload was significantly reduced. On June 2, the workers selected representatives from each department and put in a request for collective negotiations with the employer. The employer did not respond to the request but put up a notice of relocation on the factory's bulletin board on June 9. The company indicated that the workers could sign new contracts with the new company after the relocation, but did not mention compensation. This information instantly panicked the workers, many of whom worried that they would be fired, or would not be able to work in the new factory.

The frustration with factory management resulted in a constellation of bodily feelings among the workers, including anxiety, worry, fear, depression, anger, outrage, and pain. These emotions propelled them to escalate their actions. "Anger and indignation," writes Jasper (2014, 2638), "must reach a point where people are willing to take great risks for the common good." They immediately started a new round of work stoppage. This time, the workers assigned tasks and shifted the target to local government. Hoping that the government would intervene on their behalf, the workers staged actions outside the factory. The police went to the factory and arrested a dozen people, including two university students supporting the workers. On June 9, the workers gathered outside the police station to request the release of the arrested workers. On June 10, they started negotiating with the town government. The local trade union was also contacted, but failed to resolve the disputes. A staff member with the labor inspection department told the workers that "the factory must be closed down if you keep making trouble!" In the factory, public security officers and plainclothes police officers kept a close eye on the workers.

Even though the workers exerted some pressure on the employer through strikes and petitions, it was insufficient to produce a favorable response. As a result, the workers decided to occupy the factory. In the span of over forty days from June 9, they divided into a dozen groups to guard the factory. Those who were ill or had children were responsible for the day shift, others were responsible for the night shift. Everyone prepared their own meals: those with families were delivered meals by their families, while those without families took food with them.

A group of workers blocked the factory gate to prevent the employer from shipping supplies, while other groups of workers stayed in the factory around the clock to prevent the employer from removing goods and equipment. Moreover, 300 of the workers had been on a hunger strike since June 13. Meanwhile, hundreds of workers departed for the Shenzhen municipal government to make a petition. After arriving at the government, the workers were not allowed to enter, but were forced to move to a square nearby. Subsequently, the government dispatched three buses and the police tried to make people get on the buses.

Meanwhile, several workers headed for the Shenzhen Municipal Letters and Visits Office: a staff member receiving the workers asked the Longhua authorities to address this dispute as soon as possible. On June 16, the workers went to the Guanlan Street Letters and Visits Office and attempted to talk with the employer, but the representatives of the employer did not show up. A representative of the employer indicated that the employer had not broken the law, and that the workers' demands lacked any legal basis. In the afternoon, staff from the labor supervision department came to the factory and persuaded the workers to leave, pointing out that "the machines and equipment are owned by the employer," that relocation was normal business behavior, and that if the workers' prevented the relocation, then public security would intervene to maintain order.

However, some workers continued their actions: approximately 500 employees agreed to be transferred to the new factory, while 300 refused. On the morning of June 23, the workers hung banners at the factory gate, expressing their demands: "Implement the Labor Contract Law, conduct collective negotiations, safeguard labor rights and interests, uphold the spirit of central government, establish a labor negotiation mechanism, and maintain social harmony and stability. We workers unite to safeguard our rights and guard all workshops day and night despite the hot summer only in order to recover our hard-earned money!!!" It was a powerful emotional appeal widely circulated on the Internet. They lined up in the factory and held their banners, which were soon destroyed by the police. On the morning of June 25, the police took some workers away from their home, and the workers surrounded the local police station trying to get them released.

Several female workers explained to me that they felt terrified during this time and that "plainclothes police officers were stationed downstairs to keep a close watch on us." Some disappointed workers decided to go to Guangzhou and seek help from the provincial government. On June 29, around 100 workers gathered and organized sit-ins outside the Bureau for Letters and Visits of Guangdong Province, but no officers received them. In order to save money they slept in a nearby small park. This lasted for a week, until June 6, when the provincial government told Shenzhen police to send them back to Shenzhen. The workers were escorted to vehicles by the police. In the Shenzhen factory, over 200 workers continued to guard the machines, but when power was cut by the employer, the workers felt too hot to continue, and a pregnant female worker guarding the factory miscarried at four months due to poor health.

## Three Spaces of Appearance

The entire protest event relied on the concerted efforts of worker, sympathetic citizens, activists and the media to enlarge the space of appearance. Their appropriation and improvisation of physical and virtual spaces opened up a multiple front of resistances. When the workers started to strike, block access to the factory, stage sit-ins and hold gatherings outside the local police station, launch hunger strikes, and guard the factory, the original meaning and nature of these spaces shifted: The factory was transformed from a production base where they are exploited, to a stage for the workers to perform on; the physical spaces outside the government departments and police stations were also temporarily used as sites where the workers could make claims. Concerted actions had also emerged from these sites where a "complex interdependence of domination and resistance" (Pun 2005, 194–95) was constituted.

In recent years, scholars have increasingly emphasized the relation between political struggles and spatial transformation, but there has been little work done on the particularity of spatial strategies in China (Sewell 2001; Miller 2000; Keith 1997). More specifically, the field of China protest movements rarely pays attention to dimensions of space and acts of spatial appropriation (Nicholls et al. 2013). One exception is Zhao Dingxin's book *The Power of Tiananmen*, in which he analyzes how the spatial configuration of the built environment influenced the mobilization of the Tiananmen protest in 1989. In a recent article, he further proposes that built-environment-based spatial strategies "are crucial for participant mobilization with weak organizational involvement" (Zhao 2013, 233).

### State Space

The Artigas workers chose to gather at the gates of government departments (including street offices, letters and visits offices, trade unions, and police stations) to make claims. One of the main reasons for doing so is because, in mainland China, the state remains the crucial site for actualizing citizenship rights and welfare provisions. It is a relatively acceptable way to lay claim to the state. This performative action has profound cultural implications. In mainland China, humble petitions to the government, which follow an established set of procedures in "appropriate" ways, are the most familiar way to foster the condition of appearance. Petition offices, people's congresses and courts, which are designed to enact a particular performance of state power, are more frequently converted into temporary spaces of appearance where people come together and interact. Although organized protest is severely limited, these official institutions can be "reworked" to provide the space for and increase the legitimacy of mass gathering. These practices constitute a strategic appropriation of "state spaces" of profound symbolic meaning.

In mainland China, the built environment of government departments is the most accessible area through which protestors can reach government officials. The government buildings usually have a square from which crowds of people are banned: these state spaces and buildings (including government gates, squares, and nearby streets) tend to be heavily monitored. Performative power, however, emerges when workers engage with and appropriate these spaces. Massive bodily presence around these spaces is persuasive and can constitute tangible sources of power (Sutton 2010; Peterson 2002). Mass gathering around government offices can be seen as an *exercising of freedom* that expands upon state-imposed norms of visibility, where the audiences include officials, ordinary citizens, and the media. Random, nonviolent, and petition-based mass action provides an important mode of political expression:

> In a way, the collective assembling of bodies is an exercise of the popular will, and a way of asserting, in bodily form, one of the most basic presuppositions of democracy, namely that political and public institutions are bound to represent the people, and to do so in ways that establish equality as a presupposition of social and political existence. (Butler and Athanasiou 2013, 196)

As a practice that follows traditional Chinese cultural scripts, petitioning is a more prescribed and permitted form of performative politics in terms of transmitting the message of respect and obedience. Usually petitioners reiterate and demonstrate compliance with regard to state norms. Since the workers regard the governments as potential allies, their actions around state spaces are generally more restrained, cautious, and moderate. Since collective petitions are a form of quasi-legal action, the governments will not expel the petitioners immediately but tend to take a wait-and-see approach. However, the scale of the Artigas workers' petitions was too small to pose a threat, and this partly explains why the upper-level government did not immediately intervene. Ultimately, the workers did not produce a sufficient performative force to trigger favorable intervention; instead, the government arrested the workers, confiscated the bank cards of workers making petitions, and repatriated them in a forceful manner.[18]

*Factory Space*

Compared to collective petitioning, factory occupation, a way to put the body on the production line in its insistence and vulnerability, is a kind of *disruptive* action that enables the workers to subvert their assigned positions and speak up. Compared with state spaces, the factory provides a more convenient and accessible space for exerting performative power. Unlike the 1990s laid-off workers of state-owned enterprises who occupied the factories in the name of "protecting public property" (Chen 2004), the new migrant workers occupy their factories in the name of "legitimate (or legal) rights" (*hefa quanli*). There are different ways for workers to wage their struggle to retain control of the factory. Apart from strikes, workers can set up barricades to block access to the factory, or block spaces around the factory. However, disruption works better if the factory remains productive. When the employer no longer relies on the workers' production, or plans to abandon the factory—as in the case of Artigas—disruptive actions are much less effective.

In order to recover wage arrears or compensations, the workers prefer to occupy facilities inside the factory or to prevent the equipment or raw materials from being removed. There are a number of factors prompting the workers to occupy the factory, including an absconding boss, bankruptcy, or a relocation or acquisition which produces unpaid salaries or layoffs. In a factory supplying Japanese TDK in Dongguan in 2013, the workers stayed in the factory for four months demanding compensations (*Labor Newspaper* 2013; NetEase Finance 2013; *Singtao*

2013).¹⁹ In December 2012, workers at the Foshan Nanhai Xianghe shoe factory staged work stoppage and guarded equipment after the factory's production line and equipment were transferred to Chengdu (Liu 2012). In April 2015, thousands of workers in a shoe factory in Panyu District, Guangdong, staged a strike and slept on the grounds of the factory to prevent the employer from removing goods, due to their dissatisfaction with the compensation and social security funds caused by relocation (*Bastille Post* 2015).

Factory occupation symbolizes the workers' refusal to be exploited. Through the act of occupation, the logic of private ownership is contested, and the occupied factory becomes a temporary site of collective discussion, self-management, and solidarity. When they referred to the workplaces as "theirs," the Artigas workers invoked a broader collective sense of ownership and belonging. In short, the symbolic meaning of seizing a factory is that it belongs to the workers, and that they reclaim the right to keep it.

*Consumption Space*

The body, Butler argues, is "constituted in a sociality that exceeds us" (2011), and thus has its "invariably public dimension" (2004, 26). In other words, it is "outside itself, in the world of others, in a time and space it does not control" (Butler 2009, 52). Compared with a heavily guarded space of the state and the factory, sites of shopping and commodity consumption provide a more deterritorialized space of appearance from which to expand their audience base and become visible to a broader public. Consider the cross-border connection of the UNIQLO protests: they involved a Hong Kong company and the global fashion brand, and Shenzhen is adjacent to Hong Kong with its relatively liberal media culture, making it possible to extend the time and space of appearance. Consequently the protest event was formed into images and narratives and soon spread via the media, which fueled a series of global responses and formulated a politics of exposure in support of the workers. The extension of the space of appearance was made possible by what Butler (2011) calls the attempt to "appear to one another" and to establish relations:

> [W]e appear to someone, and that our appearance has to be registered by the senses, not only our own, but someone

else's, or some larger group. For the Arendtian position, it follows that to act and speak politically we must "appear" to one another in some way, that is to say, that to appear is always to appear for another, which means that for the body to exist politically, it has to assume a social dimension—it is comported outside itself and toward others in ways that cannot and do not ratify individualism.

Activists went to UNIQLO stores in cities around the world to protest. Since these stores are often situated in metropolitan business centers, large numbers of consumers witnessed these events. In similar cases, workers and supporters stood at the gate or inside the store, with the company's logo or products as the background, shouted slogans and held up such banners as "Resistance Against Unscrupulous Enterprises," "Sweatshop," "Stop Corporate Greed," "Job with Justice," and "Fulfill Corporate Social Responsibility." They also submitted a statement to the store manager, distributed leaflets to consumers, and circulated images of the protest on social media.[20] All these concerted actions made public the protest and extended its temporal and spatial boundaries. To conclude, the transformed state, factory and consumption spaces constitute "the multiple arenas of reactions and transgressions of the subject that crisscross and surpass the boundaries of conventional understandings of resistance" (Pun 2005, 194).

## Bodily Vulnerabilities

Creating a space of appearance requires intense collective bodily presence and bodily endurance, while bodies exposed to a police force are highly vulnerable and at risk (such as was the case with a female worker's miscarriage during the occupation). Since the workers' bodies were exposed to resourceful opponents, they became tired, sick, and exhausted, especially in the face of the employer's delaying tactics and police repression. During the entire process, the employer and the police sought to weaken the worker resistance by exploiting their bodily exposure and vulnerability.

The workers' bodies were precarious, but were also persisting, "insisting on their continuing and collective 'thereness'" (Butler and Athanasiou 2013, 197). In both sequences, the workers had to endure physical and emotional suffering caused by the exposure. In the first sequence, the workers guarding the factory had to sleep on the workshop floor in the cold winter. They slept and lived there, taking care of each other. In the second struggle, the workers were exposed to different physical challenges: the 100 workers making petitions in Guangzhou did not expect the provincial government to delay giving a response, and they felt physically and mentally fatigued. The workers staying in the factory slept on the floor or even on the equipment of the sweltering factory, while having to face constant harassment. During the protests, the police intimidated the workers, monitored them in the workshop, and arrested them. One respondent commented, "It was exceedingly terrible back then. I saw people passing [the factory] take photos, and the police immediately arrested them, searched their bags, confiscated their mobile phones, and sent them to the local police station . . . The police asked them if taking photos was 'interesting' without anyone paying attention to you." According to another worker, "plainclothes police officers were everywhere and looked for someone in our residence, so we dared not go outside for two to three days. They [the employers] knew our addresses, led the police to our residences, and arrested people in the name of inspection late at night. We felt highly terrified." The employer installed surveillance cameras inside and outside the factory and cut off power from time to time in order to force the workers to abandon their action. This strategy produces certain effects on the bodies: several workers fainted and could not continue. "The workers staying in the factory like us suffered," a female worker told me, "they [the employer] deliberately switched off the air conditioning, but we still dared not to stay away from the machines." Another worker recalled that "the employer kept broadcasting and repeating statements with speakers in such a high decibel that our ears almost could not stand it." All these experiences caused a proliferation of fear that articulated the process of subject-making in the face of risk. Fear contains and "shrinks bodily space," and restricts "bodily mobility in social space" (Ahmed 2004, 64). This is part of the reason why the workers' actions were ultimately confined to the limited space of factory and residential areas.

Although the protestors performed resistance over their bodies, the very bodies for which they struggled are not ever quite their own but are embedded in a social network that exceeds them (Butler 2004,

26). In light of the lived experiences of Artigas workers, we can see that the bodies need to be taken care of in order to continue their protest. However, this could not be done by the workers themselves, who lacked resources. Instead, they attempted to place their bodies in a loose kin and ethnic network of relationships, sought external help, and used public platforms to ensure their bodies' survival. *Tongxiang* (native-place) connections, which are familiar to Chinese migrant workers (Pun 2005), were reconstituted by the workers—most of whom came from Guangxi province—to provide the most intimate support and protection. In order to maintain their physical strength, the workers took advantage of the convenience that their residence was close to the factory to take turns guarding the factory. Those guarding the factory prepared their own meals and those with families had their meals delivered by their families. Around the factory were cheap restaurants, shops, and fruit stands, which helped the workers to maintain their occupation.

This body's relationality was manifest not only in the workers' mutual care and affective commitment, but extended in the support networks formed through public appearance and media communication. As Butler (2011) points out:

> [A]s biological creatures who seek to persist, we are necessarily dependent on social relations and institutions that address the basic needs for food, shelter, and protection from violence, to name a few. No monadic body simply persists on its own, but if it persists, it is in the context of a sustaining set of relations . . . the space of appearance does not belong to a sphere of politics separate from a sphere of survival and of need.

For the workers petitioning in Guangzhou, the urgent problems to be solved were sleep and the supply of water and food. Starting on June 29, at first they were sustained by other workers' donations and lived in a small hotel, with four people sleeping on the same bed. However, their funding only lasted four days, and with no government response, they had no choice but to sleep in a small park nearby; and eventually even this was denied them. During this period, the workers had to gather at the government building during high daytime temperatures with money for one meal only. In order to raise funds, the workers used a donation box to raise money on the street, but this was stopped by the police. By July 3, the workers were physically and mentally exhausted, but remained through the weekend while government officials were off duty. The workers decided to obtain funds by initiating an online "crowd-funding" campaign, which provided them with daily basic spending requirements. The donations, however, were just enough to help the workers to survive the weekend. Some citizens also sent food and medical items to the workers.

## Conclusion

The Artigas workers' activism raises profound concerns about the pronounced precarity experienced by Chinese migrant workers. In mainland China, the body remains an indispensable resource for migrant workers' defense of collective persistence. With the profound changes in capitalist needs associated with the precarization of work, the vulnerable body of migrant workers faces increasingly insecure conditions of employment, life and struggle. Under the current production regime that is rooted in the deprivation of transient rural migrants, the laboring bodies of migrant workers are closely monitored, controlled, and exploited, and are treated as disposable. This logic of disposability, as intensified by "the shift toward a norm of a more flexible and precarious work" (Phillips and Mierres 2015, 11), is demonstrated in the enterprise's refusal to assume responsibility, and the government's unwillingness to intervene. The logic has also intensified the destruction of workers' collective livability with their rights to the future being violated.

This chapter has attempted to show how these workers use their bodies to fight this logic, and to elucidate the dynamics behind their actions. It situates their performative politics in the recent context of labor resistance, and conceptualizes their actions as the desperate attempt to overcome escalating precarity. In order to make their demands audible and visible, the workers—driven by the collective sense of fear for being deprived of a livable future—drew on an array of performative resources at their disposal. In particular, I emphasize the close relationship between the precarious body and the configuration of political space and describe how the body serves as a temporary site of political self-expression; how collective bodily presence exerts limited yet crucial performative force; how protesting bodies lay claims to and transform built environments into evanescent spaces of appearance; and how the distinction between public and private is overcome by various forms of concerted actions that emerge from the sites.

The analysis presented in this chapter illustrates how state responses shape the outcome of protest. Yet it has avoided the central question about the *conditions of performative possibility* for state intervention. More specifically, what has not been explored so far is why a protest event occurs, and how it unfolds within the boundaries of state tolerance. When, how, and under what circumstances does the repressive state react positively to the people? How does the Chinese state—characterized by its multiple layers of bureaucracies—engage with protestors? And how do protestors increase the legitimacy of their action by deploying symbolic and institutional resources available in state structure and political tradition? How do they address broader audiences? These questions constitute the primary interest of the next chapter, which focuses on the *strategic* dimension of popular politics.

# Part II

# Politics of Articulation

3

# Engagement with the State

If performative politics is about reshaping what is to be seen, when, and by whom (Fabricant 2009), under what circumstances do Chinese protestors assert their voices and show their grievances publicly? This chapter addresses the salient features of popular protests in mainland China, features that call attention to protestors' engagement with the state in the process of configuring performative politics. My analysis takes an interactive political-process approach informed by Tilly and Tarrow (2007) to discover the mechanisms shaping why a protest emerges and how it unfolds, as well as its local political opportunities, constraints, and outcomes at a "micro-social level of individuals and their interactions" (Jasper 2014, 645).[1] Popular political activities inevitably take place within limits set by political institutions such as the state, which can inhibit or facilitate their development (Tilly and Tarrow 2007, 83–84). The contentious mechanisms and processes associated with such interactions involve not only claim makers but "targets, public authorities, and third parties like the media and the public in sequences of interaction." (Ibid. 10). If the protest outcome partly depends on the combination of multiple factors such as political contexts and social bases, what are the mechanisms and conditions that limit or enable people in specific institutional settings to make claims on governments and link them to others? What are the available "contentious repertoires" embedded in state structures, and the dramatic actions they adopt to construct a recognizable identity and to elicit favorable state responses? How do protestors interact with other political actors, in particular the state, to bring a new situation into being? How do they respond to the regime's opportunities, constraints and threats? How does the state hierarchy react to the claims? I will draw on cases from two distinctive protest trajectories that have mobilized a certain set of political effects.

The argument that will be put forward is that the state, despite its attempt to depoliticize and neutralize popular political activities, is disposed to create, accommodate, and co-opt forms of performative politics. It still figures as the main receiver of contentious claims and plays a key mediating role in monitoring local governance and "certifying" popular protest. Where state narratives dominate almost all public speech, decisive changes in political opportunity structure, in particular cracks from within the state, have encouraged the people to bring their discontents to higher levels. Meanwhile, protestors have also created a degree of political agency by engaging with the state in creative ways, most commonly in terms of the appropriation of its symbolic resources (such as discourses, slogans, and directives) that provides necessary legitimacy and leverage for struggle. However, those groups have also taken advantage of the new media environment to increase their visibility; they have attempted to exploit the inherent tensions between the center (*zhongyang*) and peripheral or local power networks; and finally, they have staged and engaged in a range of disruptive activities so as to trigger positive intervention. All these practices are characteristic of the unfolding of performative politics in the post-Tiananmen period, one characterized by an ambivalent, symbiotic, and interdependent relation between popular politics and the state.

In light of the above, this chapter focuses on the shifting institutional context of state authorization, where the state and its agents formulate a peculiar political relation with protestors who are characterized by different modes of being dispossessed and strategies of government-connected contestation. This chapter delineates some of the features of the entanglement of the state and protestors, with an emphasis on how the former has opened up new possibilities—however limited and precarious—for the latter to make rights claims performatively through a series of contentious interactions and negotiations. People's rights struggles, as manifested in a multiplicity of expressive activities, scenes, and relations, cannot produce effects without what Tilly and Tarrow (2007, 70) call the "constitution of collective actors," and the activation of "identity boundaries" that already exist. Instead of seeing the Chinese state as uniformly centralized, repressive and intolerant, this chapter explores the complex ways protestors seek out different performative strategies and modes of interaction among multiple divisions and alliances, which are central to mainland China's political formation in the post-Tiananmen period.

## Alliance with the Center

The becoming of political subjects is located within the specific context of governmental configuration, where governmentality is understood as "relations within social institutions and communities and . . . relations concerned with the exercise of political sovereignty" (Gordon 1991, 2–3). In mainland China, the restructuring of state-society relations has also made state surveillance more difficult, and left local governments with fewer resources to deal with popular discontent. The proliferation of mass demonstrations, strikes, and sit-ins across the country has prompted the state to become more aware of the need to rebuild popular support by accommodating protest. As Sigley (2006, 52) observes, "the socialist market economy does not demand the 'retreat of the State': it simply requires the State to intervene in different ways, one that combine neoliberal and socialist strategies." There has been a tradition of a benevolent ruler dispensing justice in ancient China, which has increasingly regained momentum in recent years. Although popular input with regard to policymaking was limited in the 1990s, mounting social unrest has led the state to pay more attention to institutional reforms. Since the Hu Jintao and Wen Jiabao administration, the state's policymaking has become more people-centered, with a populist tinge, addressing the need to pay more attention to mass discontent and follow a more people-friendly development model (Lin 2006). To regain regime legitimacy, the state has repeatedly emphasized its commitment to improving the welfare of the people, and promulgated directives warning local governments against power abuse. It has sought to explore new strategies to meet popular demands, and strived to become more efficient and service-oriented. In the sphere of politics, the state's shift of focus in policymaking has provided an avenue of legal and symbolic resources for protestors to negotiate governmentality.

The shifting relation of institutional power within the state hierarchy explains why performative politics operates on the border of the state's claim to legitimacy, which has had a profound impact on the form of contentious interaction. Since local governmental misbehavior has directly accentuated the suffering of people, it has increasingly become the prime target of discontent. Rather than creating new identity boundaries between "us" and "them," most contentious politics "activates or deactivates existing boundaries" (Tilly and Tarrow 2007, 80). This is also the case in mainland China, where the imagery of "evil local cadres vs. benevolent center" has been played out in many contentious episodes. Local officials are portrayed as what Laclau (1990, 69) calls the "antagonistic elements" that are presented as anti-community and anti-party. In constructing an oppositional identity and a sense of "us," protestors often call into question the legitimacy of local governments that claim to represent the people. They have frequently come into direct conflict with local authorities, and consequently they have demanded intervention from above.

In the face of intense surveillance and rampant repression by local officialdom, one crucial performative strategy is to seek potential allies from within the hierarchical state, and invoke the support of central leaders. This, however, requires an active reconstitution of the center as a positive political actor that can receive and certify claims. This strategy is not new: in Chinese history, there has been a long tradition of attracting the center's attention and support against municipal authorities (Perry and Li 1997). In the present context, the political forms of struggle remain determined by the *attachment* to the state. The invoking of the state's sovereign power enables protestors to perform at lower political risk. Even at local levels conflicting interests among governments and agencies at different layers, or between different departments, may also create openings for shaping ad hoc alliances (Cai 2010). To bring together a coalition, making claims that can be certified by the center is crucial:

> *Certification* occurs when a recognized external authority signals its readiness to recognize and support the existence and claims of a political actor . . . Certification thus changes both the new actor's strategic position and its relation to other actors that could become its oppressors, rivals, or allies. (Tilly and Tarrow 2007, 75)

Meanwhile, in order to deflect charges of anti-party, protestors frequently frame their actions in terms of rights defence or protection, and refrain from criticizing the CPC rule: instead they present themselves as being obedient to the CPC. As contentious episodes unfold, protestors are desperate to locate sympathetic allies within the state hierarchy who can offer favorable policy information or even intervene on their behalf. In Chinese political tradition the center has always enjoyed a more positive image than local officialdom, and has been seen as a potential ally to counter local power. Since the 1990s the restructuring of the state has further facilitated the conditions for such strategic, *invisible* alliances.

Nevertheless, the structural opening in itself is insufficient to facilitate struggle; one also needs to consider the *political* dimension of the configuration of state power, namely the growing emphasis on the task of stability maintenance (*weiwen*). In the 1980s, despite the loosening of state power, social stability was built on the state's effective control over society. Since the 1990s, with the radical reconfiguration of the structure of governance, the state-society linkage has been reshaped. In the present conjunction the center's growing concern for regime legitimacy in the wake of the 1989 incident has generated more top-down pressure on lower-level governments. The center has repeatedly denounced local cadres for misconducts and policy violations, which offers incentives to popular politics. Strikes are illegal in mainland China and demonstrations require official approval from the police, yet the center has left a space for isolated struggles to take place—as long as these protests are bounded in scale and non-regime-threatening. Although public disturbance is undesirable from the standpoint of the state, compared with local governments, it is more tolerant of popular protest that does not pose a direct challenge to the regime. The contradiction between local authorities' pursuit of growth and the state's concern for legitimacy has opened a crack within the hierarchy for protestors to exploit. The internal division within the center, however, suggests a double-edged sword, as Ching Kwan Lee observes against mounting labor unrest:

> Placing strict limits on workers' collective and autonomous organization, labor laws only allow for workers' individualized legal mobilizations, while the state uses these as a "fire alarm" mechanism that alerts local government to particularistic and particularly egregious labor violations . . . When the volume of labor disputes points towards certain serious

> abuses by the employers, the central government resorts to another round of legislation requiring more stringent labor protection . . . The promulgation of stringent labor laws, despite the strong state-capital alliance at the local level, suggests that the Chinese state at the center does not have homogeneous interests with regard to workers. (Lee 2016, 321)

The inadvertent alliance with a sympathetic bureaucracy also requires a tacit understanding among the people. Usually protestors are careful not to direct their attack at the CPC, while combining multiple tactics to arouse sympathy from officials in different tiers within the hierarchy. Despite their mixed feelings toward the state, protestors in general have a trust in its willingness and ability to solve their problems. They tend to view the center as "a source of legitimacy, a symbolic backer, and a guarantor against repression" (O'Brien and Li 2006, 68). Driven by the common belief that the center has benevolent intentions but cannot always find out what is happening below, Chinese protestors tend to believe that their mobilization helps check local misconduct, and that protests have become one of the ways the center gets to learn about wrongdoing (Ibid. 29). They do not demand radical regime change; rather, they seek support from higher-level authorities to increase their chance of success.

A shift in the method of maintaining stability has also created opportunities for protestors. The center's restriction on local governments' use of coercive means in dealing with mass incidents, for example, has weakened local officialdom's capacity and propensity to suppress protests. Local governments have been asked to solve conflicts at the initial stage, which implies that taking coercive measures may push lower-level governments into a vulnerable position. Under strong political pressure to maintain social stability, lower-level governments have become more cautious about adopting coercive measures to deal with unrest, because it is too risky to local cadres' careers. The shifting of governmental interests and of state-capital alliance has combined to reshape the mode of response to social conflicts:

> The search for change should begin with potential openings and shifts in state-capital alliances, and the dynamics of political-economic transformation in China . . . First, the

imperative of stability preservation, in addition to economic growth, has compelled local governments to play a more balanced role in brokering capital-labor relations, breaking a uniform pattern of pro-capital stances, especially in sensitive cases . . . Second, as local governments rely more on landed capital, land sales, and finance-driven speculative projects for revenues, officials may be more willing to discipline industrial capital that causes labor unrest and that tarnishes their performance record in stability maintenance. (Lee 2016, 330)

These new circumstances seem to have given Chinese people more space to make contentious claims. To avoid punishment from above, some local governments have changed their modes of response and become more willing to negotiate with protestors (Perry and Selden 2000). These emerging spaces and realignments explain why Chinese protestors generally support regime power and balance their actions with demonstrating obedience.

## Performative Use of State Norms and Disruptive Actions

Norms and conventions play a crucial role in the enactment of performative politics (Zivi 2012, 16). A performative perspective addresses the contingency of political conventions and norms, and the ways in which such norms can be transformed through reiterative performances (Rose-Redwood and Glass 2014, 13). Since the regime's hegemony is inherently unstable, it needs to re-enact the legal and political norms, which allows for the possibility for invoking them in order to influence government action. The law is initially employed by the state as a means to control struggle, and it is the very existence of state norms, laws, and claims on sovereignty that must be repetitiously invoked to legitimize and authorize forms that political subjectivity takes. Paradoxically, legal norms, which correspond to the state-imposed model of political normativity, enable the people to constitute themselves as political subjects in ways that appear "apolitical," by demonstrating that they have acted in the name of legal rights. These seemingly compliant, non-political and ritualized actions that repeat state norms, as encouraged by the opportunity structures, are crucial performative practices that allow Chinese protesters to claim agency and bring their political subjects into being. Here Judith Butler's argument is instructive:

> Butler's key argument is that the performative act of doing is precisely what brings the performer into existence through the repetition of the deed. The crucial point, for Butler, is that the political "subject" only comes into being—whether individually or collectively—in the performative act of political reiteration. The subject who performs a political action does not precede the performance but is rather constituted in and through it. (Rose-Redwood and Glass 2014, 8)

Despite the continuous reference to party and legal norms, the performative force and effect generated by collective actions often exceeds expectations. As Zivi (2012, 19) argues, "rights claims cannot be perfectly captured in terms of a set of conventions and rules . . . from the perspective of performativity, rights claiming is both a rule-bound and a rule-breaking practice that opens up the possibility of the new." While many such practices draw on a range of available, moderate repertoires tolerated by the state, some rights-seeking tactics are daring and confrontational, and involve violence that threatens public security. Peaceful petitions or marches, as forms of *modular* performance, can turn into more aggressive forms of direct actions when local authorities take a hardline approach. Chinese protesters "employ a variety of 'troublemaking' tactics, such as demonstrations, sit-downs, and highway blockades" to draw attention (Chen 2012, 4). Tactics such as setting up roadblocks and taking over government buildings can constitute a form of "political theater," where people come together as a collective force, turning any place into an arena for contestation, and calling the state to open up decision-making process. In China, the function of political theater is "to be heard," and the real audience is the authorities (Esherick and Wasserstrom 1994, 55). In some cases, their militant actions can force an emergency moment where the rule of law becomes temporarily suspended. Theatrical actions such as attacking state agencies, breaking into government buildings, or destroying public property have increased. The stripping of a party secretary in the street, as evidenced in the spectacular environmental protest in Qidong, represents a bold kind of radical tactic calling into question undemocratic decision-making.

Disruptive action often blurs the distinction between petitioning and disorder. "Every theatrical and political sequence," writes Hallward (2009, 149), "must invent its own stage." Disruptive tactics invent theatrical stages by causing chaos (*luan*) and signaling to the state that local officials have abused their power (Cai 2008). The bold, intensely visual display of condoms and alcohol found in Qidong government offices symbolizes the moral critique of power abuse. In some cases, the upper-level authorities respond by reversing decisions and disciplining local cadres. Such positive response encourages protestors to escalate the level of disruption beyond the confines of local authorities.

## Media as Space of Appearance

The media in mainland China plays a central role in enlarging the space of appearance, enabling protestors to address a wider audience and exert more pressure on authorities. Since extensive media coverage can often magnify the voices and bring lasting attention to the issue and prompt intervention, protestors have sought media coverage to increase visibility, which is "the element in which social sorting of people takes place, relegating some social groups into invisibility" (Brighenti 2010, 51). When media visibilities are increasingly incorporated into social action (Peterson 2002), new possibilities of performative politics are opened up.

The performative power of the media is unleashed in the context of state reconfiguration. With the spectacular growth of the media industry since the 1990s, people have wider access to state information, and more channels are made available to voice their discontents. While still facing harsh constraints, the extended media landscape has become more open to exposing scandals, to criticizing local governance and to discussing policy options favorable to the people. In the past decade, the center has urged local governments and the media to facilitate greater "information transparency" to monitor local governance. With the center increasingly emphasizing "public opinion supervision," the role of media in exposing local misconduct has become all the more important.

In mainland China, the media has become a decisive arena for protestors to formulate their politics of visibility. For the body of the dispossessed to generate political effect, it must enter the "visual and audible field" (Butler 2011). For Butler, media access offers a means of "transposing" the scene and exercising freedom:

> The street scenes become politically potent only when and if we have a visual and audible version of the scene communicated in live time, so that the media does not merely report the scene, but is part of the scene and the action; indeed, the media is the scene or the space in its extended and replicable visual and audible dimensions. One way of stating this is simply that the media extends the scene visually and audibly and participates in the delimitation and transposability of the scene. (Ibid.)

The partially liberalized media system has provided an important "stage" for protestors or activists to perform what Deluca (1999) calls "image events." As the following case studies on the Wukan protests and Honda worker strikes will illustrate, when dramatic images are spread out, the audience is broadened, allowing protestors to enter a wider visual field, and to gain international certification from "external actors" such as the foreign press and NGOs. Both struggles acquire an impressive international following, with new external actors weighing in and producing pressure on the state to recognize and negotiate with claim makers.

Image events can also scandalize authorities by making claims toward quasi-governmental and nongovernmental actors. The media controlled by upper-level authorities enjoy some degree of freedom in disclosing the misconduct of officials at lower levels. State media (such as CCTV and Xinhua News Agency) have become more open in dealing with local discontents: especially when the petition channels are blocked, people can approach the media and utilize their coverage. State media coverage is perceived by protestors as an expression of state recognition and certification, and a signal that "other media can do follow-up reporting." Some media practitioners even conduct "cross-border supervision" to extensively report events that have occurred in other provinces. Another key factor is overseas media. In the past few years, more and more overseas media have dispatched reporters to mainland China, who enjoy more freedom in reporting conflicts. When official media do not report, overseas reporters are warmly welcomed by the crowds.

New media forms, notably the Internet and mobile phones, have also reconfigured the distribution of the sensible, and enabled dissidents to evade censorship and construct alternative frames of perception. They have constructed their media spaces and produced images to sustain outrage and pressure. They have also deployed various tactics to turn the media into potential supporters. The circulation of dramatic images has often exceeded the local, and expanded what Rancière calls the realm of perception, visibility, and audibility. As Butler writes: "If there is a crowd, there is also a media event that forms across time and space, calling for the demonstrations, so some set of global connections is being articulated" (Butler and Athanasiou 2013, 197). Since widespread media coverage and heated online discussion often arouses enormous public sympathy, the government has sought to limit the power of image events. At any rate, the new media environment has reconfigured the ways in which grievances are heard and seen, and enhanced the organizing capacities of protestors in general. They use mobile devices and social media to disrupt the relation between the visible and the invisible. In both Wukan and Honda's sites of contention, the protestors created "a coalition of participants, supporters, and sympathizers at a much higher scale" (Tilly and Tarrow 2007, 75).

## Reappropriating "Mass-Line" Tradition

In addition to performative uses of state norms, the CPC's discursive commitment to socialism, despite its profound ambivalence in reality, has also provided useful resources for performative politics. In many contentious interactions, protestors are inclined "to work within the Party-State system," and "to use—and creatively extend—the ideals and norms of the state orthodoxy" (Cheek 2008, 21). Although the gap between official discourse and reality has generated deep disillusionment among ordinary people, the regime has not entirely abandoned its socialist tradition, but has "relied for its rule on the political legacy and ideological forms of the past" (Wang 2003, 57). In these circumstances the socialist legacy—including a set of ideals, vocabularies, practices, and party norms—has continued to be employed by Chinese dissidents performatively to challenge the lapses from official promises. They frequently "speak out against the abuses of power by using the norms and values embodied in Marxism-Leninism-Mao Zedong thought" (Cheek 2008, 21). There remains a visible, residual Maoism in popular politics. Permeated by the emphasis on egalitarianism, clean government and social welfare, the socialist heritage has opened up a reservoir of moral resources available for them to interpret and justify their actions. In many scenarios of struggle protestors have employed socialist discourse to legitimize their claims and reduce the risk of suppression. Moreover, the socialist tradition also has provided a "script" for performative politics. In some cases protestors have adopted the tactics, slogans, symbols, and organizational skills of past movements to stage political activities (Chen 2008). State-firm workers, for example, deliberately adopt particular rhetorical idioms or narratives inherited from the socialist past (Lee 2007b, 25–26, 114–20).

The state's "mass-line" tradition, with its emphasis on CPC-mass courtship and popular participation, as well as on flexible handling of specific local problems (Lin 2006, 185), has continued to facilitate popular politics. Although the regime has prevented mass movements in the wake of the 1989 incident, the impact of the mass-line tradition remains visible. For example, the state has allowed a certain procedural flexibility for protestors to make skip-level petitions and bring their grievances to upper-level authorities. This flexibility has also encouraged them to stage activities to trigger intervention. However, given the decentralized system and potential costs involved, higher-level intervention is rare and conditional. Authorities at municipal, provincial, or central levels do not usually interfere in small-scale unrests, so protestors need to cross a "threshold," that is, they need to create a state of emergency, to trigger intervention. This explains why many protestors choose to employ disruptive tactics in a way that higher-level governments cannot ignore. Upper-level governments will only decide to get involved in a few exceptional cases, where governments of different levels have failed to resolve conflicts with their available resources, or where the pressure to maintain stability and legitimacy is mounting as a result of suppression. As Cai (2010) suggests, disturbances that involve a large number of participants, serious casualties, or are widely covered by the media are more likely to trigger such interventions. In these cases the higher-level interventions involve the issuing of an urgent directive to lower-level governments, publicizing opinions through official media, or by forming a "work team" comprising party cadres and officials, and going to the site of disturbance to investigate the case and communicate with protestors directly. Disruptive actions are highly risky but are likely to generate an immediate impact and force the state to come up with a swift solution. Rural rights activists, according to O'Brien and Li (2006, 102), "strive to ensure that popular policies are carried out. And sometimes they succeed. Illegal levies are rescinded, manipulated elections are overturned, land seizures are reversed (or paid for), diverted funds are returned, victims of official violence are compensated, and rogue officials are brought to heel." When the state actively intervenes in worker struggles, Friedman (2014, 1011) observes, "they typically do not side completely with capital, but rather will seek to enforce compromise."[2] The intervention from above is not frequent and exceptional. When such intervention takes place, the practices of protestors have created a political synthesis, that is, the point of contact between the state and the people and the threshold on which popular power exceeds the constraints imposed by the state.

Figure 3.1. Map of Guangdong Province. The map was created by the author via the software Mapbox.V4.3.0, www.mapbox.com.

The following sections describe and analyze two events relevant to the unfolding of performative politics in mainland China. All the features of performative politics referred to—such as performative engagement with the central-local divide and the media, reiteration of state norms and discourse, alliance with the center, and the appropriation and reinvention of socialist traditions—are found in the cases presented below. Both cases illustrate the way performative politics can work to intimidate the state into making concessions.

*The Revolt in Wukan*

The contentious episode which unfolded on September 2011 in Wukan in Guandong Province, a coastal fishing village with a population of roughly 13,000 residents, exemplifies how the people have staged forceful actions so as to prompt the state to intervene and hold local officials to account. Many peasant rebellions associated with land dispossession have invoked Wukan as a model of defiance. Although the incident was widely portrayed by foreign media as a symbol of defiance against the CPC, its ultimate outcome was directly brought about by way of contentious negotiations with higher-ranking officials.

The villagers in Wukan had sought support from within the bureaucratic system: they had moved around the multi-layered administrative hierarchy of Guangdong to find sympathetic officials to support their cause. Wukan is part of the subdistrict of Lufeng city, a county-level city within the prefecture-level Shanwei city. From June of 2009, a group of aggrieved villagers had started to petition authorities at different levels to pay attention to the issue of farmland seizures and village cadres' corruption in Wukan, yet their appeals had been ignored. Wukan's frustration with land expropriation, however, is not an isolated case. In rural areas of mainland China the conversion of farmland into non-agricultural use in the name of economic development has been rampant, and has thus become the main source of tension after rural tax reform. Rural land, though nominally owned by the ill-defined "agricultural collectives," has been effectively controlled by village cadres, who have sought to benefit from leasing or selling the land for property development and for attracting investors. Since village cadres hold the deciding vote regarding land use, they have often abused their power and colluded with property developers to grab farmland without proper compensation. Although the state has repeatedly urged local governments to protect farmers' land rights and share the land-related income fairly, the enormous benefits from farmland conversion for government revenues and the opportunities for corruption have made it difficult to hold local cadres to account. This has created an opening for struggle. Since the frustration with local governance has run deep through rural areas, the resistance in Wukan has produced lasting resonance in other places suffering from similar longstanding abuses of power.

As in many popular political practices in mainland China, the villagers had sought to exploit the central-local divide to their advantage. They started by appealing to upper-level authorities in order to seek intervention from above. However, after exhausting all the authorized channels to address their grievances, the frustrated villagers had little expectation that the dispute would be settled through permitted means. Since local officials were unwilling to make concessions, the villagers had to resort to more disruptive tactics to apply pressure on the bureaucracy. Drawing the immediate attention of upper-level authorities and the media to propel intervention is a common tactic employed by Chinese protestors, and Wukan was no exception. The conventional form of peasant resistance ranges from transitory gatherings, collective petitions, and march demonstrations, to sit-ins, traffic blockades, and collective boycotts or refusal to pay. The more disruptive actions then include attacking government buildings and supply cooperatives, smashing police vehicles, surrounding purchasing stations and cadres, and carrying dead bodies to government buildings (Bernstein and Lu 2003). In the case of Wukan, they used some tactics inherited from the past, supported by innovative practices. The villagers held meetings to deliberate upon the issue, and decided to escalate their action by staging a mass rally that higher-ranking leaders could not ignore. On September 21, 2009, thousands of angry protestors took to the streets and knocked down the wall encircling a vast plot of land requisitioned by village cadres. They marched and chanted slogans. The numbers involved showed their strength and reinforced their moral legitimacy. Such actions are the manifestation of a gap in the sensible: "A demonstration is political not because it occurs in a particular place and bears upon a particular object but rather because its form is that of a dash between two partitions of the sensible" (Rancière 2010, 39). Moreover, for Butler, mass demonstration is a powerful performative that is yet to be captured by the law:

102 / The Politics of People

> Demonstrations are one of the few ways that police power is overcome, especially when they become too large and too mobile to be contained by police power, and when they have the resources to regenerate themselves. . . . This time of the interval is the time of the popular will . . . one that is characterized by an alliance with the performative power to lay claim to the public in a way that is not yet codified into law, and that can never be fully codified into law. (Butler 2011)

Disgruntled villagers marched to the Lufeng municipal government, holding up protest banners and shouting in unison "down with corrupt officials" and "return our land." Supported by strong clan structures within the village, the action was forceful and spectacular. Protestors erected roadblocks with tree trunks and covered the pavement with broken glass and bricks to keep out officials and the police force. Outraged villagers besieged government buildings, overturned police cars, and attacked the police station until riot police moved in. What happened at Wukan exceeded the limits imposed by the state.

Figure 3.2. The Villagers in Wukan Held Banners Bearing Their Signatures. They demanded the government to take action over illegal land grabs and "restore the truth" (*huanyuan zhenxiang*). Photo credit: Reuters.

The demonstration is not only an action but "a collective *inter*action" drawing different actors into contentious processes (Tilly and Tarrow 2007, 70). The rally was risky but it proved successful in generating more pressure on the local government. Although several villagers were arrested amid growing tension, new opportunities had been created at the upper levels. In Guangdong's administrative hierarchy, Wukan's cadres were not directly accountable to the provincial authorities, but to their local superiors at municipal and county levels instead. Under growing pressure from the villagers, the county administration decided to remove the village chief and party secretary from their positions to pacify the protestors, while the villagers refused to retreat unless other demands were fulfilled. In the occupied village, residents organized patrol teams, sneaked in supplies, and formed an ad hoc organization to negotiate with government representatives. Local governments, however, tried to silence the protesters and prevent them from approaching the provincial leadership. Several of the village representatives were subsequently named as criminal suspects and detained by police. On December 11 the conflict was dramatically escalated by the sudden death of a village representative in custody, forcing police and party cadres out of the village. Suppression triggered more clashes. As a result, the police sealed off the village in an attempt to cut off the villagers' daily supplies. Villagers began holding daily meetings to discuss countermeasures.

In the face of police blockade and domestic media censorship, the villagers made a concerted effort to gain access to foreign media. This can be seen as an attempt to reshape "the relationship between seeing, hearing, doing, making, and thinking . . . a conflict between a given distribution of the sensible and what remains outside it" (Rockhill 2004a, 4). As the event unfolded, it was obvious that foreign media and the Internet played a central role in exposing the misconduct of local cadres and generating persistent pressure on higher-level authorities. Due to Wukan's geographical proximity to Hong Kong and the expressiveness of the protest, the news was circulated widely to and through the media overseas and prompted heated discussion in Chinese cyberspace. Despite the police blockade and surveillance, a growing number of foreign reporters and sympathetic citizens managed to enter the besieged site to cover the protest, and were provided with free food and accommodations. In an attempt to encourage favorable coverage of their action, the villagers assisted foreign reporters in interviewing protestors and helped set up a media center to facilitate real-time coverage. A group of young villagers also used social media—in particular QQ, Weibo, and blogs—and mobile phones to disseminate information beyond the locality and to coordinate activities. All these joint efforts triggered an intense process of diffusion that effectively sustained media attention and attracted international support.

Like most popular political activities in the post-Tiananmen period the Wukan protest was aimed at locality-specific grievances and targeted local officials responsible for land use. The rally was bounded in scale and did not threaten the regime. As Hess suggests, "By positioning themselves against corrupt local cadres who are violating the center's policies rather than the regime itself," the "claimants can assert moral leverage in interactions with the state, minimize personal risk, and maximize their likelihood of victory" (Hess 2015, 182). In Wukan, there had been a deep distrust of local cadres and hope for intervention from above. Blaming local officials for damaging social harmony, the protest had never sought to overthrow the regime—in fact, the Chinese national flag was raised over the occupied site. In Chinese political tradition, protests have to be recognized as "patriotic" in order to be recognized by the state (Gladney 2004, 351). Throughout the process the target was strictly limited to "corrupt officials." The villagers had also been careful not to criticize the central government, displaying their loyalty to the regime by holding banners reading "We love the Communists" and chanting 'Long live the Communist Party' in unison. To minimize the risk of suppression, Wukan's protest leaders, who were acutely aware of the potential threat to the regime, kept emphasizing that the rally was not intended to challenge CPC rule, and called on the central government to come and investigate the issue. They upheld the directives and policies of the CPC, framed their demands as being in step with the legal rights endorsed by the regime, and urged villagers to abide by the law and regulations. According to Cai (2010, 15), a protesting group's position "will be strengthened if its issue is tied to other salient issues in a mutually beneficial way (that is, solving one issue helps to solve the others)." In the case of Wukan, we also saw an effective use of issue linkage to increase the chance of favorable intervention from above: beside the issue of land expropriation and compensation, the protestors related their grievances to problems of corruption and rigged elections for the village committee that held the power to control the sale and allocation of land. By doing so, the villagers were able to place pressures on their adversaries and consolidate their bargaining position.

The villagers' actions were successful in drawing provincial leaders' attention. The protest rally broke out at a time when the then-provincial party secretary of Guangdong province, Wang Yang, was seeking promotion to a top-level leadership position and thus wanted to avoid anything that would damage his prospects for promotion. Wang Yang attempted to defuse the unrest through negotiation and conciliation instead of suppression. To come up with a resolution, the provincial leader dispatched a working group to Wukan to conduct an investigation and negotiate with village representatives, bypassing the county-level administration that Wukan villagers no longer trusted. During the negotiating process the village representatives put forth three demands: the immediate release of three villagers detained by police and the return of the body of a protest leader who died in police custody; recognition of the authority of the ad hoc village committee; and a solution to the land dispute in accordance with the law. The provincial delegates swiftly agreed to make concessions and promised a probe into the alleged abuses, which brought an end to the protest. As a result, corrupt cadres were sacked, the controversial property project was frozen and elections were held according to the rules and regulations, with the protest leaders elected to the village committee to redistribute the land. One of the protest leaders was named the party secretary of Wukan.

## The Honda Worker Strike

On May 17, 2010, a strike erupted at the Honda parts plant in Nanhai, a district of Foshan city, also in Guangdong province. More than 1,800 workers from the factory joined the strike to demand higher wages, paralyzing all of Honda's production chains in mainland China. Although the struggle was mainly driven by young migrant workers' demand for wage rises to maintain their livelihood, the demands they put forward also involved reorganizing the trade union. In mainland China unions are subordinate to the leadership of the state: they have been tightly controlled by different layers of the state and enterprise management, and thus have failed to offer an effective avenue to protect labor rights. "When collective disputes arise," Lee (2007a,

246) observes, "the unions' priority is generally to defuse potential protests, communicate workers' demands to the government, and prevent any escalation of tension, for example, by persuading workers to apply for demonstration permits." However, the Honda strike, which would provoke widespread worker resistance beyond its locality, created a new political space for the workers to voice their discontents directly to management and circumvent the pro-management unions. The outbreak of the strike, which attracted widespread coverage from domestic and overseas media, encouraged workers elsewhere and triggered a strike wave in 25 factories across the country, with 38 strike actions occurring between May and August (Elfstrom and Kuruvilla 2014, 453–80). Japanese-invested automobile production lines in the Pearl River Delta region were most affected, with Honda's assembly factories forced to halt production because of the shortage of supplies. Although these strike actions were largely unorganized, sporadic, and isolated from each other, they forced a state of emergency and ultimately triggered state intervention.

Chinese workers have found different ways to organize themselves as a political force, and create dramatic political sequence that exerts pressure on the state. The Honda strike was marked by the militant workers' flexible appropriation of conventional and new scripts to stage resistance. Their militancy was expressed in both linguistic and nonverbal forms of performativity. For Rancière, democracy is "first and foremost the invention of words through which those who do not count get to be counted, thus blurring the well-ordered partition of speech and silence which constitutes the community as a 'harmonious animal,' an organic totality" (cited from Citton 2009, 137). In mainland China, the vocabularies of socialism allow workers to speak up against the undemocratic regime. Socialist slogans and symbols, for example, were frequently employed by the workers to seek moral justification and frame grievances. During the strike the workers "walked around the factory singing patriotic songs and shouting patriotic slogans" (Meng and Lu 2013, 472). The striking workers also drew on socialist discourse to criticize labor exploitation by foreign capital (Gray and Jang 2014), and adopted some elements manifested in past struggles. In Foshan the workers called on people to join a "collective walk," similar to the tactic employed by a mass rally against a chemical factory in Xiamen in 2007 (Beja 2011). Nationwide media also offered external support and increased visibility. Even the official media showed sympathy for the workers' action before being restricted by the central government. In order to gather firsthand information from the striking factory, the magazine *Caijing* went so far as to intervene in the bargaining process by inviting a prominent labor law scholar to serve as the striking workers' legal advisor (Wang 2011). This process had contributed to an enlargement of the space of worker dissensus, namely "the splitting up of sensible appearances themselves . . . The political always consists of splitting up the common space and adding additional issues on it" (Rancière 2014, 1718).

From a Rancièrean perspective, "[t]o become a political subject is to be heard and seen, and politics is the process of reconfiguring the ways in which subjects are heard and seen" (Davis 2010, 91). The Internet, a favored means of mobilization in mainland China, was crucial to reconfiguring the way of seeing and hearing, especially after domestic coverage was curtailed. The striking workers involved in this strike wave were "a new generation of young, tech-savvy workers" (Martin 2015), whose organizational capacity had been enhanced by appropriating social media to disseminate information, share experience, discuss protest strategy, mobilize action, and seek support during the strike. Before the strike the two leaders chose to hand out leaflets

Figure 3.3. The Honda Worker Protest. In Foshan, the workers took a "collective walk" to draw attention. Photo credit: Reuters.

to fellow workers. A QQ group was established the night before the action, where participants discussed all kinds of things related to the strike action, such as "when to meet, when to walk out and how much pay we want" (Barboza and Bradsherjune 2011; Beja 2011, 3). As the strike unfolded, however, the protestors avoided using QQ in favor of text messaging to escape web censorship. Information about the action was quickly spread by mobile phone to fellow workers in other production units to facilitate communication among workers. These technologies were deployed to publicize the workers' plight to prospective supporters, including uploading videos to social media to demonstrate the suppression by management and the unions. Partly due to the tactical appropriation of media resources, the Honda strike lasted until June 4, and was brought to an ended after the workers were promised a pay-raise package. In addition to the engagement with media resources, the workers sought to seize this emerging legal space to negotiate with the management and seek legal protection from the regime (Meng and Lu 2013).

On May 20, 2010, negotiations took place between management and the worker representatives elected by the strikers themselves, yet the dispute remained unresolved. In late May, with the continued stoppage of factory production, the local government and factory management decided to adopt a hardline approach to suppress the strike. Meanwhile, domestic media had been ordered to play down their coverage of the strikes to avoid copycat actions. These tactics had failed to force an end to the work stoppage, however. The persistence of worker militancy, which caused immense economic losses on the part of manufacturers, exerted more pressure on upper-level authorities to intervene. In mainland China, struggles carried out in the name of livelihood or the rights of the vulnerable tend to enjoy a degree of tolerance. The state's promise to create a harmonious and stable environment for economic development, as well as national leaders' call for improved working conditions, also offered symbolic support for struggle. In the case of Honda strike, although lower-level officials and the pro-management unions sought to deter the strikers with threats and violence, they began to shift their modes of response after the disruption drew the attention of higher-ranking leaders. With the escalation of unrest, the state, driven by its concern for regime legitimacy and by a fall in foreign investment, soon realized that repression alone did not seem a viable option to contain the strike.

A more flexible approach was needed to defuse the protest. Provincial leaders' accommodating attitude toward tackling the strikes was decisive at this point: during the strike the party chief of Guangdong, Wang Yang, openly called on enterprises to improve their treatment of workers, and expressed support for resolving dispute through collective negotiation. On May 29 the Standing Committee of the Central Politburo, the highest-level political organ of the Chinese state, held an emergency meeting, and required that "all levels of government intervene in negotiations between employers and workers, that the workers' interests be protected" (Wang 2011). Guangdong's party chief was called in to brief the politburo. As a result of the intervention of top-ranking leadership, the situation was reversed. What followed was a dramatic shift in the lower-level government stance from outright repression to accommodation. The Honda management, which had previously relied on coercive measures to deal with the strike, had come under heavy pressure from the state to settle the conflict through negotiation. The Chinese chief manager of the Guangzhou Honda joint venture partner, who was also a member of the National People's Congress, was called into the negotiation process with the workers. Factory production was temporarily resumed on June 1. After rounds of negotiations, both management and the strikers made concessions to settle the conflict: all demands regarding union representation were dropped, while management accepted a revised wage package and brought an end to the strike.

## Conclusion

The political significance of performative politics should be situated in a particular relationship of the forces unleashed during the process of state reconfiguration since the 1990s. This chapter has looked at the specific condition of possibility and constraint for performative politics, in particular the shifting and ambivalent role of the state in configuring new patterns of political interaction. The analysis presented in this chapter addresses the ambiguity of the Chinese performative context, where there are no opposition parties or an effective legislature, and the state-society relation has evolved a distinct trajectory. In mainland China popular politics has evolved an intimate relationship with the state, and the distinction between two is not self-evident.

Although existing studies have attested to the way "persistent collective acts produce an aggregate impact on high-level authorities that makes policy changes possible" (Cai 2006, 117), there has been an arguably instrumentalist and rationalist tendency that privileges predetermined opportunities, incentives, costs, and benefits, without situating popular struggle within the broader political dynamics of state re-legitimation, and taking into consideration the performative possibilities created by the redeployment of state norms and symbolic resources. In existing studies, opportunity tends to be reified in terms of formal structure of power, or as derivative of institutional, rather than something being created and enacted in concrete expressive practices through which individuals become rights-seeking subjects. Even if some scholars recognize that "contentious interaction takes place within limits set by political opportunity structure, regime controls, and available repertoires" (Tilly and Tarrow 2007, 84), it is necessary to point out that the opportunity structure is not completely frozen or predetermined by party elites, and controls are constantly contested and redeployed by protestors performatively. These contingent practices, rather than the static structure alone, create possibilities of agency and political spaces for struggle. The predominant focus on material interest and economically driven actions in the field of Chinese protest movement studies (for example, Cai 2006; O'Brien 2008) runs the risk of militating against a *political* analysis that takes into account the subversive effects of expressive actions. This chapter argues that although the structural condition of state intervention is crucial, it has to be understood in terms of the state's legitimation crisis, *and* the counter-hegemonic practices of the people that create and exploit the crisis.

If most of the protests in mainland China are marked by a lack of *horizontal* articulation among different groups, Hong Kong represents a distinctly different way of articulating performative politics. Compared to mainland China, the enclave offers a more favourable strategic condition where popular political activities are embedded in a multi-party structure, and enjoy more freedom to formulate alliances. Due to the different institutional context and political culture, the political form of popular mobilization and interaction with the state can often entail different levels of disruption and intensity. The next chapter describes the ways political activism is performed in a postcolonial context of legitimation crisis. What are the fundamental contradictions in Hong Kong? How do Hong Kong protestors create and sustain their spaces of appearance and encounter? How do they escalate actions and organize themselves in the face of political risks? How do participants negotiate differences, make decisions and formulate solidarity? The next chapter seeks to address these questions by shifting the analytical focus to the internal organizational practices and tendencies characteristic of the two spectacular events of public space occupation.

4

# The Two Occupy Movements in Hong Kong

In September 2014, the Hong Kong Federation of Students (HKFS) launched a general class boycott to protest against the resolution of the National People's Congress Standing Committee (NPCSC) regarding the upcoming Chief Executive and Legislative Council elections in Hong Kong, which were seen by the opposition as "depriving Hong Kong people's democratic rights." The student action escalated with protestors besieging Civic Square at the government headquarters. After the police arrested many student leaders and activists, thousands of protestors swarmed onto the streets of downtown, shouting loudly "release the students" and "we want true democracy." The police could not disperse the swelling crowd, even using pepper spray. The protestors resisted the pepper-spraying with umbrellas, which immediately became a global media spectacle and amplified the disobedience across the city. Failing to disperse the crowd that evening, the police fired teargas bombs at the protestors, who spread to other areas and occupied other urban centers of Hong Kong and Kowloon Islands. The occupied streets quickly became a space of gathering resistance to state power. The movement developed into a full-scale political protest, with an estimated one million people taking part.

The protest rally against the electoral arrangements, described by the media as "to throw an egg against a rock," did not come out of nowhere. Over the past decade, Hong Kong has been undergoing a process of radicalization and a dramatic shift in protest tactics, with an increasing number of people protesting self-consciously in the style of the Occupy movement. The inspiration for this copycat act is Occupy Wall Street (hereafter OWS) and the emerging Occupy movements

Figure 4.1. Map of the Hong Kong Special Administrative Region. The map was created by the author via the software Mapbox.V4.3.0, www.mapbox.com.

across the world. Before the NPCSC decision was announced, a group of scholars, politicians, students, and activists had planned to launch a large-scale protest movement in the name of "civil disobedience." However, the organizers did not expect that some 200,000 participants would turn out, and that the confrontation would continue for 79 days. Its explosive intensity and magnitude—which turned Hong Kong into a lawless city during the time of occupation—also surprised many. The protest movement paralyzed the city's major roads in the urban center, and its images spread across the global media.

Beijing authorities and pro-government media in Hong Kong severely condemned the protest action and referred to the role of "external forces." Amid widespread sympathetic media coverage in the West, a commentary in *The Telegraph* claimed that the protest posed "an existential threat to the Chinese Communist Party." (Ambrose 2014) The threat, though weakened by a leadership crisis, was deeply felt. On November 9, Chief Executive Leung Chun-ying met Xi Jinping, and stated that the protest was "the largest mass incident" since Hong Kong returned to China. Xi Jinping was quoted as saying that "Some tried to 'shake the sky' and attempted to take Hong Kong away from the authority of the central government in the name of political reform. We will never agree and they will not succeed." One commentary claimed that Hong Kong has "entered an uncertain period and it might be the start of a new era" (Yang 2014, 46–51).

What exactly was this "new era"? The movement had unfolded against the three dominant configurations in Hong Kong: "one country, two systems," the rule of law, and economic development. Although on the surface the protest movement has been motivated by the desire for a more open electoral arrangement, it was also driven by the territory's mounting tensions with mainland China since the 1997 handover. In the 1980s, during the negotiations between China and Britain over the territory's status, Beijing authorities established an alliance with the business class in Hong Kong. The official promise of maintaining "the capitalist society of Hong Kong for 50 years without change" and Hong Kong's "prosperity and stability" served to perpetuate the city's capitalist order and the oligarchical political structure left behind by the British, permitting the business elite's to continue to hold on to political power.

For many people in Hong Kong, the post-handover arrangements have continued to privilege the elite class, and the government's focus has been on economic development. Government policymaking, the Legislative Council, and the procedure of nominating and electing the Chief Executive, all remain dominated by the pro-Beijing coalition, which has treated the full implementation of universal suffrage as a threat to the status quo. Although the central government has sought to maintain Hong Kong's economic situation since the handover, rising inequality and dissatisfaction with government policies have continued to undermine the legitimacy of the regime. The frustration with the restrictive framework set down by the regime, mixed with a growing sense of discontent with the elite class, has produced an anti-government sentiment intertwined with anti-China nativism.

Since 2003, the territory has witnessed a new cycle of protests staged in the name of "protecting Hong Kong." The 2014 Occupy Central movement, with its intensified antagonism toward the regime, can be seen as the peak of this ongoing sequence vis-à-vis the Chinese state.

Hong Kong's Occupy movement has created a form of what Harcourt calls "political disobedience" (Harcourt 2013) with regard to the "one country, two systems" configured by the Chinese state. Occupy Central has increasingly become a symbol of anti-establishment politics in Hong Kong's political landscape since late 2011. This sequence first took shape around October of 2011, when a group of protestors occupied the space under the HSBC headquarters for 11 months (until evicted by the police on September 11, 2012), echoing the emerging global Occupy movement at that time. It became one of the longest-running occupations in Hong Kong. Although the scale of the 2011 occupation in Hong Kong was small and did not pose any threat to the status quo, the persistence of the occupation of urban public space and the democratic experiment conducted by the occupiers transformed the mode of popular political contestation in Hong Kong. Even though the movement finally failed, it has left a legacy for subsequent protest movements in Hong Kong: protestors occupy a public space, perform direct democracy, and engage in self-organization, as a political form against the state. Two years later, a brand new Occupy Central—with its focus on the limited electoral arrangements for choosing Hong Kong's future leader—came into being with a spectacular popular participation. Although the two scenarios of Occupy Central were different in their demands, compositions, and goals, both have been linked by disobedience against the dispositions of the neoliberal state. However they have split over tactics and ideologies, and both lacked a sustained leadership. If the resurgent global Occupy movement demonstrated "a rebirth of the political" (Mitchell 2013, xi), its implications for Hong Kong are far from self-evident and need to be understood in its own contexts. Despite some obvious differences, the two Occupy Central movements do share things in common: not only do they express the same desire to introduce democratic participation and decision-making, they also share a tendency toward "leaderlessness," as manifested in the resistance to organizational hierarchy and conventional political representation, as well as the lack of formal leadership structure.

Since the 1990s, the leaders of Hong Kong's social movement have been increasingly co-opted into the sphere of partisan and parliamentary politics, leading to the loss of autonomy and the instrumentalization of social movements. The subsequent "depoliticization" of partisan and parliamentary politics—characterized by the hierarchal organization and bureaucratization of political parties, elitism, and separation from the people—has prompted local social activists to search for a more democratic form that would be independent of conventional politics, with less emphasis on leaders' representative capacity and more on popular participation and spontaneity. The new social movement organizations have increasingly performed direct democracy, adopting a relatively open and decentralized decision-making approach involving popular mobilizations. They have also built up a range of issue-based, ad hoc alliances flexible in different situations (Ng 2013, 186–87, 197–98). It is in such an emerging space that the two Occupy movements performed their democratic experiments.

In a recent article on Occupy Central, Graeber and Hui showed how the first Occupy Central movement influenced the second, and argued that the 2014 Occupy movement marked a "genuine watershed" (Graeber and Hui 2014). However, what is absent from their account is how the limitations of the ostensibly spontaneous movements produced the opposite effect to their aims, and how the seemingly leaderless structure failed to build a mandate for effective political intervention. Despite their attempt to situate Occupy Central within a global context of protests, these questions were avoided.

This chapter provides an account and comparative analysis of the Occupy Central movements of 2011 and 2014. This research is based on field studies, analysis of media and movement discourses, and interviews with dozens of participants. Contrary to the romanticized notion of a leaderless movement and the celebration of Occupy Central as a spontaneous movement "without leaders and without the need of leaders" (Ma 2014, 2), the organizational problems that persisted throughout the occupation processes suggest that different lessons can be drawn. The first Occupy Central "set seeds of possibility, gave a sense of new modes of organizing, of direct democratic expression" (Graeber and Hui 2014), and its leadership and organizational problems resurfaced in the second Occupy protest. The historical and sociocultural conditions that facilitated a "leaderless" and "spontaneous" movement, and the consequences of these tendencies, require critical analysis. The case of Hong Kong, with all its ambivalence about hierarchy and representation, raises deep questions about the privileging of tactics over strategy in the context of the global wave of Occupy movements.

## The 2011 Occupy Central: Hong Kong as an Occupy Offshoot

The first Occupy Central in mid-October 2011 was influenced by OWS. The American movement's critique of financial capitalism, social injustice, and collusion between business and government fitted in well with the major issues of discontent in Hong Kong, such as corporate hegemony, "small-clique elections," and the functional constituencies of the Legislative Council that protect the status quo. Although in Hong Kong the government did not bail out financial institutions, the OWS slogan of "we are 99%" did offer an expedient protest frame to articulate local grievances. On October 5, 2011, a group called Socialist Action[1] organized a gathering to support OWS, and criticized the Hong Kong government for favoring business interests and ignoring social inequality. Another activist group, Left 21, also called for an Occupy Central action on Facebook. Since Central is the political and economic center of Hong Kong, "Occupy Central" symbolized that the protest was targeting Hong Kong's capitalist elite.

In the beginning, Left 21's purpose was to provide a platform for an "anti-capitalist" movement. In a city that has long "embraced capitalism" (Ma 2007) and where the left has long been weak since the suppression of the 1967 riots, this attempt was unusual and difficult. The group intended to articulate Hong Kong's local grievances through the rally, yet it did not have a clear idea about what to do next. It had never intended to undertake a prolonged physical occupation of the city's financial center. On the afternoon of October 15, the pedestrian area under HSBC headquarters was filled with crowds. Anti-capitalist banners were put up, and some 300 protestors came to the site, including activists, students, office workers, the unemployed, and curious tourists.

Political groups came from a wide spectrum, including the radical wing of pan-democrats' People Power and the League of Social

Figure 4.2. The Slogans Read: "Anti-MPF & Capitalism," "Down with Real Estate Hegemony, Strive for Worker's Rights." The occupiers protested against the problems associated with capitalism, such as the oligarchy of the real estate conglomerate. Author photo, November 10, 2011.

Democrats. Some of them took part in the annual July 1 rally and other protest movements against controversial development projects. Their demands were diverse and echoed Hong Kong's local problems: there were grievances with regard to housing prices, MPF schemes,[2] compensation from the banks on the loss of Lehman Brothers-related Minibonds, as well as demands for public housing, universal suffrage, and labor rights. A core group of participants began their occupation and ended up living there. In the pedestrian area, a public space of approximately 3,000 square feet under the HSBC headquarters, there were more than a dozen camps. The underground radio group FM101, which was forced to move because its lease had expired, provided generators, camping equipment, and sofas in preparation for long-term occupation. Those who stayed were mostly young people aged 17 to 30: some went to school and worked during the day and passed the nights in the camps. At night, when most people attended, the site took on the appearance of a carnival. Despite being labeled as an "anti-capitalist" rally, the squatters at the site had never attempted to physically attack capitalist institutions; rather, they protested against the problems associated with capitalism and attempted to establish a non-hierarchical autonomous collective inspired by OWS. A makeshift encampment and a new form of communal sharing were created. Participants shared food, supplies, and daily resources and constructed a living room, kitchen, computer area, and a library. They ate, chatted, watched films, listened to music, and even played badminton, in an effort to build up "non-capitalist" lifestyles and relationships. Some occupiers—in particular those advocating anarchism—said they intended to bring an element of everyday life into the site and saw it as a long-term fight against capitalism. Participants debated the problems of capitalism every night. Some discussions focused on Hong Kong issues, such as inequality, labor exploitation, and the capitalist monopoly of resources and politics. The mix of playfulness and critique, and their refusal to be co-opted by the political class, had attracted many younger people.

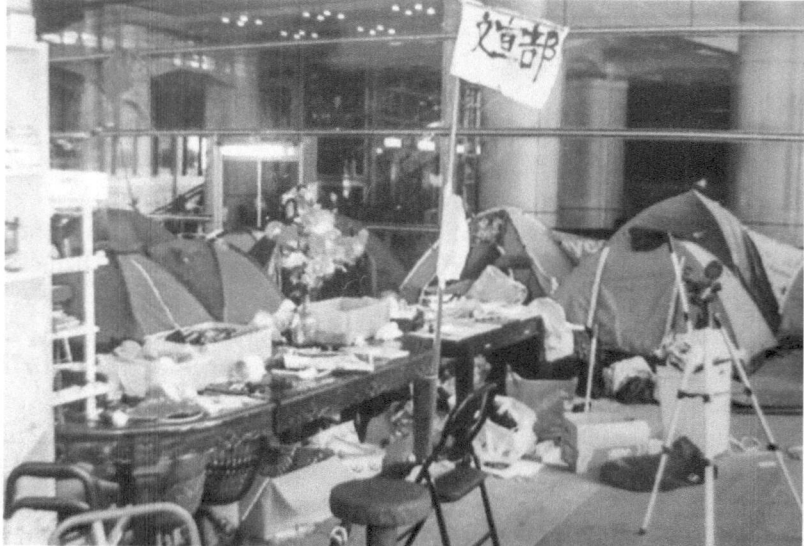

Figure 4.3. The Propaganda Department Area Set Up by the Occupiers. Anyone—with the consent of the participants on the ground—could make use of the occupied space. Author photo, December 23, 2011.

At the initial stage of the occupation, Occupy Central was widely reported by local media, most of which sympathized with the rally. However, compared to past protests, the scale of Occupy Central was far from impressive and it did not obtain a critical mass in support of its cause.[3] Capitalism, after all, has never been a significant political issue in Hong Kong. The jobless rate was relatively low at the time of occupation,[4] and the effect of the global economic crisis on Hong Kong was somewhat limited and only resulted in losses to Lehman Brothers' investors. With the intervention of the government, the banks that sold these products compensated most investors. In contrast to what happened in the United States and Europe, Hong Kong's financial institutions did not encounter serious problems, and the government did not have to save the banking industry through public funding. Therefore, despite mounting discontent with the collusion of political and economic elites, the rally was not expressly directed against financial institutions and the government. Although some socialist-minded participants called for a class struggle against capitalism, the rally never identified a specific target (Harcourt observed the absence of "adversary" in OWS, while this tendency seemed even more apparent in the Hong Kong case, Harcourt 2013). It also did not produce any tangible effect on the political mainstream or shift its language. Since the protest never amounted to a threat to the status quo, the government and HSBC remained tolerant and did not immediately evict the occupiers.

The most striking feature of Occupy Central is that it opened up a new space of direct democracy for participants—many of whom were discontented with Hong Kong's mainstream politics—to reject conventional politics and explore new forms of social organization. Without an obvious leader and a concrete goal, the occupiers formed a small community and started a social experiment seeking new ways of governing themselves. Anyone—with the consent of the participants on the ground—could organize study groups, show films, and hold music performances in the occupied space. The occupiers attempted to create an atmosphere of openness and friendliness by throwing parties and holding open discussions. With the withdrawal of Left 21, the occupation was increasingly dominated by the anti-capitalist anarchism of FM101 members. According to one of its members, the purpose of occupation was "clear at the beginning." However, hardly any effort was made to put up a united front, attract potential allies, or formulate concrete demands against the system. "We live here and this behavior is resistance to the model of capitalism," one occupier said. They practiced a lifestyle that did not depend on money and consumerism. However, it had become increasingly difficult to sustain long-term communal life in the occupied space, as the participants had to deal with problems of food supplies, sleeping conditions, and spatial limitations. Some people returned to the site after eating or slept in the makeshift tents after showering at home. Several days after the occupation, with people coming and leaving at different times, the number of occupiers was reduced to about fifty. Although the active members of Occupy Central had called for the complete overthrow of capitalism, the demand never succeeded in attracting many participants.

Despite its reluctance to embrace a leader, Occupy Central was not exactly a "leaderless" protest. Its core participants had been struggling to achieve leaderlessness, while paradoxically *leading* the entire occupation toward a more anarchistic style. Despite the refusal to assume leadership of Occupy Central, the FM101 members, who gave the scene a particular anarchic quality, were active in cultivating a non-authoritarian ethos, emphasizing the strength of direct participation, self-management, resource sharing, and collective decision-making in the occupied space. Some participants explained that although FM101 had been keen to achieve the goal of leaderlessness, they were actually the "invisible leaders" of Occupy Central. Drawing on the anarchist tradition and the practice of OWS, the members of FM101 refused to elect leaders and designate representative spokespersons, criticizing the vertical hierarchy and domination of the government, partisan politics, and traditional social movement organizations. They emphasized that participants' autonomy could not be restricted by any political parties or organizational leaders. Everyone, they insisted, had an equal opportunity to express their opinions, and differences in opinion should be respected. Their position was that decision aking with regard to the occupied space should be open to all and based on what they called "absolute consensus."

Although FM101's anarchist practices attracted supporters, the occupied site was increasingly divided by factionalism. Some Lehman Brothers customers, usually aged above fifty, supported Hong Kong's opposition parties and did not oppose capitalism. The anarchists did not agree with these Lehman Brothers investors and believed they were self-interested and cared only for their personal benefits. Some participants deliberately treated the occupation purely as a chance for experiencing an alternative communal life and had no desire to overthrow capitalism. These factions coexisted, but never united. It was a community without a sense of solidarity and commitment, and most occupiers lacked a sense of loyalty to the community. Although trade unions and social movement groups frequently organized activities on the ground, they never worked with the occupiers to formulate policy demands. In the following months, the occupation remained divided and unable to propose a unified, concrete agenda. Instead of focusing on the politics of anti-capitalism, what characterized many of the occupiers was opposition to the "one country, two systems" policy; however most people on the ground had little idea that the protest would have an impact on Hong Kong's popular politics.

Occupy Central's leaderless tendency did give many participants a sense of empowerment and provide them with a rare opportunity for experiencing alternative lifestyles, yet as time went on, this specific strength was increasingly offset by the absence of an effective leadership central to any popular mobilization. Occupiers were loosely "united" by an intense dislike of banks and corporations, but paradoxically this imposed severe limitations on the political possibilities available to them. The "absolute consensus" principle, which required that all occupiers consent on matters under discussion before implementation, paralyzed the occupation and the possibility of an articulation with regard to wider sociopolitical issues and contexts. Most interviewees admitted that the consensus model promoted by the anarchists was "extremely inefficient," and that the occupiers had spent too much time discussing how to hold meetings, the order of agendas, and basic procedural details. Moreover, since the occupied site was open to all and filled with groups and individuals from diverse backgrounds, it was difficult to cultivate a sense of solidarity and maintain a firm commitment to the ad hoc "community." Once new members joined in, past decisions—except those associated with uncontroversial daily affairs—were reversed and even rejected. Some occupiers complained that the refusal to engage with partisan politics had prompted the occupiers to withdraw from the political mainstream, thus turning them away from political structures. As a result, the occupation failed to ground its vision in concrete goals and strategies regarding broader social transformation. By early 2012, three months after the occupation, the encampment had lost its impetus. Although it had raised deep questions about Hong Kong's capitalist configuration and its link with politics, it failed to pose any challenge to the status quo, and eventually the remaining occupiers were evicted by the police. In August 2012, media surveys showed that 23 percent of citizens supported Occupy Central, 47 percent opposed it, and 55 percent agreed with the forced eviction. In the last few months of occupation, the protesters became increasingly isolated. Partly due to the weakness of the leaderless form and the lack of engagement with mainstream society and politics, the 2011 Occupy Central never obtained mass support: however, its experiment had inadvertently paved the way for another leaderless movement in Hong Kong that would confront the state in more radical and serious ways.

## The 2014 Occupy Central: A Locally Focused Movement

The 2011 Occupy Central presaged a new kind of protest movement in Hong Kong, and the notion of what it meant to organize a civil disobedience movement changed as a result. Although it failed to achieve the goal of overthrowing Hong Kong's capitalist system, the occupiers' determination to remain in the public space indefinitely and to experiment with direct democracy set a precedent for political activism in Hong Kong. The Occupy movement of 2014 has been characterized as a "sudden and unexpected revival of 'Occupy Central'" (Graeber and Hui 2014). However, compared to the first movement the second Occupy Central was more homegrown and locally focused, and was much more widely supported by pan-democrats, activists, and a large segment of the population from across the political spectrum. It was also much more resourceful and wide-ranging than the first movement, and attracted the attention of global media. In contrast to the first Occupy Central, the second occupation was not concerned with social and economic inequality, but focused on the implementation of a one-person-one-vote electoral system. The effect it had on the occupied districts was significant: roads were blocked, schools were closed, businesses—in particular small shops and retailers—were shut down, and government operations were suspended. Social order was severely disrupted.

The second version of Occupy Central could be considered a "post-Occupy Central" movement for two main reasons. First, although it was originally organized as a peaceful popular protest, and nonviolence was a core principle of the founders, after two student organizations broke into the Civic Square at government headquarters and were arrested by the police, the rally soon became dispersed and chaotic, prompting acts of violence. The crowds—some of them were supporters of far-right nativist groups and opposed to the pan-democrats—occupied the roads without following the instruction issued by student leaders, nor did they follow through on the ideas of Tai Yiu-ting, the co-founder of Occupy Central, who emphasized the values of love and peace (hereafter OCLP). When one protestor was asked if the movement could still be called "Occupy Central," he replied, "Occupy Central is a campaign of failure. Participants would be arrested and it is the end of the story, isn't it? It is a total failure. I would not support it. We stay here with everyone and we will not leave without government concessions. This makes better sense to me." This explains why OCLP leaders later emphasized that the movement was an "Umbrella Movement instead of a peaceful Occupy Central"

Figure 4.4. The Students Attempted to Occupy the Civic Square. The student action escalated with protestors besieging Civic Square at the government headquarters. Photo credit: Reuters.

campaign. Since the entire movement was derived from his idea on civil disobedience, some occupiers even suggested that Occupy Central "only belonged to Tai Yiu-ting" and that "Occupy Central never happened." However, the protest deviated from Tai's scripting of it.

The 2014 occupation was characterized by a flexible and fluid leadership structure. However, although the student leaders attempted to play down any differences between the protests camps, the movement was plagued by a lack of coordination between different factions and a deep division of leadership as the movement unfolded, which often led to tensions among occupiers. Although OCLP and student leaders had urged protestors to unite to better press their claims, their influence soon waned, and they were unable to organize the crowd. From the first day of confrontation, complaints were made that the movement had been "hijacked" by groups who were trying to "plant their flags." The refusal to be "hijacked" ran deep throughout the occupation. Although Tai Yiu-ting, more politically experienced than the militant protestors within the movement, emphasized that he was only a "founder" and "facilitator" and not a leader, he exercised a de facto leadership role in the preparation of the campaign. The OCLP leaders originally planned to kick off the protest on October 1, the National Day holiday, and cause limited traffic and business disruptions in the city's financial heart, with the idea being to pressure the government into accepting their demands for open elections. However, the radical tactics of the HKFS and Scholarism groups transformed the campaign into a protracted anti-government struggle and generated a shift in leadership toward the student leaders. After OCLP joined the protest and started a civil-disobedient campaign, its leaders were heavily criticized by student participants for allegedly "kidnapping and controlling" the movement. The original leaders of the movement were quickly marginalized by student leaders, and their influence confined within the Admiralty zone of Hong Kong. The two student groups, in particular HKFS, took the lead, particularly after the police used teargas in an attempt to clear demonstrators.

Compared to Scholarism, a rising school pupil-led protest group known for its leading role in an anti-national education campaign, HKFS was more experienced in street politics, having played a key role in the history of Hong Kong student activism. Founded in 1958, it participated in "Defend the Diaoyutai Islands" campaign, and after the 1989 Tiananmen protests it joined with the opposition and became

Figure 4.5. A Slogan Poster Writes: "I Boycott Classes, Because I Love Hong Kong." Author photo, October 22, 2014.

more involved in various kinds of activism in Hong Kong. At the time of the 2014 occupation, HKFS consisted of 14 members from different colleges, with an average age in their twenties. The resurgence of student activism in this protest movement was a sign of the paradigm shift that had occurred in the Hong Kong political landscape.

The shifts in the leadership of the 2014 protests undermined the organizational coherence of the movement and led to the emergence of seemingly "spontaneous" factions. Protest actions in different zones often spiraled out of control. On September 28, after the police had fired teargas into the crowd, HKFS immediately urged protestors to retreat amid safety concerns: however, instead the protest escalated and spread to different areas such as Admiralty, Causeway Bay, Wan Chai, Tsim Sha Tsui, and Mong Kok. The protests at Admiralty and Mong Kok, in particular, had their own themes and characteristics. Things had remained largely peaceful at the two camps on Hong Kong Island, but although HKFS and Scholarism attempted to control the occupiers at Admiralty, they found it increasingly difficult to exert effective control in other areas. The spatial dispersion of the protest and the violence that ensued undermined the public support for the protest in Mong Kok. Those who took to the streets were ambivalent with regard to the student leaders. Many spontaneous protestors, who previously did not know each other, formed new relationships and solidarity groupings at the occupied zones. The tactics of direct democracy, self-organization, and encampment that characterized the global Occupy movement were quickly adopted by the occupiers. They assigned task groups, shared resources, and designated areas for discussion, sleep, and study. They set up resource, medical, food, and recycling stations, and brought in supplies through appeals via social media. The pan-democrats took a back seat at this time. Although they set up tents in the occupied areas, occupiers were wary of political parties and some suggested that the pan-democrats and other groups had "blocked the real voice of Hong Kong people."

Across the protest sites, occupiers were divided over the status of "representatives" and leaders of the movement. Some protestors maintained that a leaderless movement would make the protests more difficult to control. Some radical factions, mostly at Mong Kok, even questioned the notion of representation and leadership and resisted being led by the students. Protestors at the Admiralty zone generally identified with HKFS or Scholarism as the movement's "representative" or "leader" charged with engaging in dialogue with the government. However, many occupiers and groups emphasized the autonomy and spontaneity of the movement. A student in Admiralty said that "People listen to what they [HKFS and Scholarism] said. However, they are not the real controllers of this campaign. They just act as a bridge for talks with the government. We, the occupiers, are the real character of the movement. We are independent individuals, and we try to figure out how to deal with problems and take responsibility by ourselves. This is the spirit of the masses." Some called the OCLP leaders and student groups "advocators" and "promoters," instead of "leaders" or "representatives" of the movement. Others questioned the idea of vertical forms of leadership and conventional political lines. One occupier in Mong Kok said that "[i]n fact, we did not have specific leaders. They were just spokesmen. If they could convince us, we would follow them. It was simple as that . . . everyone can be his (or her) own leader, and they decide their stay or acceptance." Although HKFS assumed a de facto leadership role after the clash with police, it never enjoyed sufficient power to make and implement decisions across the occupied areas.

Some occupiers attributed this organizational weakness to the leadership style of student groups, claiming that they often changed their stances, and that the messages they delivered were inconsistent. Others suggested that student groups had never come up with a clear road map. Under these circumstances, the movement, as it unfolded, had struggled with growing factionalism. At the occupation area of Admiralty, the focus of global media attention, there were four main organizations: HKFS, Scholarism, the pan-democrats, and OCLP. The latter two groups had urged protestors to minimize disruptions and were thus regarded as moderates. Despite differences, these groups attempted to maintain a united front in the form of a decision-making assembly, in which HKFS took the lead. The assembly, however, was not effectively coordinated. The assembly's decisions, which required lengthy discussions among representatives of the four groups, frequently

Figure 4.6. A Poster Reads: "Recovering Mong Kok, Umbrella Revolution." The nativist group attempted to take over the leadership in Mong Kok. Author photo, October 22, 2014.

met resistance from the people at protest zones. The platform for expression of opinions, called *dahui* or *datai* or the "main stage," was later be challenged by far-right factions. According to one occupier, "no groups in this movement could be identified as the assembly." For many participants, while OCLP "initiated" the movement and the students carried it on, the agendas and tactics were continually and often spontaneously reconfigured by different groups.

In contrast to the Admiralty zone, where the supporters were mostly students, office workers, and young people, the occupied areas of Mong Kok and Causeway Bay had a far more complex composition, political identity, and protest orientation. The protestors and groupings at these two sites apparently had different opinions regarding the leadership and protest tactics of the movement, the attitude toward China, and the function of the assembly. In the occupation area of Mong Kok, radical groups such as Civic Passion, People Power, and Proletariat Political Institute were active, and rejected conventional partisan politics and representation. These non-aligned groups, in particular Civic Passion, had adopted a more confrontational approach

Figure 4.7. An Occupied Zone in Causeway Bay. Author photo, November 3, 2014.

toward the police and were hostile to the assembly. The nativist group (usually referred to as *bentupai*, "home-soil faction"), which refused to support the moderate solutions offered by the assembly, attempted to take over the leadership in Mong Kok, where the support for the pan-democrats, HKFS, and OCLP was not high.

Some participants complained that the assembly was not representative, and sometimes when student leaders expressed their opinions on the stage, they were booed. When OCLP volunteers attempted to remove barricades and minimize disruptions, they frequently met resistance from other groups. The nativist leader, Chin Wan, called upon his supporters to oppose the student groups, and to confront the police. For some occupiers the Mong Kok and Causeway Bay areas were the battlefields "conquered by the crowd." They insisted that instead of following protest leaders, "people decide the direction of the movement." One occupier stated that "[i]n this movement, we do not have representatives, we simply do not need them. The government can talk to the masses directly instead of choosing representatives. That's why we often said, 'The people picked up by the government [HKFS] did not represent us. They can't represent us." One protestor indicated that "many people were trapped [by the notion that the movement should have leaders]. Hong Kong people, during this Umbrella Movement, have shown to others that leaders are not necessary." Occupiers in Mong Kok tended to ignore directions by the assembly. The OCLP leaders, for example, urged occupiers to keep away from residential and commercial districts, but protestors in Mong Kok insisted on blocking the roads and disrupting people's daily routines in order to maintain pressure on the government. One protestor in Admiralty said that he expected that HKFS could lead the movement to "precisely and completely speak for us, tell the government what we want, and allow Hong Kong citizens to know the purpose of this movement." However, he thought that the student leaders had failed to properly communicate with the protestors in all the protest zones. According to a survey conducted in late October, only 35 percent of respondents indicated that when student organizations' instructions were different from theirs, they would abide by the student representatives' decision, while 32 percent would not follow them. Among the three occupation areas, the percentage of those who supported student leaders at Mong Kok was only 28, while 39 percent did not support them (Tang 2014). The occupation was also split by different protest demands, with some occupiers seeking to abolish the Legislative Council's functional constituency seats first, and others demanding that the Chief Executive should step down immediately.

In early October, the gap between the assembly and the crowds had widened. The movement remained disunited, while its protest tactics had become more fragmented and disorganized. Its message had also become more diffuse and at times confusing. Scuffles and conflicts had continued to break out between protestors and police, and between occupiers and those who opposed them across the protest sites. The scenario had gone far beyond what had been envisioned by the OCLP founders. Although the crowd in Admiralty was more controlled, the assembly had a difficult time restraining the Mong Kok protestors, but would later move across to Admiralty. The more combative participants—some of whom were Civic Passion supporters—were involved in several disturbances. Some armed themselves with weapons. The government played a waiting game, in the hope that the movement would run out of steam.

The occupiers remained divided about what to do next. At Admiralty, OCLP and pan-democrats had proposed to withdraw, yet HKFS was hesitant. Some occupiers, conceding that the government was unlikely to make concessions, said they would follow the assembly if it called for a retreat. Many, however, were critical of the idea and still believed that it was inappropriate to disperse without gaining government concessions. On October 25, the assembly was joined by the Alliance of Supporting Students Protests, which comprised a radical nativist group called Defense of HK Freedom. The radical faction in the assembly insisted that occupiers should stay until the government abolished the functional constituency of the Legislative Council. The moderate groups did not agree with this proposal, and this prompted the assembly to hold a referendum in the three occupied zones. The proposed referendum, however, failed to unite the movement, and instead undermined the authority of the assembly. A protestor at Causeway Bay said that "We don't need to vote to come up with a decision, we have voted with our feet already." Some suggested that without sufficient discussion, the assembly's decision was a "betrayal of the masses." One Mong Kok occupier complained that HKFS "[h]ad never consulted the participants of Mong Kok on the referendum . . . They did not try to communicate with us. We have waited for their suggestion; however, they did not offer it. Thus, we think that HKFS and the assembly cannot represent us." Due to the lack of consensus on the issues to be voted on, the ballot was abruptly cancelled. One occupier at Causeway Bay asked "Why don't we have a representative? Looking back at past rallies, such as 'protecting the Choi Yuen Village action,' anti-high-speed rail movement, and the anti-national education campaign, the participants at the time were often betrayed by the so-called representatives, who sang, encouraged the public, and raised money. At the peak of these movements, some councilors and activists would express passionate, but useless, opinions. They claimed that we had victory at the moment, but it was actually a failure." According to another occupier, "We have not gotten what we demand and the action has not been successful. We cannot thus leave the place . . . time is not the criterion. This campaign is thus different from the past." At a forum held by Civic Passion in Causeway Bay, one citizen grabbed a microphone and said, "We do not resist the assembly, but in fact, we oppose withdrawal. We can see that the activities held by the assembly hinted at withdrawal. Sometimes we are too sensitive, but we are aware that the revolution will not be successful when we go home. Some people said that it is OK to lose this time, and we can look forward to the next . . . it is not so. If we go home, it will be the end, and such activity will never return again in the future." A survey conducted in late October 2014 showed that most occupiers did not want to end the protest.

In the face of unruly—and sometimes aggressive—crowds and a split in leadership, HKFS encountered "the most serious identity crisis as a social movement group since the return of Hong Kong . . . no social movement groups or leaders can completely represent the crowd in the same movement" (Ke 2014). One legislator admitted that the movement "did not have a unified direction, the groups could not construct their power, and they did not have a deliberation framework, not to mention the decision-making ability" (Isabella 2014). On the night of November 8, without discussion with the assembly, a group of protestors attempted to block access to government headquarters, but was stopped. The main stage, which had been controlled by the assembly since the occupation started, met mounting challenges from hostile protestors, many of whom were aligned with Civic Passion. The crowd criticized the main stage for suppressing their voices and called for "the end of one voice on the main stage and return to the opinion of the masses." They shouted at speakers on the stage and chanted the slogan "You don't represent us," and attempted to tear down the stage. The "Marshal Team," which was set up by Occupy Central and student groups to maintain order at rally sites, became the target of attack by the radical factions.

On November 19, masked protestors broke into the Legislative Council building without notifying the assembly, which precipitated a leadership crisis in the movement. The leadership crisis of the 2011 Occupy Central had resurfaced in a different fashion. Despite the assembly's efforts, support for the protest had waned from mid-October. The movement had been expected to end in some ways, but protestors had failed to come up with an exit strategy. A survey conducted in mid-November showed that nearly 55 percent of respondents did not support the movement, which was much higher than the approval rating (27.8 percent). Nearly 83 percent indicated that the occupation should be stopped, with only 13 percent wanting it to carry on. Moreover, 68.1 percent supported the police clearance of the protestors (*Hong Kong Economic Journal* 2014).

In mid-November, the movement entered its final phase. The assembly called for a siege of government headquarters at Admiralty in an attempt to sustain momentum. The final show of resistance, however, ended with a bloody conflict with police, with scores of protestors injured and arrested. The two student groups were blamed for this development. Despite the extensive global media coverage it received, the movement had ultimately failed to bring about political change.

## Far-Right *Bentupai* and the Tactical Use of "Leaderlessness" and "Spontaneity"

At later stages of the occupation, those advocating "leaderless" and "spontaneous" actions tended to become more hostile to OCLP and student leaders, especially in Mong Kok's occupied site. Many of them argued that only more militant action, such as new occupations, could force concessions from the government, as opposed to the ethos of nonviolence nurtured by the OCLP. This growing split among the protestors highlighted the deeper divisions within Hong Kong's opposition groups from 2012, when the far-right nativist group Civic Passion was formed. Although OCLP and student groups also mixed their demands for election reform, they had distanced themselves from the outright anti-China campaign of the nativists. The nativist groups articulated a more radical agenda and xenophobic ideology—they not only advocated Hong Kong independence, which moderates regarded as unrealistic, but also specifically targeted Chinese immigrants, tourists, and parallel traders. At the same time, they accused the pan-democrats of being "pro-China" and of failing to protect Hong Kong's interests. Although the advocates of the "leaderless" and "spontaneous" doctrines were not all far-right supporters, the influence of those groups was visible during the protests.

Amid growing anti-China sentiments, the "China factor"—that is, the imperative to assert a "pro-China" or "anti-China" line—strongly reconfigured Hong Kong's protest movements. Before the 2014 occupation, the far-right nativist factions had been a visible presence on Hong Kong's political fringe, and the rejection of assembly and leaders was a tactic repeatedly employed by these groups to disrupt the rallies organized by the pan-democrat camp. Mong Kok became a base for the far-right factions' aggressive politics, where Civic Passion's

Figure 4.8. The Pro-China Group Held Their Rallies in Mong Kok. Author photo, October 22, 2014.

online radio programs and live talk shows often drew large crowds. With the success of its social media-savvy publication, *Passion Times*, and a comic-book-style magazine, many youngsters disaffected with the established political parties joined Civic Passion's campaign to remove the Admiralty-based organizers from power. The smear campaign launched by Civic Passion and other like-minded groups against OCLP and student leaders, fueled by allegations of their "hijacking" and "selling out" the movement, intensified when the protests failed to achieve any significant results.

## Comparison of the Two Movements

The two Occupy protests were similar in terms of their political form and self-organizing culture. When OCLP's campaign was initiated in early 2013, it directly adopted the name "Occupy Central" that was coined by the activists in 2011. What they also shared was a willingness to experiment with direct democracy and try to establish a common platform for a range of grievances through the seizure of public spaces, something which was in both cases supported by online organizing.

Despite their similarities, however, it would be an exaggeration to place too much stress on the continuities between them. In many respects, the two occupations were distinctly different from one another. They had different organizers, motivations, interests, and political agendas. In the 2011 occupation, the organizers (notably Left 21 and some activist groups) echoed the protest theme of OWS and focused mainly on socioeconomic justice and financial capitalism. That protest was animated by anti-capitalism and anarchism, but encompassed diverse values. In the 2014 occupation, however, anti-capitalist and anarchist ideologies were largely absent. Instead of a struggle against economic inequality, the movement called for local autonomy, and its antagonism was mainly directed against Chinese rule rather than Hong Kong capitalists. The protest organizers of 2014 did not share the political ideology of the occupiers of 2011, especially with regard to their anti-capitalism. Indeed, the initial organizers of the 2014 Occupy Central had asserted that the protest would minimize economic damage. The movement's main goal was the establishment of an autonomous liberal democracy, something that was accentuated and intensified by the nativist politics that had unfolded since 2010.

In terms of leadership, both occupations have eschewed a traditional leadership hierarchy, but they developed completely different structures and orientations. In 2011, the occupation did not have a visible leadership though it was de facto coordinated by a small group of young activists and artists, who publically eschewed any sort of leadership role. By contrast, the 2014 occupation was characterized by an intense struggle over leadership. Moreover, the balance between different leading groups was more complex and unstable. The second occupation, with its distributed and fluid leadership structure, was initiated by a group of middle-aged academics, pastors, and respected opposition figures, and then eventually taken over by student groups. Compared to the 2011 event, the initiators of the 2014 campaign were more politically experienced, older, and better connected. Eventually this older group was shunted aside by student leaders and an intergenerational leadership structure was created. The student leadership, however, was fragile and opposed by militants and far-right nativist factions within the movement, who refused to form a united front.

The two occupations were also constituted by very different groups of participants. In 2011, the main participants were left-leaning activists and younger people, and very few opposition politicians or celebrities were involved. Moreover, it failed to win over the public. The protestors in 2014, however, attracted a much broader demographic, and received global media coverage and support. The participants came from across society, attracting students, office workers, unionists, religious groups, professionals, and social workers. Compared to the student protestors and militants of the far-right factions, the participants from OCLP were generally middle-aged and relatively self-restrained. Unlike the situation in 2011, the 2014 campaign successfully mobilized the media, celebrities, opposition lawmakers, and prominent public figures to support their cause. By way of example, the involvement of media tycoon Jimmy Lai was an important factor in the popularity of the 2014 campaign. Again, unlike the 2011 protestors, the leaders of the 2014 movement actively engaged in dialogue with the government in the hope of pressuring the authorities to make concessions. They also employed more varied tactics and increased the scale of the disturbance. The 2011 occupy protest was limited in participant number and scale, and mainly operated around a business building, while in 2014 the protest had greater human resources and succeeded in paralyzing the city. In order to pressure the state to respond, the protestors blocked key roads and business districts and erected barricades, causing chaos around the occupied sites and disrupting daily life in the city.

The two occupations were also driven by, and came out of, different political contexts. The 2011 event was influenced by the global Occupy movement and privileged spontaneity, while the 2014 occupation operated with a high degree of preparation and public consultation, and utilized a high-profile, 20-month-long civil disobedience campaign coordinated by the core groups. Compared to their 2011 counterparts, the 2014 organizers carefully orchestrated the protests and specifically targeted the central business district. A large number of high school and college students and professionals (lawyers, social workers, medical staff) were mobilized to support the campaign. OCLP even ran an unofficial referendum on the election. The student groups also made preparations: Scholarism had organized an occupation-style campaign against a national education curriculum two years before the event, and HKFS triggered the protest with a week-long class boycott. Moreover, unlike the negative attitude toward the mainstream media that prevailed in 2011, the leaders of 2014 frequently held news conferences and interviews, which extended its reach globally.

Due to the different sizes of the two movements, the protestors had also come up with different tactics and strategies to deal with different contingencies. Since the 2011 occupation only had some dozens of regular participants and did not constitute a threat to the state, it was tolerated by the government and police were not directed to clear the protest site. There was no tactical escalation among the occupiers. All matters were discussed and determined by a few participants. The situation set up by the protestors in 2014 was completely different: during the occupation, the government had attempted to divide the movement, clear barricades, and crack down on the protesters. There were violent clashes, and protestors were always dealing with the threat of being evicted. Some sympathizers in mainland China were arrested. Protestors sought to regain lost ground and escalated their actions, but after two months of occupation the OCLP leaders decided to surrender to police.

## Conclusion

Despite their differences the two occupations can be seen as part of a broader movement against the state: indeed, the experiment with direct democracy, through the practice of popular participation, encampment, consensus making, and new modes of self-governance, produced a distinctly new political form vis-à-vis the state, which I found inspiring and imaginative. However, as the experiences of the two movements demonstrate, the absence of effective leadership was counterproductive to the formation of a united front. Graeber and Hui make the point that "the results [of Occupy movements] depend on complex alignments between often overlapping forces," but their analysis, driven by a romantic notion of direct democracy, did not go further to identify what these forces were, how they interacted, and what kind of alignment (or non-alignment) had appeared around the occupations. If the first Occupy Central failed primarily because its occupiers were obsessed with the alternative lifestyles created by the impromptu collective, and did not engage with broader society and political structures, the second Occupy movement seemed to be paralyzed by the failure to unite different groups under coordinated leadership. In the 2014 Occupy movement, one of the crucial problems faced by occupiers was that no one took responsibility for the actions of crowds, and there was no obvious leadership group with whom the authorities could negotiate. While both the 2011 and 2014 occupations developed out of the crisis of the "one country, two systems" doctrine, they failed to develop a strategic plan that would initiate and sustain an effective protest movement. The case of the Hong Kong movements shows how the privileging of tactics over strategy, and of spontaneity over leadership, can give rise to a politically short-sighted culture of "defiance for the sake of defiance" and "disruption for the sake of disruption."

The process of occupation had also produced a variety of creative activities and spectacles through which protestors become cultural producers. In the occupied zones, protestors utilized the resources available in everyday life to construct the meaning of the movements, turning the spaces of appearance into a temporary site of cultural performances. It is logical to ask what the role these cultural practices can play in constituting forms of political subjectivity. The Occupy movements illustrate the ways culture can become a resource for performing resistance. They also demonstrate the increasing aestheticization of popular political expression. How can cultural resistance be made possible in the Chinese context? How do artistic engagements inscribe political demands and reconfigure visibility? The next chapter turns to more aesthetic forms of dissent, looking closely and directly at the creative capacities of Chinese protestors.

Part III

Cultural Resistance

5

# Political Protest as Artistic Practice

## Aestheticization of Protest

Previous chapters have described and analyzed the performative politics associated with or characteristic of protest movements and popular political activities in mainland China and Hong Kong, and demonstrated how they generally take forms that attempt to enhance their visibility. This is particularly the case with examples taken from mainland China, but even the two Hong Kong protest movements that I considered in the previous chapter eventually took on a strongly performative dimension, specifically so as to gain the attention of the global media. This performative politics can be contextualized, both generally and specifically, in terms of the development whereby sociocultural (and by extension, political) space is increasingly "media-saturated." For protests to work effectively, they have to produce themselves, in creative ways, as spectacular audio-visual performances. Dramatic scenes, actions, and artwork now play an important role in increasing the public visibility of protests.

Contemporary protest events increasingly go hand-in-hand with creative and artistic initiatives. As Reed writes, contemporary protest "involves an inescapably aesthetic dimension" (Reed 2016, 1824), and that movement aesthetic texts present information in compact, often highly memorable and emotionally charged ways (Ibid. 2018). All the protest events in mainland China and Hong Kong that feature in this book involve a degree of artistic creativity and innovation, as manifested in the creative production and display of cultural symbols. In recent years, this aestheticizing tendency has been accentuated. In addition to the creative appropriation of the body, banners, and

144 / The Politics of People

Figure 5.1. Some Improvised Artworks in the Occupied Zone. Author photo, November 2, 2014.

slogans to draw public attention, protestors in mainland China and Hong Kong have also learned to utilize a variety of cultural materials and symbols in order to express their discontent.

Creative and artistic practices do not just constitute an alternative mode of expression: they also have the potential for creating profound affective responses on the part of their audiences. These artistic performances and spectacles can become powerful public statements. If these artistic practices represent an increasingly important dimension of Chinese and Hong Kong's performative politics, then how do they constitute a symbolic challenge to the state? This challenge, as Reed (2016, 1977) suggests, is to some extent an *aesthetic* question about cultural form that needs to be taken into consideration in the analysis of popular politics. Reed argues (2016, 1845) that "To speak of protest as artistic expression is to invoke two related phenomena: on the one hand, it is to speak of the (fluid) role of artistic texts in movements, on the other it is to speak of protest events themselves as artistic texts." This chapter will consider the specific role that art and aesthetics plays in mainland China and Hong Kong's protest movements and popular political activities.

## Art as Performative Practice

If we recognize that contemporary protest has a strong aesthetic dimension, what needs to be considered is how artistic practice reformulates the visibility of protests and reconfigures their relation to regimes of public perception. Rancière's work on the "aesthetic" approach to politics provides a useful analytic lens through which to understand the performativity of protest-aesthetic configuration in China. For Rancière, the politics of aesthetics revolves around the altering of what he calls the "horizon" and "coordinate" of perception and experience. Politics, he claims, is "an aesthetic affair" (Rancière 2009b, 277), because "it is about what is seen and what can be said about it, about what is felt as common or private, and about experiences of time and space" (Ibid. 283). It is concerned with "who has the ability to see and the talent to speak" (Rancière 2004, 13), and reconfiguring the "perceptual and aesthetic coordinates" of a community. He argues that politics is tied up with reorienting people's perceptual space and sensory experience. As he writes, politics "is first of all a way of framing, among sensory data, a specific sphere of experience. It is a partition of the sensible, of the visible and the sayable, which allows (or does not allow) some specific data to appear; which allows or does not allow some specific subjects to designate them and speak about them. It is a specific intertwining of ways of being, ways of doing and ways of speaking" (Rancière 2010, 152). Because a normative regime usually "presupposes a prior aesthetic division between the visible and the invisible, the audible and the inaudible, the sayable and the unsayable" (Rockhill 2004a, 3), politics sets out to reconfigure such an imposed division or what he calls the "distribution of the sensible"; here "distribution" refers "both to forms of inclusion and to forms of exclusion," and the "sensible" refers to "what is . . . capable of being apprehended by the senses" (Rockhill 2004b, 85).

The concept of the distribution of the sensible is particularly useful for understanding how protest art reconfigures public perception in China. Because the state enjoys an enormous advantage over protestors in terms of access to news media and the ability to control the distribution of images, protestors have to utilize new methods to reconfigure public perception and sensory experience. Through generating a *conflict* over the distribution of the sensible, critical artistic practice can be seen as an act of political *subjectivization* that suspends the normal coordinate of perception and breaks with the normative construction of meaning. As Rancière articulates it: artistic practices can "create new modes of sense perception and induce novel forms of political subjectivity" (Rancière 2004, 9).

From the perspective of performative politics, artistic practice is central to democratic struggle (Mouffe 2013). When a mass protest is dominated by highly charged artistic components capable of creating an alternative aesthetic experience, then state-imposed distributions of the sensible become more open to public contestation and reconfiguration. Protest art can open up novel political possibilities by rendering visible those issues that were previously ignored or excluded, enlarging the space of appearance and dissensus, and reconfiguring the ways protestors and their demands are heard, seen, and perceived. It can, in short, offer space for political resistance that can undermine the dominant social imaginary (Ibid. 1362).

Following on from Rancière's work and ideas, this chapter will deal with the following questions: What exactly are the performative role and function of creative and artistic practices in Chinese and Hong Kong's protests? How do critical artists and protestors in mainland China and Hong Kong produce alternative protest cultures and create opportunities for asserting oppositional identities? What are the artistic processes through which protest events, sites, and subjects come to be made visible? And finally, how do these artistic practices transform the grounds and possibilities of protest politics in mainland China and Hong Kong?

## Struggle for Visibility in Mainland China

### Attention-Grabbing Expressions

Compared with the street art common in Western countries (which often feature puppet shows, rock music, dancing, graffiti, poetry, and face painting), because protest activities in mainland China are under constant surveillance, the form and content of street art tends to be limited and repetitive. Ever since the suppression of the protest movement in 1989, freedom of expression and public order in mainland China have been strictly supervised by the state. Moreover, official restrictions on cultural activities have restricted the development of protest art. In mainland China, disseminating and displaying protest materials on the street is highly risky; it is very difficult for protestors to engage in critical artistic practices and create an alternative artistic space. Street art is strictly controlled by public security, and protestors on the streets in mainland China are usually ordinary workers and peasants who generally lack the ability to produce sophisticated or creative artwork. Though some urban protestors have created artistic work, this has required considerable time, space, and mutual support among the participants. This is perhaps why protests in mainland China do not feature much artwork or stage performance. Moreover, protests in mainland China usually focus on short-term material interest rather than wider ideological issues, which can limit the range of and requirement for artistic creation.

Despite these factors, Chinese protestors have attempted to use different artistic and audio-visual texts and techniques in order to gain the attention of the public and the media. In recent years the media in mainland China has paid more attention to protest events (Li and Yang 2013, 54), and protestors have employed various objects and resources to reconfigure their public visibility. Increasingly, pictorial forms are being introduced into protest activities. The most common of these is the deployment of mundane objects to stage "artifactualized performance" (Johnson 2009, 27), including eye-catching slogans, symbols, colors, posters, banners, clothes, ribbons, masks, and caps. By way of example, a woman in Jilin held an inflatable doll with "Law" and "Human Right" written on it and stood at the gate of the local government to attract the attention of officials. In another case, several students in Guangzhou made doghouses and lined them up in the center square to protest against high housing prices. Villagers who have lost their land gather to wave the national flag, and retired military personnel wear their uniforms and sing military songs. The value of these figurative protest forms is that they bring about the creative reduction of complex issues to visual symbols and performative practices that are attractive enough to grab attention and simple enough to remember. These attention-grabbing exercises do not require the bystanders to wrestle with complex ideas, but instead tell a story quickly and dramatically.

The workers and peasants in mainland China generally tend to use simple posters and banners written with slogans that connote deep sentiments in a few memorable words or symbols. Posters and banners are unsophisticated and inexpensive and are easily recycled and circulated. Poster imagery can tell a story quickly and speak to audiences of limited literacy (Reed 2016, 1920). By contrast, environmental protestors tend to create more sophisticated materials: they make use of hand-made or modified costumes, decorated with graphic arts and creative signs, to gain visibility and, by extension, publicity. For instance, anti-PX campaigns employed visual signs such as skulls to signify the danger of environmental pollution, or the use of ribbons to express the message of peace. Some protestors also exploit public spaces to write graffiti on sidewalks, bus stations, or walls of residential buildings, a form of art that takes "anonymous advantage of visible public spaces to convey a brief message" (Jasper 2014, 838).

*Street Performance Arts*

Creative and artistic practices during protests are much less confrontational in mainland China. Instead of causing physical damages, property destruction, or bringing about public disorder, the creative and artistic practices employ more implicit and subtle ways to express discontent. Street performance art is an emerging protest tactic that has become increasingly popular among Chinese protestors. Such performative forms of protest minimize confrontation and help protestors evade censorship. Because these aesthetic displays and performances often adopt comedy and black humor to express demands in implicit ways, it is difficult for the police to find an excuse to intervene.

Performance art-as-protest in mainland China is usually created to minimize political risk. A notable case is how rural migrant workers have staged wage protests through a series of eye-catching street performances to arouse public attention. In 2013, two girls dressed as cartoon "Super Heroes" held signs demanding wages for their father in Zhengzhou, Henan Province. In another protest in Beijing, migrant workers put on the costumes of "Angry Bird," "Garfield," "Donald Duck," and other cartoon figures to ask for salaries to be paid. In Shaanxi, two migrant workers rented costumes to play two well-known figures in Chinese history, Di Renjie and Yuan Fang. In Wuhan, more than forty migrant workers danced Gangnam Style to protest unpaid salaries. These forms of creative resistance add a lighter moment to protest activities, and this can serve to ease the tension caused by the protest action and enlarge the space to express their appeals under specific restrictions of time and space (Wei 2014, 109).

However, the majority of popular protests by workers and peasants have not been able to develop sophisticated aesthetic forms. By contrast, protests organized by educated urban groups often employ expressive forms with strong visual effects and stage spectacular performances in public spaces (Ibid. 107). Live performances are important for their *gathering* function of assembling people (Jasper 2014). Young urban protestors often use fancy dress, dancing, and singing to attract public attention. For instance, two young women wore black veils and bra props and held banners to protest against the Shanghai Metro Corporation, which attributed sexual harassment to the clothes women wore. In Beijing, a group of women wore large size underwear to sing and dance on the street to protest against sexual discrimination in business advertisements. In Shenzhen, a group of young men gathered at the gate of a Chinese medicine shop selling bear gall, performing the pain experienced by bears when their gallbladders are removed. In 2015, on the eve of the Guangxi Yulin Dog Festival, a group of dancers pretended to be stray dogs and circulated the images online in an attempt to attract the attention of the public.

These street performances are attempting to exert pressure on the government. What distinguishes them from other protest tactics is that the performers do not challenge or attack the state directly, but *reconfigure* the ways their demands are heard and seen. Their aim is to awaken public consciousness about a wide range of issues that require state intervention. For example, a group of people gathered in front of a court in Beijing to sing a song they wrote themselves, to draw attention to the issue of domestic violence. In Guangzhou and Shanghai, a group of protesters wore blood-stained bridal dresses at shopping malls to call on the government to legislate against domestic violence. There are many other well-known cases that are widely reported by the media. A group of female college students staged a drama in front of the local government to protest that women who sat for the civil service examination were asked to take off their pants to sit the exam; four young women shaved each other's hair off to protest against the Ministry of Education's standard that discriminated female students. A group of women wore pajamas and stood on a sofa in the street of Shanghai to protest the harm that overwork was causing to family life. Unlike conventional disruptive protest tactics that attempt to intimidate authorities and target officials into concessions, these artistic resistances attempt to widen public consciousness about what they consider to be important issues.

For cultural minorities in mainland China, artistic practices can also provide alternative forms of expressing their discontent, and homosexual groups, who in recent years have become more politically active and vocal, have utilized creative street performances to "dramatize" their concerns. Wei (2014) reports that Chinese homosexual communities have flown kites with rainbow patterns at parks or scenic spots, distributed roses wrapped in leaflets supporting homosexual marriage, and have staged homosexual couples taking wedding pictures or kissing each other on the street, in order to attract the attention of bystanders and extensive media coverage.

## Hong Kong's Protest Art

### The Aesthetic Turn

There has been a flowering of movement-based artistic expression in Hong Kong since the handover in 1997. During the Occupy Central movement in 2014, aesthetic performances were diversified, sophisticated, and attention-grabbing. Hong Kong's unique cultural and political circumstances have produced a completely different set of visual performances compared to mainland China, for three main reasons. First, Hong Kong enjoys much greater freedom of speech and assembly and fewer restrictions on street art, giving rise to bolder and more daring creative forms. Second, unlike the precarious conditions that inform popular political activities in mainland China, protestors in Hong Kong are largely free to stage artistic productions in a variety of public spaces and places. Third, and again unlike the situation in mainland China where protesters are typically workers and peasants, those participating in Hong Kong's recent protest movements are often comprised of students, teachers, academics, social workers, office workers, and professionals from the cultural and creative industries. The protestors possess more cultural capital and are more creative in their use of protest culture. Moreover, the historical relations between mainland China and Hong Kong have produced a deep-rooted cultural imagery that feeds artistic creation. The rise of nativist movements in Hong Kong has further stimulated intense affective and creative energies, which are generally more widespread and sustainable than the short-term, localized, and issue-specific protests of workers and peasants. In other words, Hong Kong protests are more likely to be characterized by a strong sense of cultural belonging to a wider affective community, and thus find it easier to attract more sympathizers.

Hong Kong's aestheticizing of its protest movements and activities took shape after the July 1 protest in 2003. During that protest, some professional and amateur artists adopted creative clothes and protest posters to impress and move an audience in entertaining ways. In 2006, the demolitions of Star Ferry Pier and Queen's Pier inspired a new form of artistic activism, where a "lengthy cycle of oppositional actions interwove imaginative interventions, occupations, and investigative reportage, creating 'temporary affective spaces' around the piers" (Rimini 2013, 465). During this period, under internal and external cultural influences, creative and artistic practices played a crucial role in expanding the movement's public visibility. For instance, during the WTO meeting held in Hong Kong in 2005, the dramatic protest staged by Korean peasants—in particular their adoption of the kneeling ritual—exerted a far-reaching influence on Hong Kong's performative politics. During the anti-high-speed rail movement in 2009, six protesters held rice and knelt once every 26 steps for 15 hours daily. They walked around the Legislative Council for three days, attracting extensive public attention and sympathy. Since then, Hong Kong protestors have gradually learned to make use of streets, government buildings, and specific occasions (such as press conferences or graduation ceremonies) to stage protest arts. In 2011, anonymous protest graffiti was spread across Hong Kong in support of the Chinese artist-activist Ai Weiwei. Since then, deploying artworks and street performances to "free" public spaces has also become a component of Hong Kong's protest culture.

*The Art of Occupation*

The Occupy Central movement in 2014 can be seen as a turning point for artistic activism in Hong Kong. The process of occupation and community building opened up an autonomous space and time for artistic creation where protestors could express themselves freely through a myriad of practices. The 2014 occupation provided an opportunity for a reconfiguration of public space. The public spaces previously controlled by the government and businesses became sites of dissensus. All the available resources and spaces in the occupied zones—including government and commercial buildings, roads, overpasses, bus stations, barricades, shop windows, and traffic signs—were appropriated so as to make the demands of the protestors more visually available. During the movement, some streets were renamed, and part of a government building was transformed into a spectacular "Lennon Wall."

As the movement developed, the occupied areas became a large outdoor exhibition area, attracting all improvised artistic forms drawn from past social movements—graphic arts, graffiti, secondary creation, music, and performance arts. Unlike the situation in the past, however, protestors were given time and space to improvise and innovate cultural materials and symbols. As a result, there was a creative explosion of political art, and the artworks created by protestors were more diverse and complicated in style. The protesters created sculptures, installation art, and multi-media forms that facilitated the movement's struggle for appearance: these artistic practices not only reconfigure the ways protestors and their demands were heard and seen, but also played a central role in increasing the movement's visibility and access to publicity.

What distinguished Occupy Central from other protest movements in Hong Kong's history was the *innovation* and *intensity* of the artistic creations. The participants drew inspiration from popular culture and everyday life—sticky notes, umbrellas, flowers, ribbons, Hollywood movies, icons of politicians, pop music, and cartoon characters were all used to express discontent, often in a makeshift and improvised manner. As Wei writes, "Through the application of symbols, speeches, and concepts commonly used" the protestors "could not only reinforce the mobilization and communication effect, but also creatively express their movement's appeal" (Wei 2014, 108).

One example of the way that the movement participants used everyday items as a resource can be seen in the way in which the umbrella is utilized as a "cultural artifact" (Jasper 2014, 878). Although the umbrella is a mundane daily object, it is associated with the idea of sheltering and self-protection, which can be recontextualized for

Figure 5.2. A Spoofed Image of the Hong Kong Chief Executive Leung Chun-ying. The protestors drew inspiration from popular culture and expressed discontent in overtly playful style. Author photo, October 22, 2014.

political ends. When protestors used the umbrellas to deflect pepper spray and tear gas, they invested the object with symbolic meanings such as "courage" and "defiance." In the 2014 Occupy movement, an installation of a "wooden man" statue holding a yellow umbrella became an icon of the movement and was widely disseminated in the global media. The umbrella was re-appropriated in various creative ways to put across political messages and attract audiences. For example, when the protestors collectively raised umbrellas on official occasions or during public ceremonies, the symbolic act was read as an act of defiance.

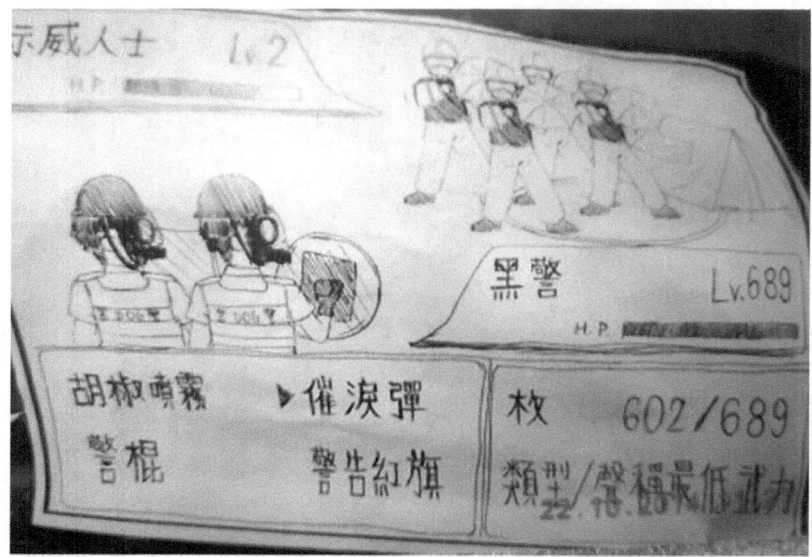

Figure 5.3. A Comic Storytelling Drawn by the Protesters to Describe the Clash with Police. Author photo, October 22, 2014.

Figure 5.4. The Political Use of Daily Objects (Yellow Umbrella). The umbrella is recontextualized to signify courage and defiance. Author photo, October 22, 2014.

In addition to the subversive use of the umbrella in political mobilization, protestors invented other new forms of artistic action. During the 2014 occupation, all kinds of daily objects (such as bottled water, balloons, umbrellas, dolls, chairs, models of human body, and tents) were put to work to express discontent. These objects were deployed in creative ways. For instance, a group of people climbed the famous Sierra Leone Mountain to hang a big yellow banner reading "I want true general elections." As the mountain supposedly symbolizes "the spirit of Hong Kong," the dramatic act of climbing to the peak and appropriating popular cultural icons (such as Spiderman) turned it against the government. The huge yellow banner with its slogan soon became popular and copies were made and hung throughout the city.

## Temporary Affective Space

Occupy Central's aesthetic practices have also created a temporary affective space across the three occupy zones. In the aftermath of a teargas incident, the growing body of protest artworks expressed emotional responses such as anger and solidarity with the protestors. These practices mainly utilized images of heroes, villains, and victims, along with satire and caricatures. Images of the vulnerability and pain suffered by people added to feelings of resentment and sympathy. When the movement failed to achieve its goals, disappointment was expressed pictorially and textually. A double-decker bus, barricades, and the Lennon Wall were appropriated to display posters and adhesive notes with messages of support and appreciation.

The protestors also employed music to reconfigure ways of speaking. During the occupation, protestors employed familiar popular songs as anthems of solidarity and unity, and, to add a lighter tone to the protest, protestors sang these songs in unison, which created a festive atmosphere. Some interviewees confided that when they sang songs and waved their mobile phone lights at the rally, they had a strong feeling of "belonging to this place and these people." As Jasper writes (2014, 848), "music . . . absorbs the entire body in ways that can put people in ecstatic moods. Singing together . . . gives people a feeling of mutual solidarity that words and images alone cannot . . . This joyful mood is the central pleasure that encourages participants to return to future events."

## Critical Artists and Dissidents

The term "critical artists" refers, in a general sense, to professional or semi-professional artists whose practices express political dissent, and attempt to establish a link between art and politics in a plurality of ways (Rancière 2004). This form of art might not be directed at any specific political target, but functions to subvert the existing configuration of power. According to Rancière, the politics of critical art is founded on "the play of exchanges and displacements between the art world and that of non-art" (Rancière 2009a, 51). He defines critical art as "a type of art that sets out to build awareness of the mechanism of domination to turn the spectator into a conscious agent of world transformation . . . to change the configuration of sensory givens and forms of a world to come, from within the existent world" (Ibid. 45–46). The task of critical artists is to render visible power relations and to delegitimize the existing forms of domination. In the mainland Chinese context, the task of critical artists has been to create a space of dissensus and alternative aesthetic experiences within the state-imposed distribution of the sensible.

The development of mainland China's critical art must be situated in the context of a state-dominated cultural scene. Since 1949, the CPC has exerted tight ideological control over cultural and artistic production. In the early period, art was highly politicized and seen "primarily as a reflection or expression of political forces" (Sullivan 1999, 712). Art was viewed as an instrument in service of the CPC rule.

The situation began to change after Deng Xiaoping came to power, which ushered in a period of comparative economic and cultural liberalism. There was a remarkable outburst of artistic activity in the 1980s. While the function of official art, which had been closely monitored, continued to promote official ideologies, a new artistic culture emerged that reflected contemporary social and political issues in an indirect manner (Gao 2001, 242). This coincided with the opening up of public-sphere discussions and debates across the country, and some artists started focusing on current issues censored by the state. During the occupation of Tiananmen Square in 1989, artists and artwork played a central role in transforming the square into a temporary space of appearance and dissensus. During this period, art provided not only a form for critical expression, but it also became a symbol of countercultural struggle.

Mainland China's art scene, however, has seen significant changes since the Tiananmen Square protests. Art was perceived as a potential threat to the state, and those artists who participated in the protest were interrogated and sometimes punished (Sullivan 1999, 717). State monitoring of and intervention in the art scene intensified. Critical art had become problematic for the state, and "the socially critical side of avant-garde art could not be expressed directly . . . Work of this sort would be banned, so it could not be displayed publicly . . . many artists began painting with a cynical attitude" (Andrews and Gao 1995, 269–71). In this repressive atmosphere, non-official exhibitions of controversial artworks were closed. Some art magazines sympathetic to dissidents were shut down or reorganized, "closing off their most important access to the audiences for their art" (Ibid. 240).

The state continued to reshape the distribution of artworks in an attempt to eliminate all critical contents, tightening its control through a range of practices and policies. Cultural institutions made efforts to co-opt non-official art through official exhibitions from the late 1990s onward, leading to self-censorship and a *depoliticization* of the art scene. Some artists targeted non-state outlets, resources, and venues: unemployed independent artists increasingly turned to foreign markets. The environment for artistic creation completely changed as a result of commercialization and state clientelism.

## Chinese Artists' Struggle for Visibility

Because the Chinese government is not well-disposed to contemporary art (Yang 2013) and in particular critical artistic forms, artists have had to find ways to reduce political risk and to take advantage of the opportunities made available by the new market conditions. However, because the state has strictly forbidden artists to participate in protest activities, contemporary artwork generally has not been produced in the context of, or featured in, popular protests. While some artworks do show sympathy to protest activities and events, they are not usually part of those events or organizations.

The growing importance of commercial success since the 1990s has further alienated artists from the ordinary people. In the aftermath of the Tiananmen protests, even though some artists showed sympathy for political dissidents, they seldom engaged in anti-government activities. Chinese artworks have seldom been critical of the authorities, nor have the artists tried to organize themselves as a political force against the state.

However, these political and commercial restrictions and contexts do not necessarily mean that independent artists cannot construct critical artwork. Although artistic censorship remains pervasive, some artists have devised strategies for expressing dissent in the state-controlled cultural environment. Since the late 1990s, there have been flourishing unofficial art scenes in the suburban areas of major cities. Some artists now focus on sociopolitical topics and use popular images, installations, and paintings to voice and represent dissent (Li and Yang 2013). Their art addresses a variety of issues, such as the living condition and lifestyles of ordinary people; the relation between cultural values, history, and urban change; or consumerism, the plight of laid-off workers, the economic gap between rural and urban areas, class differentiation, housing demolitions, the problem of food safety, and environmental pollution. Some art takes state policies and regulations (censorship, family planning, and housing) as its object of critique. Generally speaking, though this critical art does not directly target the state, it does engage with broader social problems caused by state policies.

Some critical artists have actively sought alternative outlets and resources—particularly from within the new media milieu—to increase the visibility of their work. For instance, some performance artists choose official occasions or exhibition venues that will attract media attention. In 2007, performance artist Liang Kegang wore ancient instruments of torture to represent "house slaves." He protested against real estate developers during the China Housing Fair, and this caught the attention of the mainstream media. In another well-known case in Beijing, a group of artists protested against the forced eviction of artist communities. In recent years, Chinese artists have become more adept at using video art and social media to circulate their work. Ai Weiwei, for example, produced a series of documentary films on civil liberties and human rights and circulated them on social media. All these practices have contributed to the expansion of the space of artistic dissensus, but it should be noted that this space is extremely precarious in the face of a repressive state which does not tolerate critical expression. If artistic practices are seen to be openly political (for instance, by supporting Hong Kong's Occupy Central movement), then the artists are warned or punished by the authorities.

## Hong Kong's Artistic Activism

Ever since the July 1 protest against the national security bill in 2003, the artists of Hong Kong have played a more prominent role in popular protests. They have not only participated in various movements, but have also created art in support of protest activities. The rise of nativist identity politics, for instance, has been accompanied by the proliferation of political art that attempts to engage public attention.

In the context of Hong Kong's tense relation with mainland China, the task of these politically engaged artists has been to build up critical awareness on a range of issues, such as civil rights, local identity politics, the preservation of local cultural traditions and historical

Figure 5.5. Artists Attempted to Portray the Participants in the Occupied Zone. The movement attracted many professional artists, who offered their talents to the movement. Author photo, November 2, 2014.

sites, and the ills of capitalism. For instance, during the protests that sought to preserve the Star Ferry Terminal and the Queen's Pier in 2006 and 2007, some artists staged a series of performances and art installations in public spaces in support of Hong Kong's cultural heritage. In 2008, a group of artists deliberately chose the space controlled by large businesses to highlight the problem of corporate hegemony. In 2011, some artists showed support for Ai Weiwei through exhibitions or performance art staged in public places, directly targeting the issue of freedom of speech in mainland China. In their protests against community housing demolitions, some artists used graffiti and video art to record the life of villagers. Some moved into the villages that were about to be demolished to organize various artistic activities and created artworks together with local residents. More recently, Hong Kong's artists have produced a great deal of movement-based and movement-supportive art. For instance, Occupy Central attracted many professional artists, who offered their talents to the movement. Some established a visual archive of the creative objects produced during the movement; others produced documentaries, movies, dramas, dance works and visual art.

*Reconstituting Workers' Sensory Experience*

A new kind of worker-oriented artistic set of practices has emerged in mainland China. The most famous case is the establishment of the New Workers Art Troupe (NWAT) in 2002, formed by some migrant workers, amateur artists, and music teachers who hoped to represent the lives and voices of migrant workers through art and music.[1] The troupe initially produced pop and folk songs with simple lyrics that represented the experiences and feelings of migrant workers, and criticized capitalist exploitation of workers. These songs, which were performed at factories, construction sites, and schools, offered a "bottom-up" perspective on socioeconomic conditions in mainland China, and posed a challenge to the dominant form of commercialized, state-sponsored popular music.

NWAT's artistic work is closely interwoven with members' activist practices. Their appeal is clear: through popular artistic forms, they hope to develop critical self-awareness of worker subordination and shape class identity (Cui et al. 2013). In a political environment in which workers' voices are silenced, NWAT has staged a "Workers' Spring

Festival Gala," which provides a platform for workers to perform and express their voices on social media and television. NWAT has also organized a series of artistic activities and initiatives that reconfigures and represents workers' sensory experiences. In recent years, NWAT has produced documentaries, films, and dramas to record the lives of migrant workers. Through the support among workers and labor NGOs, NWAT established a community shop, school, and theater. These practices provide a community space for workers to exchange ideas, and it has also attracted scholars and college students who do volunteer work.

Appealing to the vast majority of workers is not the only way in which the group carries out its critical work. In addition to the formation of the various collectives, initiatives, and workshops, NWAT's artistic practices also include the creation of cultural institutions such as the Culture and Arts Museum of Migrant Labor. This museum, which was an idle factory, collects many items from the daily lives of workers and records their culture and history. The museum attempts to counter the silencing of workers' voices by providing an alternative, worker-oriented set of stories and histories.

Since performative politics always responds to specific modes of governmentality, its expressive forms are necessarily contextual. What forms of dissent protestors take to contest local governmentality, what cultural resources they use, and what effects they generate depend primarily on how they exploit the condition of possibilities available in local settings. The next chapter turns to the "carnivalistic" mode of political engagement in Macau, looking closely at the subcultural formation facilitated by Internet communication. What are the locally grounded practices of dissent enacted by the people in Macau to reallocate their mode of appearance, and articulate oppositional identities? What are the media resources, opportunities, and strategies through which to perform Macau-style popular democracy since the transfer of sovereignty? This is the next chapter's mission.

6

# Macau's Cyberpolitics

Macau's postcolonial trajectory after being returned to China in 1999 has been shaped by the "one country, two systems" doctrine. and by a tendency to maximize the city's economic and cultural capital, predominantly by way of Macau taking on the more or less official status of the gambling center of China. Formal politics is very much a top-down process of governance, with a strictly limited system of elections overseen by and effectively subject to the dictates of the CPC. The rapid proliferation of new media, however, has to some extent brought about a more participatory and open mode of communication and association.

This chapter will describe and analyze the relation between new media culture and popular political activities in Macau since the handover. In doing so, it is necessary to consider the ways in which digital communication network and culture facilitates, informs, and contributes to the development of Macau's performative politics. In contrast to traditional media, it can be argued that the cyberspace of the Internet allows for a more interactive, autonomous and creative form of popular political practice that poses a challenge to the establishment (Dyer-Witheford 1999; Best and Kellner 2001; Liu 2009). Internet users in Macau not only use cyberspace to obtain information, communicate, and mobilize, it has increasingly become a space of cultural creation and group formation. Macau, which began accessing the Internet just a few years ahead of its return to China, has been characterized by a culture of cyberpolitics, which is outside but on occasions also articulates with and into conventional political spaces and processes. Before considering this political cyberculture in detail, it is necessary to provide an account of the specific political, historical, and cultural contexts that inform contemporary Macau.

## New Postcolony, Old Colonial Structure

Located at the mouth of the Pearl River Delta and bordered to the north by Guangdong province, Macau was a Portuguese colonial territory which has, since the handover, quickly been integrated into global gambling networks. Macau is now referred to as the "Las Vegas of the East": it is the only part of China where gambling is legal, and to facilitate its economic development the state has, since 2001, enthusiastically opened the region to casino businesses from the United States and Hong Kong. This strongly capitalist expansion has been overseen by local pro-Beijing elites and sanctioned by the state. With the liberalization of the gambling sector in 2002, the speed and scale of Macau's casino expansion has been dramatic: by late 2006, Macau had surpassed Las Vegas in terms of revenue, and had taken on the role and status of the gambling capital of East Asia.

Since the handover, Macau's political landscape has been dominated by government-backed groups and associations, including business organizations and unions that constitute a broad-based alliance controlling civil society. The CPC-backed establishment has utilized nationalist and developmental discourses in order to promote a twined identification with Macau *and* China. Political activism is effectively restricted in the name of national unification, national interest and social stability. The first Chief Executive appointed by Beijing in 1999, Edmund Ho Hau-Wah, benefited from extensive local political connections: his father, Ho Yin, had been a wealthy banker widely regarded as the "unofficial" governor of Macau under colonial rule. Edmund Ho's popular appeal was based on the notion of "Macau people governing Macau" (*aoren zhi ao*), but the political setup was as undemocratic as its colonial predecessor. The period since 1999 has seen no fundamental change in political governance. The Chief Executive has been vested with strong administrative powers and is only responsible to the CPC. The nomination of the Chief Executive is approved by a pro-CPC committee made up of business leaders, unions, and other "chosen" groups. This "small-clique" form of governance ensures that pro-government forces control political decision-making, clearing the way for the authorities to implement neoliberal policies without resistance from the legislature (Chou 2007).

Edmund Ho benefitted from his father's connection with Beijing, which helped his administration implement a series of policies without much resistance. In his first term in office, his administration enjoyed considerable popularity, possibly allied to the situation whereby the building of the new casinos and hotel resorts created numerous new jobs. Local media outlets such as *Macau Daily News* and the TV station TDM represented the Chief Executive as a capable and reliable leader who could help Macau and its people advance their interests and well-being. The Chief Executive's agents and bureaucrats—high-ranking government officials, close aides, and prominent leaders of traditional associations—also enjoyed privileges due to their relationships with the Chief Executive, and consolidated their position within the power structure.

Despite initial prosperity, problems emerged. The gambling expansion brought about both rampant corruption and a widening of the gap between rich and poor. In the last years of his second term, Ho's popularity declined because of financial and other scandals. The most common form of corruption was by way of the allocation of land, granted to developers through closed-door negotiations with the government. Despite the government's pledge to combat corruption, it became apparent that corruption was pervasive among top-ranking government officials. Moreover, high economic growth obscured a series of structural dislocations that fueled resentment among the public, who complained that the benefits of economic growth had not been shared equally among Macau's residents. Moreover, Macau's mainstream trade unions were incapable of (and to some extent showed no interest in) protecting workers' rights and interests. With democratic rights and the freedom of the press both severely constrained, there were few opportunities for protests. However on May Day in 2007, a rare mass demonstration of workers and civil servants took place in the streets of Macau. Thousands of protesters took to the streets with banners bearing a range of slogans—Against Corruption, For Housing Rights and Better Livelihoods, Against the Influx of Illegal Labor—and calling for the resignation of Edmund Ho. An altercation with the police over the protest's route turned into a series of scuffles, leaving one citizen seriously injured by shots fired by the police (Liu 2008). The May Day 2007 protests were followed by a series of political mobilizations—spontaneous social movements organized by workers, school teachers, students, and reform-minded citizens—which have occurred more frequently in recent years.

Macau's neoliberal turn has also profoundly transformed the media sphere. Macau's mainstream media is dominated by pro-government groups and capitalist enterprises, and rarely provides coverage of issues related to governance; and audiences have little influence over media content. Most media outlets have been funded by a controversial subsidy scheme perceived to be aimed at silencing critical voices. These media rarely take lines that are counter to the interests of the status quo. During periods of social protest, the mainstream media tend to promote and support government stances. The Macau media, in particular the *Macau Daily* and TDM, have been criticized for their news censorship and pro-government orientation, and for their uncritical stance toward the gambling sector. In this political context, the Internet has become crucial to organizing public dissent.

## Network Protest

Macau's Internet space is undergoing a considerable expansion with the proliferation of online forums, blogs, instant messaging, and social media. After the transfer of sovereignty, the colonial political culture has been replaced by a different set of binary oppositions that constitute Macau's identity-forming "Us/Them" distinction (Mouffe 2002). These include the official authorities (endorsed by the state) vs. the Macau people; foreign/illegal workers vs. local workers; the casino sector vs. local people; and the pro-establishment media vs. unofficial media. The discursive frontiers between "Us" (the underprivileged) and "Them" (corrupt officials, police, pro-government groups and the media, illegal workers, and to some extent foreign casino operators) are constantly being established in cyberspace, with the latter groupings being represented as negating "our" collective identity and dignity, and putting "our" interests at risk. They have become what Hardt and Negri (2004, 55) call "network enemies."

Since 2003, online attacks on government officials and police have become increasingly bold, sharp, and direct, especially after the media exposure of the high-profile official Ao Man Long's corruption scandal in December 2006. Cyberspace is increasingly used by protesting individuals and groups for circulating information, organizing communities, and staging resistance. Macau has been marked by a new type of political "warfare" against the government: individuals and groups make use of the Internet to denigrate, mock, and oppose unpopular policies and improper administrative practices. In response, the authorities have censored online activities by preventing the use of politically sensitive words, ordering portal operators to delete postings and close down forums, and by questioning and arresting people for the alleged online defamation of government officials (Hu 2008a, 2008b).

Internet sites are also used by netizens to produce and share alternative content.[1] When a national security law was being considered by the Macau Legislative Assembly in 2008, for example, political activists used emails and Facebook to coordinate protests. Online discussion forums run by commercial sites, notably Cyber CTM and Qoos.com, remained the major channels for disseminating criticism, alternative news, and eyewitness accounts not covered by the mainstream media. Macau's online media have become one of the prime agents of sociocultural change since the handover. By way of example, local teachers, students, and professionals formed a Wikipedia group for producing Chinese entries during Macau's key social events, as a form of alternative knowledge production. In 2008, after police charged a teacher over his online posting, some Internet users established a website called "The Truth is Out There" to "recover Macau's freedom of speech."

The Macau government's official pledge to improve the wellbeing of citizens and to preserve the city's cultural heritage also offers legitimate grounds for online political mobilization. In 2004, the authorities' relaxation of a longstanding height limit on buildings in the Guia Hill area drew protests from the "Guia Lighthouse Protection Group," which was made up of a group of urban planners and conservationist who feared that the lighthouse would be obscured by new high-rise buildings. Activists used the media and the Internet as critical parts of their strategy. They set up Yahoo forums for internal communication, disseminated negative publicity, and established a campaign website to keep Macau and Hong Kong reporters informed of their activities. In 2007, a group of school teachers and social workers began disseminating critical messages about their worsening conditions through online forums, emails, and blogs, calling on citizens to support these causes and to participate in their protest action to be staged on National Day. Their messages were widely circulated online, attracted media attention, and drew many citizens to the demonstration. These network campaigns appropriated government discourses, policies, and pledges to legitimize their actions, which is very different from Macau's traditional campaigns initiated by the government's agents—namely the local unions and community groups backed by the government.

## *Egao* as Politics by Other Means

As Macau's network protests demonstrate, popular politics is linked to the problematization of the government's integrity and credibility. During the period of the government's first legitimation crisis (from late 2006 through 2007), other tactics were employed to bring these issues to public consciousness. The concept of *egao* (which can be translated as spoofing or mocking in English) is specifically used to contest the meanings of government activities and spectacles.[2] In particular, *egao* pictures, which are made through Photoshop, have increasingly become a means of problematizing governmental discourses.[3]

*Egao*, which literally means "making mischievous tricks" in Chinese, is a slang term coined by Chinese Internet users to describe a kind of subculture characterized by creativity, spontaneity, defiance of authority, and humor. It is a form of multimedia that extensively appropriates popular culture to generate comic effects. Literally, the two characters—"*e*" meaning "malicious" or "evil," and "*gao*" signifying "do" or "make"—combine to describe practices or works that "deflate" serious themes, or poke fun at authorities, sometimes imbued with a sense of defiance and disobedience. Although the definition of *egao* varies in different contexts, its literary origin is sometimes traced to the Japanese word *kuso*, which carries such meanings as "damned," "nonsense," and "mischievous tricks" (Wu 2007). *Egao* has gradually emerged as one of the most striking manifestations of cultural change in China, and has become the focus of media coverage and mass entertainment (Ming Pao 2006; Sim 2009; Eimer 2006).[4] The rise of *egao* culture has also prompted debates over its political and sociocultural significance in the region (Dang 2008; Liang 2006).

Contemporary Chinese *egao* draws on a wide range of popular cultural resources, makes fun of everything serious, and takes different expressive forms such as narratives, poems, puns, songs, images, and videos (Kwong 2008). Its popularity can be attributed to widespread image-editing software packages such as PhotoImpact and Photoshop, and then the spread of digital cameras with a video function, which made images more readily available in cyberspace. Web forums and Facebook have also contributed to its visibility. *Egao* allows people to play with power on a micro-level, sending messages of subversion as much through the mode of its address as its content. Its intent ranges from playful mockery to allusive pranks to sharp derision. Its main targets include not only high-profile celebrities and blockbuster films, but also authorities and national emblems. It makes use of innuendo, metaphor, pastiche,[5] satire, irony, mockery, and parody. In mainland China, *egao* offers an alternative avenue for sociocultural criticism,[6] but it has also been dismissed as vulgar, disrespectful and superficial, an inferior subcultural genre harmful to a healthy public culture (Huang 2010; Wang 2007).[7] Since 2006, *egao* has become more visible in cyberspace, with greater diversity in style and more political in orientation.[8]

As a form of network protest, *egao* is more entertaining and playful compared to campaign-style activities, but it is often characterized by the lack of any clear agenda. Campaign-style protest can mobilize supporters for political change, while a visual spoof contests the authoritative image of official figures, reworking and reclaiming their meanings. The former is usually formally organized and poses a more direct challenge to the government, while the latter is rarely tied to concrete goals or further action. Despite these differences, both campaign-style protest and *egao* share three features in common. First, both can be said to have emerged from the same process driven by the Macau's structural transformation. Second, both have redeployed communicative and cultural resources available in the existing network of power. And third, both express dissatisfaction and contest authorized meanings and discourses.

Although Macau's *egao* culture has been active since the late 1990s, the first spoof picture that explicitly mocked official authorities was put up during the Legislative Assembly election in 2005: a reconstructed picture, which mocked an official anti-bribery poster produced by the Commission Against Corruption of Macau (CCAC), was put into circulation in cyberspace and soon gained popularity. In the image, homonyms or words of similar pronunciations were used to mock the formal official language about corruption. The official slogan, which advocated clean and fair elections, was reformulated satirically, with the expression "Cleanly Voting Virtuous and Capable Candidates" becoming the "CCAC Harming Virtuous and Capable

170 / The Politics of People

Candidates." The image of a bear, which was originally featured in the official poster wearing a Superman suit, was reproduced but with its finger on its mouth (to suggest that people are silenced) and by wearing a belt with the CCAC logo, to signify the CCAC's impotence.

During the period of social unrest in May 2007, the Internet was used to circulate subversive images that expressed critical attitudes toward unpopular policies and to mock high-ranking officials. Online forums coordinated by Cyber CTM and Qoos.com, and more recently Facebook, have been filled with such images, which are clearly *egao* in style and sentiment. On the 17th of May 2011, a protest scene was staged in Senado Square (see Figure 6.1):

> About 30 protesters stage[d] a flash mob event in Macau yesterday to demonstrate against the monopoly of the city's internet service. Responding to calls made by a few internet users on Facebook, they gathered to protest outside the store of Macau's only internet service provider, CTM. One of the organisers, who called himself K, said he wanted to

Figure 6.1. A Flash Mob Event Was Staged to Protest Against the Monopoly of CTM. Source: Macauplanker's Facebook page, accessed August 20, 2011, http://www.facebook.com/macauplanker.

express internet users' dissatisfaction with CTM's service on World Telecommunication and Information Society Day. (*South China Morning Post* 2011)

In June 2011, a Facebook group page, entitled "Add One More Metre to Small Taipa Hill," was created to protest against a new development project that was going to obscure the hill. The page, which displayed a set of photos in which nine naked artists were piled on top of each other, went viral, but was ultimately deleted by Facebook for its alleged obscenity (see Figure 6.2). What these campaigns had in common was that they were all spectacular events developed with the intention of attracting public attention.

*Egao* can be understood as a reappropriation of popular culture: it uses media images (such as a movie posters, comics, and video game characters) to ironize and mock what is serious and authorized. By way of example, a picture appeared after the popular forum Orchidbbs.com

Figure 6.2. Macau's Local Artists Used Facebook to Disseminate Protest Spectacles. Source: Facebook page, accessed August 18, 2011, http://www.facebook.com (page discontinued).

172 / The Politics of People

(known for its political pranks) was closed down on June 4, 2008, the anniversary of the 1989 Tiananmen crackdown. The closedown soon sparked anger online, and a campaign picture originally deployed by the controversial, media-savvy American animal rights organization PETA (People for the Ethical Treatment of Animals), in which a group of naked people are covered in fake blood, was reconfigured to protest against Internet censorship. During a debate in November 2008 on national security legislation known as Article 23, a campaign was launched on Facebook which appropriated a photograph of Sun Yat-Sen, to "authorize" a protest rally (see Figure 6.3).

What often characterizes *egao* pictures is their use of authorized and iconic imagery. One common practice is to juxtapose government officials' facial expressions or body language with different scenes or characters. The political opposition group New Macau Association

Figure 6.3. Macau's Internet Users Launched a Campaign during the National Security Legislation, Known as Article 23, in November 2008. The campaign produced a dramatic flyer on Facebook in which Sun Yat-Sen, known as the "Father of the Nation," was taken up to give legitimize cause for the protest Source: Facebook page, accessed December 10, 2008, http://www. facebook. com (page discontinued).

(*xin aomen xueshe*) began publishing its official organ *New Macau* in 1992. From late 2005 onward, *New Macau* featured a section called *Concealing Daily* (*ai man ribao*), whose title satirically mimics the pro-government *Macau Daily* by reconfiguring the words "love Macau" as "love-deceiving" or "love-concealing" based on their similar pronunciations in Cantonese. The section has produced numerous satirical images, slogans, and narratives mocking government policies, official figures, and the pro-government media. These critical spoofs soon became the most popular section of *New Macau* and attracted many readers to its online content. Much of this focuses on how Macau's casino boom has promoted corruption, an issue ignored by the mainstream media. In Figure 6.4, the cover page borrows the Japanese comic strip *Full Metal*

Figure 6.4. The Dissident Publication *Concealing Daily*. It draws on the Japanese comic strip *Full Metal Alchemist* and the Hollywood movie *The Da Vinci Code* as its frame of reference to mock Macau's former Chief Executive Edmund Ho and the anti-corruption body CCAC. Source: *New Macau*'s page, accessed August 20, 2011, http//www.newmacau.org/issues/index.php?option=com_pho cadownload&view=category&id=1&Itemid=63# (site discontinued).

*Alchemist* as its frame of reference to mock Macau's former Edmund Ho, pictured in place of the original character, with words that refer to him as an "alchemist of lands," implying his role in Macau's land corruption cases. The idea of "equivalent exchange," which runs through the comic series, is evoked to mock Macau's corruption. The lower half of the page then ridicules the anti-corruption body CCAC by imitating the movie poster for *The Da Vinci Code*, renaming it *The Da CCAC Code*, in an attempt to produce an ironic effect. The Chinese words below the main icon imply the CCAC's inability to reveal the truth. Following on from the work of *Concealing Daily*, Macau's Chief Executive has become a common target on the Internet.

Two prominent cases involving alleged government corruption gave rise to a great deal of *egao* activity in Macau. The first case involved Ao Man Long, the first Secretary for Transport and Public Works, who was charged with bribe-taking, the abuse of power, and money laundering. Soon after his arrest, spoof collages were produced, made out of media images that insinuated a link between Ao and the former Edmund Ho, who was Ao's superior and approved a number of projects related to the corruption scandal. One image uses the original poster of the 2007 Chinese espionage thriller film *Lust, Caution*, which features a patriotic female undercover agent who attempts to lure the traitor (who is shown sitting on a chair) into a trap: in the *egao* version Ao and Ho are substituted for the main characters, suggesting that Ao was "seduced" by Ho (see Figure 6.5). The main title (*Corruption Off*) and subtitle (which signifies the difficulty of preventing corruption) accentuate the political meanings of the spoof poster.

A second example involves the 2002 Hong Kong crime-thriller film *Infernal Affairs*, which features the complex relationship between a police officer who infiltrates the Triads and a police officer secretly working for the same gang. The characters and plots deployed in the film provide a shared frame of references (to crime, corruption, and self-interest) with which to mock Ao and Ho, whose images are arranged in ways that call into question their relationship. In the spoof poster (see Figure 6.6), the movie is renamed as *Greedy Affairs*, with Ho and Ao as the protagonists.

In a third example (see Figure 6.7), Ao's icon is inserted into an advertisement for the financial services company MoneyGram International: the spoof version features the images of dictators and figures

Figures 6.5 (left) and 6.6 (right). Hong Kong Films Referencing Corruption Scandals. (Left) Netizens use the Hong Kong film *Lust, Caution* to allude to the close relationship between Ho and his close aid in the corruption scandal. Source: CyberCTM, accessed October 20, 2011, http://forum.cyberctm.com/forum (site discontinued). (Right) The characters and plots of the Hong Kong film *Infernal Affairs* offer a frame of reference for insinuating Ao and Ho's relationship. Source: CyberCTM, accessed August 20, 2011, http://forum.cyberctm.com/forum/viewthread.php?tid=13298&extra=page%3D577 (site discontinued).

including Osama Bin Laden, Fidel Castro, Saddam Hussein, and Kim Jong-il, as well as Lai Changxing, China's once-most-wanted fugitive. Ao is characterized as a member of the imagined "evil group." The spoof advertisement uses a title mimicking the company's slogan, and reads "The Safe, Fast Way to Send and Receive Money Worldwide," which refers to Ao's money laundering activities.

The second case involves the rationalization of the police shooting at the 2007 May Day protest by the Macau media. In a spoof poster inspired by the film *Saturday Night Fever* (see Figure 6.8), the main actor, John Travolta, is replaced by the police firing gunshots

Figure 6.7. Critiquing Corruption. An advertisement is reworked as a critique of rampant official corruption. Source: CyberCTM, accessed August 20, 2011, http://forum.cyberctm.com/forum/viewthread.php?tid=111154 (site discontinued).

Figure 6.8. Macau's Netizens turn on the Policeman Firing Gunshots on the May Day Protest in 2007, Resulting in Many Spoofs. This spoof is inspired by the 1977 Hollywood film *Saturday Night Fever*. Source: CyberCTM, accessed August, 20, 2011, http://forum.cyberctm.com/forum/viewthread.php?action=printable &tid=52756 (site discontinued).

Macau's Cyberpolitics / 177

skywards. In another set of works, the figures depicted in films such as *Spiderman* and *Hero* are substituted by images of an aggressive, angry policeman (see Figure 6.9 and Figure 6.10). The video game series *Street Fighter* was also manipulated to call attention to police violence (see Figure 6.11).

## Conclusion

Popular political practices in Macau use online networks and digital techniques that allow for the manipulation of images to voice dissent and contest the authorized meanings and discourses produced by the government and valorized and rationalized by the local media. These performative practices constitute an alternative space of appearance where some form of sociocultural and political agency can be articulated and asserted in the context of a soft authoritarian government.

Figures 6.9 (left) and 6.10 (right). Heroic Figures Used to Spoof Police Involvement. (Left) The heroic figure such as Spiderman is also evoked to portray the policeman involved in the protest. Source: CyberCTM, accessed August 20, 2011, http://forum.cyberctm.com/forum/viewthread.php?action=printable&tid=52756 (site discontinued). (Right) The spoof is inspired by the Chinese film *Hero* released in 2002. Source: CyberCTM, accessed August 20, 2011, http://forum.cyberctm.com/forum/viewthread.php?action=printable&tid=52756 (site discontinued).

178 / The Politics of People

Figure 6.11. *Egao* Allows the Two Previously Different Worlds—Popular Culture and Politics—to Converge into One Another. The themes and characters of the video game *Street Fighter* are redeployed to produce mockery. Source: CyberCTM, accessed August 20, 2011, http://forum.cyberctm.com/forum/viewthread.php?tid=52756&extra=&highlight=%E6%83%A1%E6%90%9E&page=12 (site discontinued).

The examples presented in this chapter show how collective creativity is articulated as a form of political expression and endowed with a sense of disapproval or skepticism against the governance of "one country, two systems."

# Conclusion

## For the Appearance of a Subject

> Men make their own history, but they do not make it as they please; they do not make it under self-selected circumstances, but under circumstances existing already, given and transmitted from the past.
>
> —Karl Marx, *The Eighteenth Brumaire of Louis Bonaparte*

## Trajectory

The development and forms of the protest movements and popular political activities in China open a series of questions for both intellectual and political reflection. Since the crackdown of the 1989 social movement, the Chinese political landscape has witnessed a resurgence of popular politics, characterized by a strong performative dimension and expressed by a multiplicity of practices. In order to acquire performative force, protestors need to deploy a variety of creative practices. The performative politics examined in this book is situated in the state's ensuing legitimation crisis in the post-1989 era. In the post-Tiananmen era, the relationship between the state and the people remains ruptured and contested as the state modified its neoliberal agenda and forms of governance. There has been a profound transformation of state-society relations and the logic of Chinese governmentality. The state carried out a series of economic reforms, where "mechanisms of interaction between state and market came to substitute for those between state and society" (Wang

2003, 119), intensifying the condition of neoliberalism and altering the circumstances and forms of popular struggles. With the further penetration of precarity to all spheres of life and segments of the population, the political subjects involved in anti-precarity struggles have become more diverse and fragmented—they come from almost all social groups and make a wide range of claims, and for a variety of reasons. Dislocated peasants and urban dwellers, laid-off workers, unpaid pensioners and migrant workers, aggrieved teachers, students and taxi drivers, demobilized soldiers, residents affected by pollution, and tax-burdened farmers—whose grievances are immediately associated with the state's governance and development trajectories—have become the key figure of the popular political domain in the post-1989 setting. There is a widespread sense of deprivation and unfairness among them, closely linked to development, mass layoffs, welfare problems, low salaries, excessive taxes, land expropriation, and housing demolition. The emotional experience of dispossession motivates them to reclaim their rights and liveability at multiple points of resistance. Most protests are associated with the abuse of power, and can be seen as forms of social self-protection. Many struggles are triggered by frustration with local institutions (such as trade unions, courts, and petition offices), and the intense process of dispossession induced by neoliberalism.

In the political sense, the mounting social unrest can be seen as a response to the state's disconnection from the people (*tuoli qunzhong*) that has been exacerbated by the neoliberal erosion of rights. The breakaway has generated a deep-seated legitimation crisis characterized by bureaucratic domination and the *absence of people* in the exercise of sovereignty and in decision-making processes. The crisis is also caused by its shift away from the CPC's traditional constituency (Lin 2006, 198). Many grievances originated in the state's reform program and are beyond the capacity of local governments to address. These grievances have combined to generate a political crisis with regard to the allocation of resources, social arrangements, and undemocratic decision-making carried out in the name of reform and development. Although the state has attempted to cope with the crisis through economic development and a paternalist system of social protections, its reconfiguration has also generated wider discontents and tensions that could become a threat to regime stability. More crucially, although the state has tightened its surveillance of organized activism to reduce the threat to its power, the reform measures it has implemented, in particular economic marketization and power decentralization (in both fiscal and administrative senses), have not only produced a more heterogeneous social space, but have also inadvertently offered numerous opportunities and resources for performative political practices. More labor legislations and institutional channels, for example, were introduced to regulate labor disputes, which are subsequently used by workers to legitimize their actions.

Shifting the border of the unrecognizable and the invisible has become a crucial way to negotiate this political rupture and to reclaim rights and dignity. Performative politics, which is driven by the structural disenfranchisement of access to power and aims at reconfiguring the relation between the visible and the invisible, plays a crucial role in reestablishing relations with the state and counteracting the destruction of liveability. The function of performative politics is not only to disclose a wrong, but also to demand a reconfiguration of the sensible order. Performative politics is really about the hegemonic struggle over meaning, about the expression of disagreement through innovative methods. The question is precisely one of the possibility of political expression and existence. It is through the enactment of performative politics that people render their grievances visible and constitute their identities. Performative politics enables them to create their own political realms and bring into existence a new politics of rights.

Performative politics, which can open up alternative modes of expression and frames of perception, requires an active capability to assert rights in public spaces. Compared to the episodes of protest leading up to 1989, the performative politics since the 1990s has unfolded with a set of distinctively different features, dynamics, and consequences. It is marked by the increasing prevalence of *the embodiment of protest, the occupation of public space, and the proliferation of creative resistance*. As this book has illustrated, performative politics in Macau, Hong Kong, and mainland China is manifested in variety of ways. What the three places share in common is that they focus on achieving public visibility and enact their practices against the governments in an attempt to reconfigure the ways of being governed. People in these places draw on a number of public performances that have evolved over time. Some of these performances are conventional, routinized, and normalized, while others remain transgressive, confrontational, and forbidden. These expressive practices may draw on the past (Perry 2008b) or local traditions, or be improvised by protestors themselves according to a variety of local circumstances and needs. Meanwhile, they all tend to escalate actions and resort to more disruptive forms after exhausting authorized channels. Usually people turn to disruptive actions for two reasons: in response to the use of force by local officials or firms supported by government, and because they have exhausted official channels (Cai 2008, 164). Disruptive action, which can create what DeLuca (1999) calls "image events," is aimed at a larger audience and performs politics that "revolves around what is seen and what can be said about it, around who has the ability to see" (Rancière 2004, 13). With popular grievances increasingly attributed to local misrule, the site of struggle has scattered across different localities. As a result, these practices tend to be highly localized, cellular and spatially constricted in terms of social composition, scale, and demands, and lack lateral coordination and sustainable organisation. Paradoxically, the rigidly unequal citizenship regime's continued emphasis on "social stability" and expansion of social rights, seen as the prerequisite to economic development, has also made it possible for protestors to blame local authorities for undermining social harmony. The reconfiguration of state power also provides new opportunities for unauthorized actions.

In light of the analysis presented in this book, I would like to suggest that vague references to "civil society" risk obscuring the complex ways of engaging with the state in China. Chinese protests do not simply emanate from civil society, but actively engage with the state. A performative understanding of popular politics does not treat the people as a static, fixed, and passive object on which the state projects its power (i.e., through the constitution of passive beneficiaries of social aid), or as a group of rationally motivated, self-interested individuals seeking to maximize their material benefits. Rather, the construction of political subjects involves reconfiguring the ways subjects are heard and seen by the state and the wider public, as well as efforts to enlarge the space of what Rancière calls *dissensus* (Rancière 2014, 88). The militant and theatrical power entailed by performative practices can often produce unpredictable outcomes. It also contributes to the enlargement of the space of dissent characterized by the "splitting up of sensible appearances themselves" (Ibid. 1720).

Despite being united under the arrangement of "one country, two systems," Macau, Hong Kong, and mainland China have their own political formations and styles of resistance. The three places have evolved distinct trajectories where there are significant differences in terms of agenda, identities, orientations, practices, expressive forms, and conditions of appearance, which are necessarily locally grounded and context-specific. Specifically, each region has specific political dynamics and power configurations, and ways of articulating performative politics. In mainland China, most protests are aimed at local governance and do not call regime power into question. They take place within the arena of the state to call for redress.[1] In order to trigger intervention, they have to make their way through complex hierarchies and look for potential allies and supporters. The oppositional practices in Hong Kong instead are characterized by a distinctly different modality of performativity. While mainland protesters are concerned with socioeconomic justice, in Hong Kong they mainly focus on universal suffrage and self-determination, and thus their political practices are often directed against the central state. Both Hong Kong and Macau's practices are entangled with forces of identity politics.

To be sure, the cases presented in this book demonstrate that different political landscapes can offer different conditions of possibility and restrain bodily capacities for performative politics. In mainland China, where mass assemblies are severely prohibited, protests are largely confined within the limits set by prescribed and tolerated performances, and thus transgressive acts such as protracted occupation can hardly be sustained. How to decrease the risk of repression and develop an intimate interaction with the state has always been an issue. And also, because there are no opposition parties and effective legislatures, the protest scripts tend to be attached to the state and regime-supportive. In terms of goals, mainland practices mainly focus on socioeconomic justice, while Hong Kong protests call for local autonomy and self-determination, and thus its antagonism is mainly directed against the CPC rule. The latter's main goal is establishing an autonomous liberal democracy. However, universal suffrage has never become a significant political issue in mainland China. In terms of participant number, due to the high political risk, mainland protests are generally short-lived and bounded in scale. By contrast, Hong Kong's opposition has much greater human resources and can often succeed in paralyzing the city. The participants are obviously more diverse, broad-based, and resourceful than their mainland and Macau counterparts.

Taking performative politics as the central analytical lens to dissect the struggles against precarization and dispossession, it is important to stress that the rights promised by the state are not pre-given, but realizable only in the act of claiming (Zivi 2012). Not all such acts, however, are tolerated by the state. Meanwhile, the space of appearance is not a fixed location, but something that is taking place and brought into being through concrete action (Arendt 1958, 198–99). Under the different performative conditions, people in the three places have also deployed different strategies, discourses, and resources to gain access to rights. Both Hong Kong and mainland Chinese people are concerned to stage actions that authorities do not tolerate but cannot ignore. In the relatively liberal Hong Kong, the radical actions of occupation, which formulate a "no" through the body (Butler and Athanasiou 2013), can disrupt existing norms that allocate public appearance and recognition. Sometimes the assembly of the body, which opens up evanescent spaces of appearance, can overcome the distinction between public and private.

In mainland China, however, rights-claiming is extremely risky, and there has been an invisible alliance with the center. In Chinese political culture, there is a strong tendency to operate close to authorized channels. Ordinary people generally assume that it is up to the leaders to fix things, and tend to avoid confrontation. Protestors see the state as an ally to counter local abuses, and appropriate its symbols, norms, discourses, and mass-line tradition to trigger intervention. Although the state has imposed severe restrictions on popular political activities, protestors can always find ways to contest dominant forms of visibility. They employ many non-regime-threatening tactics inherited from the past that carry smaller risks, and are careful not go beyond economic demands. One crucial strategy to forge the alliance is to demonstrate allegiance to the CPC in order to reduce the risk of immediate repression. Forms of performativity and their corresponding visibility are improvised mainly to gain the attention of upper-level authorities: rather than rejecting official notions of popular sovereignty, protestors in mainland China remain highly reliant on the state's promise of legal rights. To mobilize central power, they frequently "turn central commitments into weapons of the powerless" to challenge local bureaucracies (O'Brien and Li 2006, 49). They also seek to mobilize institutional and legal resources to advance claims that the state purports to guarantee. Despite poor law enforcement and the failure of the unions, the legal regime has at least promised a greater protection of rights, thus offering people more symbolic power. In many cases protestors have lodged repeated but futile complaints with various official agencies, before they turn to more forceful action, which transgresses permissible limits and violates the law. Sometimes they turn official events into political theaters while demonstrating compliance with state norms. Such practice can increase the legitimacy of action and enables protestors to turn the institutional-legal spaces into temporary spaces of appearance in order to be recognized and seen by authorities. The use of the body is particularly crucial in mainland China because it is charged with moral significance that can produce tremendous performative force.

Their ways of constructing official Otherness are also different. In Macau and Hong Kong, Chief Executives often become a target. In Hong Kong, there has existed a problematization of the role of the postcolonial state. Compared to Macau and mainland China, Hong Kong's political agendas are much more overt and radical and thus often confront the state. Its practices call into question sovereign power and promises, using oppositional language as their means of articulation. It challenges its authorizing conditions and authorities, expressing strong disobedience to its rule. Its protestors are more adept at combining different tactics to increase the scale of disturbance. Dramatic tensions tend to be created against both local and central governments, and most tensions embody the spirit of disobedience and pose a direct challenge to the regime. Unlike mainland China, the oppositional practices in Hong Kong are not intended to exploit the cleavage in the political hierarchy and refuse to be recognized as patriotic. Its political and material environment is favorable to a movement-type of extended occupation. The organizers are more experienced in street politics, and the movements they coordinate are obviously more well-planned and sustained. However, recent movements in Hong Kong tend to eschew formal traditional leadership and organization, leaving the question of how to unite all factions and constitute them as a collective force unresolved.

In order to force a state of emergency, popular politics in Hong Kong and mainland China sometimes involves the interruption of business-as-usual: these practices, which enable people to organize themselves and relate to one another, create alternative ways of reconfiguring the space of appearance. In contrast to the intense demand of bodily participation, Macau's performative politics is characterized by the more disembodied, subtle, indirect, and playful expression of dissent. Some of the expressions are not obviously political at first sight, and are restrained in terms of political demand and scope. Meanwhile, both mainland China and Macau protestors often uphold the spirit of the central government as a means of legitimizing their actions and holding local governments to account.

The ways of opening up political spaces and laying claims to the public also differ across the three regions. Although physical space remains a crucial site where popular politics is staged, in Macau the Internet is the preferred site for public contestation. In Hong Kong and mainland China, spatial practices tend to operate closely to state spaces. Assembling in habitual venues or laying claim to a space controlled by the government can also generate a certain performative force. In terms of spatial distribution, Hong Kong protests often target central business districts, while many mainland protests are scattered and occur in suburban and rural areas. Because public spaces remain extremely restricted in mainland China, physical occupation tends to be short-lived and isolated, lacking horizontal articulation. While in Hong Kong, it is more possible to create spaces of encounters where utopian forms of politics are enacted. The political formation also allows more multifarious alliances to take place.

The different political contexts have also entailed divergent patterns of contentious interaction and different ways of redistributing the sensible order. In Macau, the government rarely directly responds to the request of citizens, who then turn to social media to vent discontents and construct oppositional identities. In mainland China, the regime's deep concern for legitimacy has encouraged demands that the state lives up to its promises. Despite the demonstration of obedience to the regime, these demands are frequently crushed by local governments, and entail situated responses from the state. Hong Kong, by contrast, can hardly find the attempt to mobilize central power. The protestors do not intend to appeal to the bureaucracies within the state or seek their support.

As for the use of the media, all the three places have actively engaged with media resources and come up with locally grounded visibility tactics. All have sought to appeal to the public and obtain widespread media coverage, and are supported by online organizing. In Macau and mainland China, mainstream media is dominated by pro-government groups and audiences have little influence over media content. For mainland protestors, getting the attention of national media can effectively apply pressure on local bureaucracies, so protestors often approach the media for help. Compared to Hong Kong's vibrant media environment, foreign and social media play a much more crucial role to mainland protestors, especially after domestic coverage is curtailed and there is a need to secure outside support.

## The Future

This book argues that the conventional top-down explanation of popular struggle should be called into question, since it cannot affirm the capacities and creativity of the people and explain how political spaces are opened up. Their practices illuminate that politics is not simply constituted by and through the institutions of the state, but emerges from a series of performatives that are disseminated and recognized across social space. The performative practices depicted in this book result from the crisis of political representation—these actions have exposed the more deep-seated lack and failure of the representative function of the socialist state. Chinese protestors often call into question local authorities' representativeness, but far from evading representation by the state as a whole (as manifested in some European and American struggles), they generally demand a more effective and just representation and rely on the sovereign power of political authorities to recognize their existence and grievances and to change the way of being governed. They come together as a collective force, making demands on the state, and expecting it to react. Their aim is mainly to recuperate what they consider to be their rights and to be properly "counted" by the state.

There are, however, some limitations to this contentious process and scenario. Although performative politics makes possible political subjectivity, the paradox is that political subjects, particularly in mainland China, come into existence through the enactment of state norms, which simultaneously constraining and enabling its formation. Rather than seeking to delegitimize the repressive state, protestors derive their agency from the regime that constitutes them. Popular struggles are largely staged within the framework of stability determined by the state, and thus their strategy is to make sure that the game is played by the rules. With a deep attachment to the state, their forms of subjectivity are in some ways *statized*. Popular political activities operate mainly around the spaces authorized by the state, and act on the terms it defines. Most of them, however, lack a political strategy and vision. They look up to "the central government as the ultimate authority and problem solver" (Sun and Zhao 2008: 151; O'Brien and Li 2006; Cai 2006).

What is illustrated in this book is a mode of subjectivity distinct from Euro-American experiences. As a result of the state's attempt to defuse antagonism by incorporating it into state form, these protests are characterized by parochialism, statism, and depoliticization through legalization. Although engaging with the state does not imply absolute passivity, the state indeed defines which political actions it certifies and the boundary of dissent it permits. The targeting of local officials is non-regime-threatening, and so it is tolerated. Although their actions are mostly unauthorized and sometimes challenge the law, the defiant actions and illegality have been selectively permitted by the state, as long as there is no imminent threat. Despite some intermittent expressions of large-scale militancy, struggles are generally scattered and isolated from each other, and there is no longer any ambitious, sustained movement that can bring about sweeping political turbulences. Its militancy is not directed at the legitimacy of the state or the CPC. It is, therefore, difficult to envision what Dirlik (1997, 237) calls the possibility of common political projects, given that there lacks a unifying force that can articulate the frustrations of larger segments of the population. If there is any political motive, it is not about reconfiguring the regime but more a case of calling into question the representativeness and the rapacious form of governance at local levels. Despite their remarkable frequency and pervasiveness, at most these activities generate local or regional disturbances. The shifting of relationships of power remains confined to the internal bureaucracies of the state. Although the Chinese experience shares something in common with other parts of the world, such as focusing on the lack of political representation, its performative politics aims to search for the possibility of expression and recognition by state power, rather than achieving autonomy and self-governance.

Yet the Chinese state's flexibility should not be overestimated. In recognizing its "adaptive capacity" (Bernstein and Lu 2003) in taking emergency measures, and the relative stable set of ordered relations constitutive of the state, one should not be distracted from the fact that the infringement of rights and problems of dispossession are still rampant, which remains the source of discontent that fuels struggle. Indignation against inequality and injustice remains widespread. This is why performative politics, which has evolved more novel forms of engagement in the past few decades, is gathering momentum. We have also seen the increased capacity of ordinary people who are more capable of organizing and politicizing themselves and thus creating some moments when changes do occur. In formulating their spaces of appearance, the uncertainty, surprise, and shock generated by their performative politics entail an intensity that disturbs the regularity of the state. They open up the sequences of performing what Rancière calls "disagreement" with the existing form of representation, and "for the appearance of a subject" (Rancière 2010). It is, as this book has attempted to illustrate, through this contentious process that an active subject is brought into political existence. Although these fractured struggles do not constitute a once-and-for-all transformation, their performatives are decisive in exposing the gap between the state and people, between discourse and reality, and in bringing about a new syntheses of popular political actions. It can hardly be viewed as a completely "new" form of politics, but it does differ from the Tiananmen occupation of 1989. Its impact is incremental, but will continue to disturb the state in China.

# Notes

## Introduction

1. Hardt and Negri (2012); Gould-Wartofsky (2015); Calhoun (2013); Smaligo (2014); Uitermark and Nicholls (2013); Taylor et al. (2011); Mitchell et al. (2013), Panitch et al. (2012); Khatib et al. (2012). For accounts of occupations in non-Western contexts, see Sitrin and Azzellini (2012); Castells (2012); Mason (2013); Schiffrin and Kircher-Allen (2012); Gunning and Baron (2014).

2. For a treatment of the cultural in new social movement theories, see Edwards (2014).

3. In mainland China, "the most frequently used method by citizens to defend their interests against state or other public actors is making appeals to the authorities concerned" (Cai 2006, 34). A contentious episode usually begins by lodging appeals. However, such appeals frequently escalate into direct actions if their demands are rebuffed. Most petitions eventually evolve into protest actions "either because petitions fail to bring about results or because the gathering of petitioning masses easily generates unanticipated action dynamics" (Lee 2007b, 119).

4. Since the 1990s, the conventional forms have included collective petitions, mass assemblies, leafleting, collective appeals, hunger strikes, boycotts and refusal to pay taxes or fees, demonstrations, strikes, sit-ins, disruptions of public ceremonies or festivals, marches to public authorities, invasions of enclosed lands or public properties, traffic blockades, government-office blockades, surround cadres, smashing windows, and burning vehicles. See Chen (2012); Lee (2007b); Bernstein and Lu (2003); Cai (2010); Froissart (2009); Rocca (2011).

## Chapter 1

1. All the examples cited in this chapter are drawn from mainland China, exclusive of Hong Kong and Macau. The unfolding of the latter's

struggles for citizenship has taken different forms and followed different logics that will be discussed in the following chapters.

2. However, De Certeau did not discuss the different practices of walking: Pile (2013, 228).

3. In addition to expressing their discontent, some protestors wore masks to conceal their identity and due to fear of police. For instance, in April 2014, a group of teachers in Henan wore masks in their protest against the government's wage reduction.

4. Regarding how environmental activists create image events, see DeLuca (1999).

5. Anti-PX protestors in Chengdu made the gesture of crossing their arms.

6. For how dominated groups develop a sense of identity through a set of rituals and symbols, see Laclau (2005).

7. In July 2014, the crowds against the maglev train in Shenzhen collectively wore yellow t-shirts.

8. There are distinctions between how the Foxconn suicides were read by Hong Kong activists and those in Beijing. In Hong Kong, the suicides tended to be understood as a consequence of the global production regime marked by the exploitation of Chinese migrant workers. The activists were more critical of the Chinese government's role in maintaining the export growth model. In Beijing, a coalition of environmental, health, and labor NGOs focused more on Apple's health record and the exposure of its environmental pollution (Litzinger 2013).

9. For an account of the origin, context, and media coverage of Tibet's self-immolation, see the special issue in *Cultural Anthropology* (McGranahan and Litzinger 2012).

10. For an account of unauthorized mourning and remembering in Maoist and post-Maoist China, see Watson (1994b).

11. For a more detailed analysis of the different readings and uses of Mao by the Chinese state and social groups, see Barmé (1996).

# Chapter 2

1. Some workers found that the social security deductions from their wages by the company were not deposited into their social security accounts, and that the employer secretly paid the social security funds for some management staff, thus, rendering the workers indignant. To evade responsibility, the employer required the employees to pay the social security fund arrears for the company on their own, and persuaded the workers who had just turned 50 years old to resign. Some workers also noticed that the labor contracts

were invalid. In addition, the workers were dissatisfied with the compensation amount proposed by the employer and asked to receive their unpaid overtime pay, high temperature subsidy, and paid annual leave.

2. By contrast, Lee (2016, 329–30) holds a more pessimistic view about the extent to which these state-led initiatives can help minimize worker's precarious status: "The institutional foundations of Chinese worker subordination have not changed. If anything, they have become more pernicious—collusion of local government and employers leading to arbitrary implementation of labor laws . . . state monopoly of worker representation and relentless crackdowns on labor NGOs and activists who dare to assist worker mobilization."

3. Some local officials have attempted to limit the access to administrative institutions and the legal mobilization of workers, or find ways to deflect grievances because the existing laws or policies are in conflict with their interests. In other cases, local cadres shut down institutionalized channels of appeal, rig elections, and order the court to reject lawsuits filed by citizens. See Gallagher (2005; 2009); O'Brien and Li (2006); and Cai (2007).

4. Employment security, according to Standing, includes "the existence of long-term employment contracts, protection against arbitrary dismissal, compensation for redundancy." Job security refers to "the assurance that the set of tasks a person is assigned to do or develops will not be changed arbitrarily and that he or she can foresee channels of stability and mobility ahead inside the enterprise" (2017, 168).

5. According to Standing (2017, 167), labor-based security includes labor market security, employment security, job security, work security, skill reproduction security, income security, and representation security.

6. The majority of Chinese workers are, as part of their general experience on the rise of China as the workshop of the world, "forced to change their jobs frequently, due to factors that include variations in production seasons; the practice of loaning employees (*zhiyuan*) to other departments or factories; the tradition of changing workers' job specifications and labour relationships (*fenliu*); as well as an abusive labour regime that involves the use of 'constructive dismissal,' active pressure to take on unwanted tasks, and limited job security . . . factories routinely violate labour contracts to change formal workers' work, content, and locations, effectively 'selling' labourers from the original factories to other factories or firms" (Smith and Pun 2018, 6).

7. Chan and Pun (2010, 30) offer a succinct account of the context: "The suppression of wages to jump-start export-processing industries in the 1980s brought about a large influx of foreign investments to China. Accelerated in the 1990s, transnational companies and Taiwanese contractors have outsourced low-value-added production to Chinese manufacturers. Millions

of export-oriented factories are subject to order specifications of Western and Asian multinationals."

8. These same market conditions could result in, as Lee (2016) suggests, negative implications for labor solidarity. The shortening of job tenure and the fluidity of job market, she notes, could undermine the collective capacity of labor power.

9. The provision of social insurance is an indicator to measure the extent of labor informalization (Lee 2016).

10. The Yue Yuen shoe factory is owned by the Taiwanese Pou Chen Group and started to serve as a supplier for the European and American brands in Dongguan in 1988. The to-be-retired workers of this factory inquired at the local social security department, and found that their amount of social security contribution was abnormal; some workers found the labor contract they signed was illegal, or that the employer paid their social security based on the standard of "temporary workers," which was far lower than their actual incomes. Once the information was revealed, workers at all Yue Yuen factories began to stage joint strikes with other plants. Finally, the employer promised to pay back the social security funds and granted increased subsistence allowances, but did not respond to the workers' demands that including pay raises, reorganization of trade unions, and execution of collective contracts. The strikes ended after police intervention.

11. The implementation of social security involves complex factors, and migrant workers' unwillingness to buy social security results from their practical consideration, while the enterprises also evade their responsibility in various ways (Gao 2015; He and Chen 2015).

12. Apart from the illegal evasion of social security funds and housing provident funds, the enterprises selectively pay social security for the core managerial and technical staff, or pay the funds at the minimum wage standard without the knowledge of employees. This practice is very common in labor-intensive sectors.

13. The Shenzhen Intermediate People's Court issued "Guidance" regarding the trials of labor disputes, that if the enterprises' relocation within the administrative district in Shenzhen causes the workers to sever labor relations, the enterprises are allowed not to offer compensation. See Article 85: "Guidelines of Shenzhen Intermediate People's Court on Judgment of Several Problems in Trial of Labor Dispute Cases" (Wang 2015). A labor activist I interviewed offered another explanation: "Currently the labor departments and trade unions will use the Guidance as a shield, but we stress that the Guidance is neither law nor regulation, only a guidance of the Intermediate People's Court on the trial of labor disputes and an internal operating rule within the court. Thus, can such a rule be used to address labor disputes?" (July 19, 2015).

14. Over the past few years, the worker protests in Shenzhen all failed to require the employers to pay back social security funds. For instance, in April 2013, the workers of a Shenzhen toy factory sent a petition letter to Shenzhen Municipal Human Resources and Social Security Bureau, the Shenzhen Federation of Trade Unions, and the Shenzhen Municipal People's Congress Standing Committee; however, they received no response. Moreover, the workers' request for negotiation with the employer was not responded to. Therefore, in August of 2013, the workers decided to take action; however, the municipal government did not accept the case on the grounds of no operational details (Yang 2015). The provisions of Shenzhen social security specify that the "repayment" after the two-year term shall be negotiated and decided by employers and workers, but not mandatory. The provisions of paying late fees make the negotiation between workers and employers more difficult. Some workers safeguard their rights through judicial means (*Southern Worker News* 2014).

15. *Dagong* "refers to casual labor-labor that can be dismissed at will, that can be replaced by anyone who is willing to sell his or her labor for a lower price" (Pun 2005, 12).

16. See relevant reports on *Yangcheng Evening News* and *Jianjiaobuluo* (尖椒部落).

17. Such as Guangdong Pearl River Channel and *Baoan Daily*.

18. The police's reason for confiscation was "extortion" and later amended to "destruction of production discipline."

19. The Chinese media refer these cases where the factories are shut down but refuse to grant workers compensation as "zombie factories" (*jiangshi gongchang*).

20. These supporting actions are proliferated in Japan, UK, USA, Turkey, Taiwan, Hong Kong, and India.

# Chapter 3

1. The approach has been criticized for its overly "structuralist" tendency in explaining causal connections of protest events (Edwards 2014, 239–40). I suggest that the theoretical weakness could be balanced by taking into account the *performative* engagement with state institutions and norms that sometimes entail unpredictable outcomes, as well as a set of contingent, creative practices enacted by protestors themselves to produce new opportunities for public visibility. These practices can create political agency and should not be reduced to merely "a function of political opportunity structure" (Tilly and Tarrow 2007, 76–77).

2. Other short-term measures taken by the authorities include providing funds to workers, paying back wages or pensions, and reversing governmental

or managerial decisions that triggered the dispute. See Lee (2007a) and Cai (2007).

## Chapter 4

1. The group was aligned with the radical wing of the opposition, the League of Social Democrats.

2. It is a compulsory pension fund for the retirement of residents in Hong Kong. The protestors claimed that the public funds were invested in capital markets to increase financiers' benefits.

3. In Asia, 200 people joined the global Occupy movement in Malaysia and 600 in Seoul. In Taipei and Tokyo, 300 and 200 participants, respectively, joined. Sydney and Auckland had about 2,000 protestors (*Hong Kong Economic Journal* 2011).

4. At the time, the U.S. unemployment rate surpassed 9 percent. For young people in Spain, the unemployment rate was more than 40 percent, while the unemployment rate in Hong Kong was only 3.2 percent, the lowest in the past 13 years. Before the action of Occupy Central, Hong Kong's stock market had reached new highs.

## Chapter 5

1. About the experience of the founding members of NWAT, see Guo (2016).

## Chapter 6

1. For a systematic account of user as producer in the network, see Bruns (2008). "Production today," according to Hardt and Negri (2004, xv), "has to be conceived not merely in economic terms but more generally as social production—not only the production of material goods but also the production of communications, relationships, and forms of life."

2. For Debord (2002), the spectacle is alienation. But I suggest the spectacle constitutes a field of cultural struggle that has transformative potentials to the passive attitude Debord criticizes.

3. Visual spoof can be seen as a peculiar form of "inter-textuality" (Hall 1997) that draws on different texts and alters their meanings in new contexts. Through "transcoding" and arbitrary juxtaposition, the original meanings of these elements are altered.

4. *Egao* is certainly not a "Chinese" thing: the so-called "Photoshop justice" has been waged against the pepper-spraying cop John Pike, who used the pepper spray in the midst of the global Occupy movement (Jardin 2011).

5. Jameson (1991, 17) defined "pastiche" with a derogatory sense. He dismissed late capitalism's pastiche as a blind, superficial, and meaningless form of imitation, nothing but a "blank parody" devoid of the sense of humor. But my empirical object does not support such a claim; instead, some images of *egao* are not just humorous and funny in themselves, but carry a profound sense of defiance or skepticism.

6. One reason for the popularity, of course, is *egao*'s evasion of censorship that designates certain words as unacceptable and simply prohibits their use online. Compared with traditional text, spoof is less tightly policed. However, the "newness" of *egao* should not be exaggerated—in the history of modern Chinese political culture, jokes, irony, puns, hyperbole, metaphors, and comics are widely used to convey sarcasm and ridicule. Mainland China's *pi zi* literature and Hong Kong's *wu li tou* films can also be seen as the longstanding tradition in which *egao* is rooted.

7. In fact the phenomenon has increasingly spread to the media sphere. The liberal-minded *Southern Metropolis Weekly*, for example, devoted an issue that made up fake news in 2006 to show support for *egao* culture's subversion of authorities (Martinsen 2006).

8. A notable example is seen in a widely circulated post entitled "Self-created English vocabularies with Chinese characteristics," which remade a range of political vocabularies with satirical meanings (http://lightson.blog.hexun.com/46024651_d.html, accessed 4 October 2011).

# Conclusion

1. In recent years, there has been a tendency to minimize or refuse the role of the state in critical theories on protest movements, mostly drawn from relatively limited Euro-American experiences. In China and most parts of the world, however, the state and its political capacity is not shrinking. It remains indispensable and continues to serve as the main target of rights struggles. Rather than becoming completely subordinate to capitalist demands, it still plays a crucial role in mediating social conflicts, redistributing resources, and expanding social rights. Protestors may have much discontent with the state, yet they remain highly reliant on state intervention, and do not seek novel political forms that are independent of the state. For a critique of the "autonomous politics" thesis, see Liu (2017).

# Bibliography

16 Beaver Group. 2013. Social Revolt in China: Foxconn is not Alone (April 17), http://16beavergroup.org/mondays/2013/04/17/social-revolt-in-china-foxconn-is-not-alone. Accessed on October 22, 2017.
Ahmad, Aijaz. 1992. *In Theory*. London: Verso.
Ahmed, Sara. 2004. *The Cultural Politics of Emotion*. New York: Routledge.
AI (Aluminium Insider). 2017. "Proposed Construction of Zhongwang Plant in China Spurs Mass Protests." http://aluminiuminsider.com/proposed-construction-zhongwang-plant-china-spurs-mass-protests/. Accessed on May 15, 2018.
AlCircle. 2017. "China Zhongwang Says its Facilities Conform to the Highest International Environmental Standards." February 15, 2017. https://www.alcircle.com/news/downstream-products/detail/27016/china-zhongwang-says-its-facilities-conform-to-the-highestinternational-environmental-standards. Accessed on May 21, 2018.
Andrews, J. F., and M. Gao. 1995. "The Avant-Garde's Challenge to Official Art." In Deborah S. Davis et al. eds. *Urban Spaces in Contemporary China*, Cambridge: Cambridge University Press, pp. 221–278.
AP (Associated Press). 2017. "Residents of Chinese City Protest Against Aluminum Plant." *WBAL Radio*, February 14, 2017. http://www.wbal.com/article/220250/130/residents-of-chinese-city-protest-against-aluminum-plantFebruary%2014%202017. Accessed on May 18, 2018.
Arendt, Hannah. 1958. *The Human Condition*. Chicago: The University of Chicago Press.
Badiou, Alain. 2012. *The Rebirth of History*. London: Verso.
Balibar, Etienne. 2015. *Citizenship*. Cambridge, UK: Polity.
Barboza, David, and Keith Bradsherjune. 2011. "In China, Labour Movement Enabled by Technology." *New York Times*, June 16, 2010. https://www.nytimes.com/2010/06/17/business/global/17strike.html. Accessed on May 3, 2016.

Bargu, Banu. 2014. *Starve and Immolate: The Politics of Human Weapons*. New York: Columbia University Press.
Barmé, Geremie. 1996. *Shades of Mao*. New York: M. E. Sharpe.
Bastille Post. 2015. "2700 Shoe-making Workers in Panyu Occupied the Factory for Compensation." April 25, 2015. http://www.bastillepost.com/macau/6-大視野/74214-. Accessed on November 5, 2015.
Becker, Jeffrey. 2014. *Social Ties, Resources, and Migrant Labor Contention in Contemporary China: From Peasants to Protesters*. Lanham, MD: Lexington Books.
Beja, Jean-Philippe. 2011. "The New Working Class Renews the Repertoire of Social Conflict." *China Perspectives*, 2: 3–7.
Bernstein, Thomas B. 1999. "Farmer Discontent and Regime Responses." In *The Paradox of China's Post-Mao Reforms*. Edited by Merle Goldman and Roderick MacFarquhar, 197–219. Cambridge, MA: Harvard University Press.
——— and Lu Xiaobo. 2003. *Taxation without Representation in Contemporary Rural China*. Cambridge: Cambridge University Press.
Best, Steven, and Kellner Douglas. 2001. *The Postmodern Adventure: Science, Technology, and Cultural Studies at the Third Millennium*. New York: Routledge.
Bradsher, Keith. 2015. "China Turned to Risky Devaluation as Export Machine Stalled." *New York Times*, August 17, 2015. https://www.nytimes.com/2015/08/18/business/international/chinas-devaluation-of-its-currency-was-a-call-to-action.html. Accessed on November 10, 2015.
Bray, Mark. 2014. *Translating Anarchy: The Anarchism of Occupy Wall Street*. Winchester, UK: Zero Books.
Brighenti, Andrea Mubi. 2010. *Visibility in Social Theory and Social Research*. Hampshire, UK: Palgrave.
Brown, Miranda. 2007. *The Politics of Mourning in Early China*. New York: State University of New York Press.
Bruns, Axel. 2008. *Blogs, Wikipedia, Second Life, and Beyond*. New York: Peter Lang.
Buechler, Steven M. 2000. *Social Movements in Advanced Capitalism*. Oxford: Oxford University Press.
Buruma, Ian. 2001. "Cult of the Chairman." *The Guardian*, March 7, 2001. https://www.theguardian.com/world/2001/mar/07/china.features11. Accessed on October 10, 2017.
Butler, Judith. 2004. *Precarious life*. London: Verso.
———. 2009. *Frames of War: When is Life Grievable?* London: Verso.
———. 2011. "Bodies in Alliance and the Politics of the Street." *European Institute for Progressive Cultural Policies*, September 2011. http://www.eipcp.net/transversal/1011/butler/en. Accessed on November 16, 2015.
———. 2015. *Notes Toward a Performative Theory of Assembly*. Cambridge, MA: Harvard University Press.

———, and Athena Athanasiou. 2013. *Dispossession: The Performative in the Political.* Cambridge, UK: Polity.
Cai, Jane. 2006. "Online Spoofs Now Part of Mainstream." *South China Morning Post,* September 5, 2006, EDT 6.
Cai, Yongshun. 2006. *State and Laid-Off Workers in Reform China.* London: Routledge.
———. 2007. "Civil Resistance and Rule of Law in China." In *Grassroots Politilcal Reform in Contemporary China,* edited by Merle Goldman and Roderick MacFarquhar, 174–95. Cambridge, MA: Harvard University Press.
———. 2008. "Disruptive Collective Action in the Reform Era." In Kevin J. O'Brien ed., *Popular Protest in China,* pp. 163–78, Cambridge, MA: Harvard University Press.
———. 2010. *Collective Resistance in China: Why Popular Protests Succeed or Fail.* Stanford, CA: Stanford University Press.
Calhoun, Craig. 2013. "Occupy Wall Street in Perspective." *The British Journal of Sociology,* 64 (1): 26–38.
Carlson, Allen et al., eds. 2010. *Contemporary Chinese Politics.* Cambridge: Cambridge University Press.
Castells, Manuel. 2012. *Networks of Outrage and Hope: Social Movements in the Internet Age.* Cambridge, UK: Polity.
Chan, A. 2015. "Investigative Report on the Working Conditions in UNIQLO's China Suppliers." *Students & Scholars against Corporate Misbehaviour,* January 11, 2015. http://sacom.hk/statement-clean-clothes-from-uniqlo-now-uniqlo-should-improve-the-working-conditions-of-the-suppliers-in-china-immediately. Accessed on November 21, 2015.
Chan, Jenny, and Ngai Pun. 2010. "Suicide as Protest for the New Generation of Chinese Migrant Workers: Foxconn, Global Capital, and the State." *The Asia-Pacific Journal* 8 (37): 2.
Chatterjee, Partha. 2004. *The Politics of the Governed.* New York: Columbia University Press.
Cheater, A. P. 1991. "Death Ritual as Political Trickster in the People's Republic of China." *The Australian Journal of Chinese Affairs* 26 (July): 67–97.
Cheek, Timothy. 2008. "The Multiple Maos of Contemporary China." *Harvard Asia Quarterly* XI (2–3): 14–25.
Chen, Feng. 2004. "SOE Restructuring and Worker Protests." *Aisixiang,* August 26, 2004. http://www.aisixiang.com/data/3929.html. Accessed on November 5, 2015.
———. 2008. "Worker Leaders and Framing Factory-based Resistance." In *Popular Protest in China,* edited by J. K. O'Brien, 88–107. Cambridge, MA: Harvard University Press.
Chen, Xi. 2012. *Social Protest and Contentious Authoritarianism in China.* Cambridge: Cambridge University Press.

Chou, Kwok Ping. 2007. "Interest Group Politics in Macau after Handover." *Journal of Contemporary China* 4(43): 191–206.
Chun, Allen. 2012. "Toward a Postcolonial Critique of the State in Singapore." *Cultural Studies* 26 (5): 670–87.
Citton, Yves. 2009. "Political Agency and the Ambivalence of the Sensible." In *Jacques Rancière: History, Politics, Aesthetics*, ed. Gabriel Rockhill and Philip Watts, Durham, NC: Duke University Press.
Corcoran, Steven. 2010. "Editor's Introduction." In *Dissensus: On Politics and Aesthetics*, edited by Steven Corcoran, 1–24. London: Continuum.
Cui, K. et al. 2013. "New Workers Art Troupe." *Theory and Criticism of Literature and Art* 4: 67–76.
Dang, Zi. 2008. "Why is 'Egao Culture' so Prosperous?" *The Rednet*, August 2008. http://hlj.rednet.cn/c/2008/08/05/1567482.htm. Accessed on October 10, 2008.
Davis, Oliver. 2010. *Jacques Rancière*. Cambridge, UK: Polity.
Debord, Guy. 2002. *The Society of the Spectacle*. New York: Zone Books.
DeLuca, Kevin M. 1999. *Image Politics: The New Rhetoric of Environmental Activism*. New York: Guildford.
Dirlik, Arif. 1997. *The Postcolonial Aura*. Boulder, CO: Westview.
———. 2007. *Global Modernity*. Boulder, CO: Paradigm.
Dyer-Witheford, Nick. 1999. *Cyber-Marx: Cycles and Circuits of Struggle in High-Technology Capitalism*. Urbana and Chicago: University of Illinois Press.
Edwards, Gemma. 2014. *Social Movements and Protest*. Cambridge: Cambridge University Press.
Eimer, David. 2006. "The Great Parody Craze." *South China Morning Post*, August 9, 2006, EDT 13.
Elfstrom, M., and S. Kuruvilla. 2014. "The Changing Nature of Labour Unrest in China." *Industrial & Labour Relations Review* 67 (2): 453–80.
Esherick, Joseph W., and Jeffrey N. Wasserstrom. 1994. "Acting Out Democracy: Political Theater in Modern China." In *Popular Protest & Political Culture in Modern China*, edited by Jeffrey N. Wasserstrom and Elizabeth J. Perry, 32–73. Boulder,CO: Westview Press.
Evans-Pritchard, Ambrose. 2014. "Hong Kong Crisis Exposes Impossible Contradiction of China's Economic Growth." *The Telegraph*, October 1, 2014. https://www.telegraph.co.uk/finance/comment/ambroseevans_pritchard/11134755/Hong-Kong-crisis-exposes-impossible-contradiction-of-Chinas-economic-growth.html. Accessed on October 5, 2014.
Fabricant, Nicole. 2009. "Performative Politics." *American Ethnologist* 36 (4): 768–83.
Fernandez, Luis. 2008. *Policing Dissent: Social Control and the Anti-globalization Movement*. New Brunswick, NJ: Rutgers University Press.

Fewsmith, Joseph. 2013. *The Logic and Limits of Political Reform in China*. Cambridge: Cambridge University Press.

Fierke, Karin M. 2013. *Political Self-Sacrifice: Agency, Body and Emotion in International Relations*. New York: Cambridge University Press.

Fong, Vanessa L., and Rachel Murphy. eds. 2006. *Chinese Citizenship*. London: Routledge.

Foucault, Michel. 2007. *The Politics of Truth*. Los Angeles: Semiotext(e).

Friedman, Eli. 2012. "China in Revolt." *Jacobin*, August 1, 2012. https://www.jacobinmag.com/2012/08/china-in-revolt. Accessed on December 12, 2012.

———. 2014. "Alienated Politics: Labor Insurgency and the Paternalistic State in China." *Development and Change* 45 (5): 1001–018.

Froissart, Chloe. 2009. "The Rise of Migrant Workers' Collective Action." In *Social Movements in China and Hong Kong*. Edited by Khun Eng Kuah-Pearce and Gilles Guiheux, Amsterdam: Amsterdam University Press.

Gallagher, Mary E. 2005. *Contagious Capitalism*. Princeton, NJ: Princeton University Press.

———. 2009. "China's Older Workers." In *Laid-off Workers in a Worker's State*, edited by Thomas B. Gold et al., 135–58. New York: Palgrave.

Gao, M. 2001. *Century Utopia*. Taipei: Artists.

Gao, Y. 2015. "Focus on Basic Endowment Insurance for Migrant Workers: Helplessness behind Withdrawal from Social Security." *The Procuratorate Daily*, March 4, 2015. http://news.swchina.org/hot/2015/0304/20816.shtml. Accessed on November 1, 2015.

Gladney, Dru C. 2004. *Dislocating China: Muslims, Minorities, and Other Subaltern Subjects*. Chicago: The University of Chicago Press.

Glass, Michael R., and Reuben Rose-Redwood, ed. 2014. *Performativity, Politics, and the Production of Social Space*. London: Routledge.

Golder, Ben. 2015. *Foucault and the Politics of Rights*. Stanford, CA: Stanford University Press.

Goldman, Merle. 2005. *From Comrade to Citizen*. Cambridge, MA: Harvard University Press.

Gong, L. 2015. "How the First Generation of Migrant Workers Provide Themselves in Retirement When They Grow Old?" *China News Week*, July 20, 2015. http://news.inewsweek.cn/detail-1954.html. Accessed on November 12, 2015.

Gordon, Colin. 1991. "Governmental Rationality: An Introduction." In *The Foucault Effect: Studies in Governmentality*, edited by Graham Burchell, Colin Gordan, and Peter Miller, 1– 51. Chicago: The Chicago University Press.

Gould-Watorfsky, Michael A. 2015. *The Occupiers: The Making of the 99 Percent Movement*. New York: Oxford University Press.

Graeber, David, and Hui, Yuk. 2014. "From Occupy Wall Street to Occupy Central: The Case of Hong Kong." *Los Angeles Review of Books*, October 14, 2014. https://lareviewofbooks.org/article/occupy-central-the-case-of-hong-kong. Accessed on November 14, 2014.

Gray, K., and Jang, Y. 2014. "Labour Unrest in the Global Political Economy: The Case of China's 2010 Strike Wave." *New Political Economy* 20 (4): 594–613.

Gunning, Jeroen, and Ilan Zvi Baron. 2014. *Why Occupy a Square?* Oxford: Oxford University Press.

Guo, Jia. 2016. "'Entering' NWAT." *Coolloud*. http://www.coolloud.org.tw/node/86733. Accessed on January 16, 2017.

Hall, Stuart. 1997. "The Spectacle of the 'Other.'" In *Representation: Cultural Representations and Signifying Practices*, edited by Stuart Hall, 223–290. London: Sage.

Hallward, Peter. 2001. *Absolutely Postcolonial*. Manchester, UK: Manchester University Press.

———. 2009. "Staging Equality: Rancière's Theatrocracy and the Limits of Anarchic Equality." In *Jacques Rancière: History, Politics, Aesthetics*, edited by Gabriel Rockhill and Philip Watts, 140–157. Durham, NC: Duke University Press.

Haoxiana. 2014. "Social Security Problem Stimulated Workers' Violent Protest." http://article.haoxiana.com/93369.html. Accessed on June 6, 2015.

Harcourt, E. Bernard. 2013. "Political Disobedience." In *Occupy: Three Inquiries in Disobedience*, edited by W. J. T Mitchell, E. Bernard Harcourt, and Michael Taussig, 45–93. Chicago: The University of Chicago Press.

Hardt, Michael, and Antonio Negri. 2000. *Empire*. Cambridge, MA: Harvard University Press.

———. 2004. *Multitude*. New York: The Penguin Press.

———. 2012. *Declaration*. Belgrade: Argo-Navis.

He, Y., and Chen, P. 2015. "China's Basic Endowment Insurance." *Events in Focus*. http://www.eventsinfocus.org/issues/261. Accessed on November 19, 2015.

Hess, Steve. 2015. "Foreign Media Coverage and Protest Outcomes in China: The Case of the 2011 Wukan Rebellion." *Modern Asian Studies* 49 (1): 177–203.

*Hong Kong Economic Journal*. 2011. "Indifference in Asia and Hong Kong Claimed the Long-term Movement of 'Occupy Central.'" October 17, 2011.

———. 2014. "Public Opinion Program, the University of Hong Kong: 83% of the People Called for Stopping the Occupation, and Nearly 70% Suggested that Government Should Evict the Protestants. The Violence Will Leave a Negative Image for the Public." November 20, 2014.

Hu, Fox Yi. 2008a. "Censors Stalking Macau's Net Users." *South China Morning Post*, June 29, 2008. EDT 2.
———. 2008b. "Macau Netizens Fear Big Brother at Work as Security Law Looms." *South China Morning Post*, October 17, 2008, CITY 4.
Huang, Cary. 2010. "Revolutionary Humor No Laughing Matter for Cadres." *South China Morning Post*, September 1, 2010. http://www.scmp.com/article/723517/revolutionary-humour-no-laughing-matter-cadres. Accessed on December 12, 2010.
Huang, H. 2014. "Difficult Problem of 'Getting Old without Pension' of the First Generation of Migrant Workers." *South Reviews*, December 9, 2014. http://www.nfcmag.com/article/5169.html. Accessed on November 8, 2015.
Isabella, Steger. 2014. "Hong Kong Protesters Suspend Democracy Vote." *The Wall Street Journal*, October 26, 2014.
Isin, Engin F. 2008. "Theorizing Acts of Citizenship." In *Acts of Citizenship*. Edited by Engin F. Isin and Greg M. Nielsen, London: Zed Books, pp. 15–43.
———. 2012. *Citizens Without Frontiers*. New York: Bloomsbury.
Jameson, Fredric. 1991. *Postmodernism, or, the Cultural Logic of Late Capitalism*. Taipei: Tonsan.
Jardin, Xeni. 2011. "The Pepper-Spraying Cop Gets Photoshop Justice." *The Guardian*, November 23, 2011. http://www.guardian.co.uk/commentisfree/2011/nov/23/pepper-spraying-cop-photoshop-justice?newsfeed=true. Accessed on December 5, 2011.
Jasper, James. M. 2014. *Protest: A Cultural Introduction to Social Movements*. Cambridge, UK: Polity.
Jenkins, Henry. 2006. *Convergence Culture*. New York: New York University Press.
Johnston, H. 2009. "Protest cultures. In *Culture, Social Movements, and Protest*, edited by Hank Johnston, 3–29. Surrey, UK: Ashgate.
———, and Bert Klandermans. 1995. "The Cultural Analysis of Social Movements." In *Social Movements and Culture*, edited by Hank Johnston and Bert Klandermans, 3–24. Minneapolis: University of Minnesota Press.
Joseph, May. 1999. *Nomadic Identities*. Minneapolis: University of Minnesota Press.
"Just Flat Angry." *South China Morning Post*. May 18, 2011, EDT 2.
Ke, Yanjian. 2014. "Crisis and Prospect of Umbrella Movement." *Hong Kong Economic Journal*, A21.
Keith, M., ed. 1997. *Geographies of Resistance*. London: Routledge.
Khatib, Kate, Margaret Killjoy, Mike McGuire, and David Graeber, ed. 2012. *We Are Many: Reflections on Movement Strategy from Occupation to Liberation*. Oakland, CA: AK Press.
Kutcher, Norman. 1999. *Mourning in Late Imperial China: Filial Piety and the State*. New York: Cambridge University Press.

Kwong, Peter. 2008. The Tao of Spoof. *Agence Global*, February 18, 2008. http://www.agenceglobal.com/article. asp?id=1486. Accessed on January 18, 2010.

*Labor Newspaper*. 2013. "Over Hundred Workers in Dongguan Received Microblogging Subsidies and Requested 'Dismissal.'" Shanghai Federation of Trade Unions. http://www.shzgh.org/renda/node5902/node18796/u1a1843498.html. Accessed on November 26, 2015.

Laclau, Ernesto 1990. *New Reflections on the Revolution of Our Time*. London: Verso.

———. 2005. *On Populist Reason*. New York: Verso.

Lee, Ching Kwan. 2007a. "Is Labor a Political Force in China?" In *Grassroots Politilcal Reform in Contemporary China*, edited by Merle Goldman and Roderick MacFarquhar, 228–52. Cambridge, MA: Harvard University Press.

———. 2007b. *Against the Law: Labor Protests in China's Rustbelt and Sunbelt*. Berkeley: University of California Press.

———. 2016. "Precarization or Empowerment? Reflections on Recent Labor Unrest in China." *The Journal of Asian Studies* 75 (2): 317–33.

Leese, Daniel. 2011. *Mao Cult: Rhetoric and Ritual in China's Cultural Revolution*. New York: Cambridge University Press.

Li, Qiang. 2012. *Peasant-Workers and Chinese Social Stratification*. Beijing: Social Sciences Academic Press.

Li, Yanhong, and Yang, Fan. 2013. "Cultural Capital and Communicative Empowerment." *Communication and Society* 26: 33–73.

Liang, Wendao. 2006. "When People Laugh, Governments Start to Think." *Ming Pao*, September 8, 2006, P08.

Lin, Chun. 2006. *The Transformation of Chinese Socialism*. Durham, NC: Duke University Press.

Lin, K. 2015. "Chinese Strikes in Manufacturing: from Offensive to Defensive?" *Solidarity*, October 3, 2015. https://www.solidarity-us.org/site/node/4513. Accessed on November 24, 2015.

Litzinger, Ralph. 2012. "Tibet Talk—on Life, Death, and the State." *Cultural Anthropology*, April 8, 2012. https://culanth.org/fieldsights/104-tibet-talk-on-life-death-and-the-state. Accessed on May 11, 2018.

———. 2013. "The Labor Question in China." *The South Atlantic Quarterly* 112 (1): 172–78.

Liu, Serena. 2007. "Social Citizenship in China." *Citizenship Studies* 11 (5): 465–79.

Liu, Shih-Diing. 2008. "Casino Colony." *New Left Review* 50: 109–24.

———. 2009. "The Emergence of Internet Biopolitics in China." *Reflexion* 11: 57–77.

———. 2017. "Demanding State Intervention." *The New Global Politics*, edited by Harry E. Vanden et al., 234–49. London: Routledge.
Liu, Y. 2012. "Suspecting the Factory Became a Ghost Factory, Hundreds of Workers in a Naihai Factory Stopped Work." *Southern Metropolis Daily*, December 13, 2012. http://news.sohu.com/20121213/n360279983.shtml. Accessed on November 2, 2015.
Ma, Guoming. 2007. *Society of Total Urbanization*, Hong Kong: Step Forward.
———. 2014. "Delayed Democratic Return." *Ming Pao*, October 5, 2014.
Makley, Charlene. 2015. "The Sociopolitical Live of Dead Bodies: Tibetan Self-Immolation Protest as Mass Media." *Cultural Anthropology* 30 (3): 448–76.
Martín, Jorge. 2010. "China: Honda Workers' Strike—the Beginning of a New Labour Movement?" *In Defence of Marxism*, June 1, 2010. http://www.marxist.com/china-honda-workers-strike.htm. Accessed on March 18, 2015.
Martinsen, Joel. 2006. "2006: The Year in Spoofs." *Danwei*, December 29, 2006. http://www.danwei.org/magazines/2006_the_year_in_spoofs.php. Accessed on June 10, 2008.
Mason, Paul. 2013. *Why It's Still Kicking Off Everywhere*. London: Verso.
Matynia, Elzbieta. 2009. *Performative Democracy*. Boulder, CO: Paradigm.
McGranahan, Carole, and Ralph Litzinger. 2012. "Self-Immolation as Protest in Tibet." *Cultural Anthropology*, April 9, 2012. https://culanth.org/fieldsights/93-self-immolation-as-protest-in-tibet. Accessed on May 11, 2018.
Meng, Quan, and Jun Lu. 2013. "Political Space in the Achievement of Collective Labour Rights: Interaction between Regional Government and Workers' Protest." *Journal of Comparative Asian Development* 12(3): 465–88.
Miller, B. A. 2000. *Geography and Social Movements: Comparing Antinuclear Activism in the Boston Area*. Minneapolis: University of Minnesota Press.
*Ming Pao*. 2006. "Egao." September 17, 2006, P09.
Mitchell, W. J. T., E. B. Harcourt, and Micheal Taussig, ed. 2013. *Occupy: Three Inquiries in Disobedience*. Chicago: The University of Chicago Press.
Mitchell, W. J. T. 2013. "Preface." In *Occupy: Three Inquiries in Disobedience*, edited by W. J. T. Mitchell, E. B. Harcourt, and Michael Taussig, vii–xv. Chicago: The University of Chicago Press.
Mouffe, Chantal. 2002. *Politics and Passions: The Stakes of Democracy*. London: Centre for the Study of Democracy. London: University of Westminster.
———. 2013. *Agonistics*. London: Verso.
Mustafa, Daanish, Katherine E. Brown, and Matthew Tillotson. 2013. "Antipode to Terror? Spaces of Performative Politics." *Antipode* 45 (5): 1110–127.

NetEase Finance. 2013. "Hundred Workers in Dongguan Stayed in Zombie Factories for Four Months." August 14, 2013. http://money.163.com/photoview/5BNQ0025/10252.html#p=9659QFCL5BNQ0025. Accessed on November 18, 2015.

Ng, Kai Hong. 2013. "Social Movements and Policy Capacity in Hong Kong." *Issues and Studies* 49 (2): 179–214.

Nicholls, W., B. A. Miller, and J. Beaumont, ed. 2013. *Spaces of Contention: Spatialities and Social Movements*. Farnham, UK: Ashgate.

O'Brien, Kevin J., ed. 2008. *Popular Protest in China*. Cambridge, MA: Harvard University Press.

———, and Lianjiang Li. 2006. *Rightful Resistance in Rural China*. Cambridge: Cambridge University Press.

Panitch, Leo, Greg Albo, and Vivek Chibber, ed. 2012. *The Question of Strategy*. Wales; London: The Merlin Press.

Parry, Jonathan. 2018. "Introduction: Precarity, Class, and the Neoliberal Subject." In *Industrial Labor on the Margins of Capitalism*, edited by Chris Hann and Jonathan Parry, 1–38. New York: Berghahn.

Pei, Minxin. 2010. "Rights and Resistance: The Changing Contexts of the Dissident Movement." In *Chinese Society*, 3rd ed, edited by Elizabeth J. Perry and Mark Selden, 20–40. London: Routledge.

Perry, Elizabeth J. 2007. "Studying Chinese Politics: Farewell to Revolution?" *The China Journal* 57: 1–22.

———. 2008a. "Permanent Rebellion?" In *Popular Protest in China*, edited by Kevin J. O'Brien, 205–15. Cambridge, MA: Harvard University Press.

———. 2008b. "Chinese Conceptions of 'Rights.'" *Perspectives on Politics* 6 (1): 37–50.

———, and Li Xun. 1997. *Proletarian Power: Shanghai in the Cultural Revolution*. Boulder, CO: Westview Press.

———, and Merle Goldman, ed. 2007. *Grassroots Political Reform in Contemporary China*. Cambridge, MA: Harvard University Press.

———, and Mark Seldon, ed. 2000. *Chinese Society*. London: Routledge.

Peterson, Abby. 2002. *Contemporary Political Protest: Essays on Political Militancy*. Burlington VT: Ashgate.

Phadke, Shilpa et al. 2009. "Why Loiter?" In *Dissent and Cultural Resistance in Asia's Cities*, edited by Melissa Butcher and Selvaraj Velayutham, 185–203. New York: Routledge.

Phillips, Nicola, and Fabiola Mieres. 2015. "The Governance of Forced Labour in the Global Economy." *Globalizations*, 12 (2): 244–60.

Pile, Steve. 2013. *The Body and the City: Psychoanalysis, Space and Subjectivity*. New York: Routledge.

Prokhovnik, Raia. 2014. "Introduction: The Body as a Site for Politics." *Citizenship Studies* 18 (5): 465–84.

Pun, Ngai. 2005. *Made in China: Women Factory Workers in a Global Workplace*. Durham, NC: Duke University Press.
———. 2016. *Migrant Labor in China*. Cambridge, UK: Polity.
Rancière, J. 2004. *The Politics of Aesthetics*, New York: Continuum.
———. 2009a. *Aesthetics and its Discontents*, Cambridge, UK: Polity.
———. 2009b. "The Method of Equality." In *Jacques Rancière*, edited by Gabriel Rockhill and Philip Watts, 273–88. Durham, NC: Duke University Press.
———. 2010. *Dissensus*, New York: Continuum.
———. 2014. *Moments Poliques*. New York: Seven Stories Press.
Reed, T. V. 2005. *The Art of Protest*. Minneapolis: University of Minnesota Press.
———. 2016. "Protest as Artistic Expression." In *Protest Culture*, edited by Kathrin Fahlenbrach et al, 1820–2142. New York: Berghahn, 2016.
Renmin chunqiu. 2001. "Shanghai Workers Occupied a Factory." *Maostudy*, November 15, 2001. http://maostudy.org/ldarticle.php3?article=2001-11/N_shanghai.txt. Accessed on November 11, 2015.
Rimini, F. D. 2013. "Reinscribing the City." *Globalizations* 10 (3): 465–79.
Rocca, Jean-Luis. 2011. "'Old Working Class' Resistance in Capitalist China." In *Social Movements in China and Hong Kong*, edited by Khun Eng Kuah-Pearce and Gilles Guiheux, 117–34. Amsterdam: Amsterdam University Press.
Rockhill, Gabriel. 2004a. "Translator's Introduction: Jacques Rancière's Politics of Perception." In *The Politics of Aesthetics*, by Jacques Rancière, 1–6. New York: Continuum.
———. 2004b. "Appendix I: Glossary of Technical Terms." In *The Politics of Aesthetics*, by Jacques Rancière, 80–89. New York: Continuum.
Rose-Redwood, Reuben, and Michael R. Glass. 2014. "Introduction: Geographies of Performativity." In *Performativity, Politics, and the Production of Social Space*, edited by Michael R. Glass and Reuben Rose-Redwood, 1–34. London: Routledge.
Salmenkari, T. 2004. "Implementing and Voiding Control." *China: An International Journal* (2): 235–61.
San Juan, Epifanio. 1999. *Beyond Postcolonial Theory*. New York: St. Martins Press.
Schiffrin, Anya, and Eamon Kircher-Allen, ed. 2012. *From Cairo to Wall Street*. New York: The New Press.
Sethi, Rumina. 2011. *The Politics of Postcolonialism*. London: Pluto.
Sewell, H. W. 2001. "Space in Contentious Politics." In *Silence and Voice in the Study of Contentious Politics*, edited by Ronald R. Aminzade, Jack A. Goldstone, Doug McAdam, Elizabeth J. Perry, Sewell H. William, Sidney Tarrow, and Charles Tilley, 51–68. Cambridge: Cambridge University Press.

Shi, S. 2015. "The World's Factory in Mainland China was Hit by Crisis and Foreign Investors Accelerate the Withdrawal from China." *Radio Free Asia*, February 23, 2015. http://www.rfa.org/mandarin/yataibaodao/jingmao/xql-02232015103857.html. Accessed on June 20, 2015.

Sigley, Gary. 2006. "Chinese Governmentalities: Government, Governance, and Socialist Market Economy." *Economy and Society* 35 (4): 487–508.

Sim, Chi Yin. 2009. "Free Speech with 'Grass Mud Horse.'" *The Straits Times*, March 27, 2009. https://chinadigitaltimes.net/2009/03/free-speech-with-grass-mud-horse-mythical-creature-a-not-so-secret-weapon-against-net-nannies. Accessed on May 5, 2012.

*Singtao*. 2013. "Factories Shut down and on Holidays, Hundreds of People Requested Dismissal and Workers in Dongguan Put Managers under House Arrest." August 12, 2013. http://news.singtao.ca/toronto/2013-08-12/china1376299708d4641095.html. Accessed on November 24, 2015.

Sitrin, Marina, and Dario Azzellini. 2012. *Occupying Language: The Secret Rendezvous with History and the Present*. New York: Zuccotti Park Press.

Smaligo, Nicholas. 2014. *The Occupy Movement Explained*. Chicago: Open Courtm.

Smith, Chris, and Pun Ngai. 2018. "Class and Precarity in China." *Chinoiresie*, February 14, 2018. https://www.chinoiresie.info/class-precarity-in-china. Accessed on March 2018.

*Southern Worker News*. 2014. "Why it is so Difficult for Migrant Workers to Retire." August 4, 2014. http://www.hngrrb.cn/hngrrb/html/2014-08/04/content_29962.htm. Accessed on June 15, 2015.

Spivak, Gayatri Chakravorty. 1988. "Can the Subaltern Speak?" In *Marxism and the Interpretation of Culture*, edited by Cary Nelson and Lawrence Grossberg, 271–313. London: Macmillan.

Standing, Guy. 2017. "The Precariat in China: A Comment on Conceptual Confusion." *Rural China* 14: 165–70.

Sullivan, M. 1999. "Art in China since 1949." *The China Quarterly* 159: 712–22.

Sun, Yanfei, and Zhao Dingxin. 2008. "Environmental Campaigns." In *Popular Protest in China*, edited by Kevin O'Brien, 144–62. Cambridge, MA: Harvard University Press.

Sutton, Barbara. 2010. *Bodies in Crisis: Culture, Violence, and Women's Resistance in Neoliberal Argentina*. New Brunswick, NJ: Rutgers University Press.

Tally, Robert. 2013. *Spatiality*. New York: Routledge.

Tang, Alex. 2014. "Investigation on Participants of Occupation (3)—Possibility to Represent the Public by Student Leaders." *Hong Kong Inmedia* (October 30). http://www.inmediahk.net/node/3. Accessed on December 9, 2014.

Taylor, Astra, Carla Blumenkranz, Keith Gessen, Mark Geif, Sarah Lenard, and Sarah Resnick, ed. 2011. *Occupy! Scenes from Occupied America.* London: Verso.
*The Standard.* "Residents Reject Zhongwang Aluminum Plant." February 15, 2017. http://www.thestandard.com.Hk/breaking-news.php?id=84863. Accessed on May 21, 2018.
Tilly, Charles, and Sidney Tarrow. 2007. *Contentious Politics.* Oxford: Oxford University Press.
Tormey, Simon. 2015. *The End of Representative Politics.* Cambridge, UK: Polity.
Tsou, Tang. 1986. *The Cultural Revolution and Post-Mao Reforms.* Chicago: The University of Chicago Press.
Uitermark, Justus, and Walter Nicholls. 2013. "How Local Networks Shape a Global Movement." *Social Movement Studies* 11 (3/4): 295–301.
Wang, Cheng. 2015. "Guidelines of Shenzhen Intermediate People's Court on Judgment of Several Problems in Trial of Labor Dispute Cases." *Shenzhen Intermediate People's Court*, November 18, 2015. http://blog.workercn.cn/?uid-10274-action-viewspace-itemid-557175. Accessed on December 10, 2015.
Wang, Hui. 2003. *China's New Order.* Cambridge, MA: Harvard University Press.
Wang, Kan. 2011. "Collective Awakening and Action of Chinese Workers: The 2010 Auto Workers' Strike and its Effects." Translated by Ralf Ruckus. *Sozial. Geschichete Online* 6.
Wang, Ran. 2007. "The Internet Has Not Ruined Public Taste." *Southern Metropolis Daily*, January 9, 2007.
Wasserstrom, Jeffrey N., and Elizabeth J. Perry, ed. 1994. *Popular Protest & Political Culture in Modern China.* Boulder, CO: Westview Press.
Watson, Rubie S. 1994a. "Memory, History, and Opposition under State Socialism: An Introduction." In *Memory, History and Opposition*, edited by Rubie S. Watson, 1–20. Santa Fe, NM: School of American Research Press.
———. 1994b. "Making Secret Histories: Memory and Mourning in Post-Mao China." In *Memory, History and Opposition*, edited by Rubie S. Waton, 65–86. Santa Fe, NM: School of American Research Press.
Wei, W. 2014. "Street, behavior, art." *Society* 34 (2): 94–117.
"Workers Reasonably Suffer 'Shock' and Legally 'Get Hungry'?—Investigation into 'Requesting Dismissal' by over Hundred Workers in Dongguan." *Xinhuanet*, 2015. http://news.xinhuanet.com/fortune/2013-08/22/c_117056073.htm. Accessed on November 12, 2015.
Wu, Jiao. 2007. "Egao: Popular Art Criticism or Just Plain Evil?" *China Daily*, January 22, 2007, P05.

Yang, Fan. 2017. "Thousands Protest Aluminum Plant in Chinese Oil City of Daqing." *Radio Free Asia*, February 14, 2017. https://www.rfa.org/english/news/china/thousands-protest-aluminum-plant-in-chinese-oil-city-of-daqing-02142017103918.html. Accessed on May 10, 2018.

Yang, Guobin. 2005. "Emotional Events and the Transformation of Collective Action: The Chinese Student Movement." In *Emotions and Social Movement*, edited by Helena Fram and Debra King, 79–98. London: Routledge.

———. 2009. *The Internet of Power in China*. New York: Columbia University Press.

Yang, H. 2015. "UNIQLO OEM Factory Evaded the Workers' Social Security and the Parent Company Urged to Solve." *Yangcheng Evening News*, July 19, 2015. http://wap.ycwb.com/2015-07/19/content_20426748.htm. Accessed on November 26, 2015.

Yang, J. 2013. "The Puzzle and Breakthrough of Behavior." *Oriental Art* 7: 128–31.

Yang, Jianxing. 2014. "Future of Hong Kong after Occupy Central." *Hong Kong Economic Journal Monthly*, November 1, 2014.

Young, A. 2015. "Hunger Strike at UNIQLO Clothing Supplier in China Highlights Industry's Search for Lower Labor Costs." *International Business Times*, June 16, 2015. http://www.ibtimes.com/hunger-strike-uniqlo-clothing-supplier-china-highlights-industrys-search-lower-labor-1969393. Accessed on June 29, 2015.

Young, Robert J. C. 2001. *Postcolonialism: An Historical Introduction*. Oxford: Blackwell.

Zhao, Dingxin. 2001. *The Power of Tiananmen*. Chicago: The University of Chicago Press.

———. 2007. *State-Society Relations and the 1989 Beijing Student Movement*. Hong Kong: The Chinese University Press.

———. 2013. "The Built Environment and Organization in Anti-US Protest Mobilization after the 1999 Belgrade Embassy Bombing." In *Spaces of Contention: Spatialities and Social Movements*, edited by Walter Nicholls, Byron A. Miller, and Justin Beaumont, 199–218. Farnham, UK: Ashgate.

Zheng, Shiping. 1997. *Party vs. State in Post-1949 China*. Cambridge: Cambridge University Press.

Ziv, Amalia. 2010. "Performative Politics in Israeli Queer Anti-Occupation Activism." *GLQ: A Journal of Gay and Lesbian Studies* 16 (4): 537–56.

Zivi, Karen. 2012. *Making Rights Claims*. New York: Oxford University Press.

# Index

acts
  of citizenship, 30, 32, 33, 42
  See also Isin, citizenship
activist
  and distribution of the sensible, 43
  and space of appearance, 75
  artist, 151
  citizen, 32
  Hong Kong, 72, 79, 117, 118, 124, 133, 136, 137, 192n8
  image event, 96, 192n4
  in emotional protest events, 71
  labor, 43, 50, 72, 79, 160, 192n8, 193n2, 194n13
  Macau, 167
  Occupy Central, 113, 114, 118, 124, 133, 136, 137
  rural rights, 99
  unapproved mourning, 49, 50
aesthetic
  aestheticization of protest, 139, 143–161
  of bodily pain, 45
  practices, 17, 25
  See also art, Rancière, Reed
affective
  commitment, 81
  community, 151
  energies stimulated by nativist movements, 151
  engagement with death, 47
  intensity of Tiananmen protest, 14
  responses to creative and artistic practices, 144
  responses to coffin, 46
  responses to self-immolation, 44
  temporary affective spaces, 151, 155
  See also emotion, body
agency
  as derived from power regime, 14
  attention-grabbing practices as a source of, 11
  body and, 15
  embodied, 19, 24, 69
  of masses, 9
  of social change, 6
  political, 17, 20, 22, 54, 70, 88, 177, 195n1
  popular politics and, 11
  possibilities of, 9, 110
  protestors, 94
  regime and, 13, 188
Ahmed, Sara
  on fear, 80
  See also emotion, affect

214 / Index

alignment
  Graeber and Hui on, 139
  non-aligned groups in Occupy Central, 130
  with center, 93
  See also alliance, representation
alliance
  and certification, 90
  articulation of broad-based, 21
  between Beijing and Hong Kong business class, 115
  between local state and capital, 61, 92
  construction of, 24
  Hong Kong, 110, 117, 132, 186
  Macau, 164
  of Occupy Central, 121
  strategic, 6, 23, 24, 89, 91
  with center, 89–93, 184
  with performative power, 102
  with state (and government), 23, 24, 77, 90–92, 183, 184
  See also alignment
anarchism
  and Occupy Studies, 7
  in Occupy Central, 120–123
  See also leadership, representation
antagonism
  elements, 90
  for political struggle, 35
  state's attempt to defuse, 188
  to the state, 8, 116, 136
  See also identity, nativism
appeal
  and creative practices, 149, 152
  and local cadres, 193n3
  collective, 60, 191n4
  emotional, 74
  escalation into direct action, 191n3
  institutions for, 61
  to the public, 187
  to authorities, 101, 186, 191n3
  via social media, 128
  workers, 60, 61, 74, 160, 161
  Wukan protest, 100
  See also petition
appearance
  body and, 7, 19, 55
  central-local relation and condition of, 18
  media as space of, 95–97
  of political actors, 15
  of subject, 189
  performative politics and, 12
  public, 11, 81, 184
  right to, 19, 24, 55
  sensible, 107, 111, 182
  space of, 12, 15, 17, 18, 19, 21, 24, 42, 55, 62, 69, 70, 75–79, 81, 83, 95–97, 111, 139, 146, 156, 177, 184, 185, 186, 189
  struggle for, 152
  See also Butler, visibility, Arendt
Arendt, Hannah
  space of appearance and, 17, 61, 79, 184
  See also appearance, Butler, space
art
  and protest, 143–161
  as cultural form, 9
  politicized, 25
  See also aesthetic, Rancière, Reed, sensible, visibility
articulation
  horizontal, 14, 110, 186
  Laclau on, 21
  of normative language, 21
  performative, 21, 59
  through embodied actions, 70
  "we are 99%," 118
  See also identity
artifact
  "artifactualized performance," 147

cultural, 17, 152
  *See also* aesthetic, art
assembly
  and bodies, 69, 70, 76, 184
  and live performance, 149
  and space, 19, 186
  as form of protest, 191n4
  freedom of, 150
  in Occupy Central, 129–135
  law against, 69
  mask, 35
  mass, 20, 183
  public, 6, 7, 37
attention
  and artists, 146
  and disruptive action, 69
  and "troublemaking tactics," 94
  and workers, 107
  *egao*, 177
  local residents, 47
  media, 37, 39, 43, 45, 47, 50, 51, 53, 72, 95, 104, 124, 129, 143, 147, 150, 158, 167, 187
  public, 11, 13, 19, 29, 30, 35, 36, 37, 38, 39, 40, 41, 46, 53, 144, 147, 148, 149, 150, 151, 159, 171
  state (and government), 12, 15, 38, 41, 89, 90, 100, 101, 105, 108, 147, 184
  *See also* visibility, dramatic, expressive
audibility
  Butler on, 96
  distribution of the sensible and, 12
  normative regime and, 145
  of assemblies, 69
  of body, 96
  of workers, 82
  performative politics and, 12
  realm of, 12, 97
  *See also* Rancière, voice

authorities
  and bodies, 24, 53
  and Chinese artworks, 158
  and disruptive protest, 150
  and *egao*, 168–169, 197n7
  and image events, 96
  and Mao, 51
  and masks, 35
  and naked protest, 39
  and neoliberalism, 21
  and Occupy Central, 139, 185
  and protestors, 19, 21
  and rural migrants, 64
  and suicidal protest, 44
  and unapproved mourning, 49, 51
  and workers, 74, 195n2
  as audience, 94
  attention, 184, 185, 191n3
  Beijing, 114, 115
  central, 18, 188
  censorship, 167
  certification, 90
  Chinese, 31, 33
  contentious interaction, 87
  defiance of, 168
  devolution of, 59
  interference, 98
  legitimacy of, 49
  local, 16, 23, 39, 49, 90, 94, 95, 182, 187
  Macau, 164, 166, 167
  municipal, 29, 90, 91
  of assembly (Hong Kong), 132
  of central government, 115
  petition, 100
  political, 2, 20, 51, 187
  pressure on, 15, 39, 40, 41, 95, 137
  provincial, 103
  public, 87, 191n4
  speak to, 33
  state, 15, 53

authorities (*continued*)
   sympathy of, 40
   threaten with death, 40–41
   upper-level (higher-level), 11, 22, 24, 40, 92, 95, 96, 98, 101, 103, 108, 110, 184
   Wukan 105
   *See also* hierarchy
authorize
   and disruptive actions, 182
   authorized channels, 101, 182, 184
   authorized meanings, 169, 177
   *egao*, 171–172, 177
   forms of state authorization, 13, 22, 88, 93, 185, 188
   Sun Yat-Sen, 172
   unauthorized actions, 48–49, 69, 182, 188, 192n10
   *See also* certification, recognition

Balibar, Etienne
   on rights, 33
   *See also* citizenship
body
   and children, 38
   and death threat, 40
   and elderly, 38
   and funeral, 20, 46–47
   and grievability, 47–51
   and kneeling, 36–38, 151
   and mourning, unapproved, 47–51, 192n10
   and naked protest, 39–40, 171, 172
   and self-immolation, 42, 43–46, 192n9
   and suicidal protest, 41, 42–46, 50, 192n8
   and walk, 33–34, 35, 107, 192n2
   and worker protest, 55–58, 67–70, 73, 76–77, 79–83

   as source of agency, 15
   Butler on, 19, 55, 69, 76, 79, 81, 184
   embodied practices of citizenship, 29–54
   feeling, 73
   in Occupy Studies, 6–7
   media and, 96
   occupation and, 3, 184
   pain, 45
   performative politics and, 12, 17, 19–20, 101, 143, 181, 183, 185, 186
   space and, 19–21, 76–79
   vulnerabilities, 79–82
   *See also* visibility, attention, appearance, sacrifice
Butler, Judith
   on body, 7, 19, 55, 69, 76, 78, 79, 80, 96, 184
   on demonstration, 101–102
   on dispossession, 42
   on media, 96, 97
   on mourning, 47, 48, 50
   on performativity, 3, 12, 69, 94
   space of appearance, 15, 19, 55, 78, 81
   *See also* visibility, rights, assembly

Cai, Yongshun
   Chinese Protest Studies, 110
   on appeals, 191n3
   on chaos, 69
   on disruptive tactics, 95, 182
   on forms of protest, 191n4
   on government measures, 196n2 (chapter 3)
   on intervention, 98
   on issue articulation, 104
   on local officials, 193n3
   on policy change, 110
   on worker protest, 60

on protest outcomes, 8
    See also tactic
censorship
    artistic, 158
    as object of critique, 158
    evasion of, 97, 148, 197n6
    media, 13, 103
    of current issues, 156
    of mourning, 48, 49
    of online activities, 108, 167, 172
    performative politics and, 11
    self-censorship of art scene, 157
center
    as political actor, 90
    as source of legitimacy, 92
    attention, 90
    benevolent, 90, 92
    center-local relations, 18, 24, 59, 88
    claims certified by, 90
    concern for regime legitimacy, 91
    devolution of authority, 59
    in Chinese political tradition, 91
    internal division within, 91
    local cadres and misconduct, 91, 92
    local economic development, 59
    monitoring of local governance, 95
    protestors' alliance with, 89–93, 100, 104
    restriction on local government, 92
    tolerance of isolated struggles, 91
    workers, 92
    See also CPC, hierarchy, intervention
certification
    international, 96
    of center, 90
    of state, 88, 188
    See also recognition

Chatterjee, Partha
    on subaltern politics in India, 14, 22
    expressive forms ignored by, 15
    See also Postcolonial Studies, society
Chinese Protest Studies
    critique of, 8–10
    See also creative, culture
citizenship
    and struggles, 14, 192n1
    embodied practices of, 24, 29–54
    Isin on acts of, 30
    popular sovereignty and, 22–23
    regime, 57, 182
    rights, 14, 23, 59, 64, 65, 76
    workers, 57, 59, 64, 65, 76
    See also body, state
Communist Party of China (CPC)
    alliance with protestors, 23
    commitment to socialism as recourse for performative politics, 97
    control over cultural production, 156
    Hong Kong and, 183
    legality and 10
    legitimacy, 22, 180, 188
    Maoism and, 51
    Macau and, 163, 164
    mass-line tradition, 98
    obedience to, 91, 92, 184
    Occupy Central and, 115
    Wukan protest, 100, 104
    See also center, regime, stability
contention
    and law, 61
    definition of, 70
    sites of, 97
    See also Tilly and Tarrow, contentious

contentious
  actors, 54
  claims, 4, 11, 14, 88, 93
  episodes, 3, 55, 90, 91, 100, 191n3
  events, 70
  interactions and negotiations, 88, 90, 97, 100, 110, 186
  mechanisms, 87
  mobilization, 19
  politics, 90
  repertoires, 87
  sequences (and processes), 70, 71–72, 87, 103, 187, 189
  *See also* Tilly and Tarrow, contention
creative
  activist citizens, 32
  agency of masses, 9
  capacity and energy, 3, 9, 139, 151, 187
  dimension of political practice, 3
  *egao*, 168
  engagement with state, 88, 97
  forms of claim making, 24
  practices, expressions and tactics, 6, 10, 16, 17, 25, 41, 53, 139, 143–144, 146–155, 160, 163, 178, 179, 181
  production and art, 143–144, 146–155
  use of Maoist language and symbols, 51–52
  *See also* tactic
culture
  artistic protest and, 143, 144, 147, 150, 151, 152, 155–161
  *egao* as subculture, 168–178, 197n7
  in Chinese Protest Studies, 8–10, 16
  in new social movement theories, 191n2
  in Postcolonial Studies, 4–5
  media, 24, 78, 163
  occupation and, 20, 136, 139, 152
  performative politics and, 13, 14, 16–17, 196n2 (chapter 6)
  political, 51, 53, 110, 166, 184, 197n6
  popular, 51, 152, 153, 168, 171, 178
  protest and Chinese, 38, 39, 42, 46, 49, 76
  state and, 50
  workers, 161
  *See also* Jasper, Reed
cyberpolitics 25, 163–178
  *See also* Internet, *egao*, creative

death
  and suicidal protest, 42
  as accompanied by ritual, 47
  as form of protest, 44
  as site of contestation, 49–51, 103
  defiant, 42
  of self-immolation, 45–46
  of ungrievable lives, 50–51
  threat, 40–41
  value of, 42
  *See also* body
democracy
  and body, 76
  direct, 116, 117, 121, 124, 128, 136, 139
  governmentality without substantive, 11
  Hong Kong, 1, 113
  Occupy Central and liberal, 136, 183
  participatory, 25
  popular, 3, 11, 15, 17, 18, 161
  radical, 6
  Rancière on, 106

democratic
   experiment, 116, 117
   force, 21
   form, 117
   intervention, 23
   participation, 116
   politics, 15, 22
   rights, 1, 113, 165
   struggles over everyday spaces, 18
   struggle, 14, 23, 149
   undemocratic decision-making, 95, 180
dignity
   and kneeling down, 36
   and suicidal protest, 42
   in Macau identity, 166
   performative politics and reclaiming of, 181
   workers, 42, 50, 59, 69
direct
   actions, 16, 69, 94
   democracy, 116, 117, 121, 124, 128, 136, 139
   participation, 122
disobedience
   against neoliberal state, 116
   civil, 114, 124, 126, 138
   combination with obedience, 22
   *egao*, 168
   in Hong Kong, 113, 185
   political, 116
   See also disruptive
dispossession
   emotional experience of, 180
   land, 100
   neoliberalism, 180
   performative politics and, 184
   state and, 189
   suicidal protest and, 42
   workers and, 56, 57, 59 64
   See also precarity, Butler

disruptive
   actions and tactics, 68, 69, 77, 88, 93–95, 98, 99, 101, 150, 182
   disruption caused by self-immolation, 46
   "disruption for the sake of disruption," 139
   disruption of business routine and government activity, 2, 15, 20, 33, 51, 69, 77, 95, 108, 124, 126, 129, 131, 138, 191n4
   disruption of far-right nativists, 135
   disruption of norms that allocate public appearance and recognition, 184
   disruption of relation between visible and invisible, 97
   embodied practice, 70
   levels of disruption, 110
   See also body, attention
dissent
   aestheticization of, 25, 139
   and China as repressive regime, 6
   and governmentality, 161
   and rights claiming, 14
   and state rituals, 48
   and traditional festivals, 48
   and use of spaces, 54, 58, 152, 156
   body and, 24
   boundary of, 188
   critical artists and, 156, 158
   cultural forms of, 25
   dissensual spaces and activities, 43, 182
   figurative forms of, 17
   Macau's forms of, 25, 166, 177, 186
   protest art and spaces of, 146, 156, 158

dissent (continued)
    Rancière on, 182
    state's suppression of organized, 60
    through performances, 3
    workers, 55, 58, 107
    See also voice
dramatic
    actions, 11, 20, 31, 87, 155
    enactment of citizenship, 31
    events, 10
    expressions, 18
    forms of suicidal protest, 43
    images, 96, 97
    medium for expression
        discontent, 48
    memorializations of central
        leaders, 48
    political sequence, 106
    protest by Korean peasants, 151
    rituals of public worshiping, 52
    scenes, 34, 36, 143
    shift in performative politics, 14
    shift in protest tactics, 113
    tactic, 39
    tensions, 16, 185
    use of bodies, 39
    See also attention

egao 168–178, 197
    See also culture, creative,
        cyberpolitics
emergency
    and intervention, 98, 106
    measures, 61, 189
    moments forced by militant
        actions, 94
    response, 40
    state of, 98, 186
    See also disruptive
emotion
    and dramatic events, 10
    and experience of dispossession,
        180
    and image of self-sacrifice, 46
    and kneeling down, 37
    and labor action, 73, 74, 80
    and movement aesthetic texts, 143
    and mourning, 47
    and protest, 70
    and protest artworks, 155
    and protest movement of 1989, 13
    and self-immolation, 45
    anger, 36, 69, 73, 155, 172
    anxiety, 73
    aroused by striking images, 18
    compassion, 37
    depression, 73
    dissatisfaction, 35, 46, 47, 52, 78,
        115, 169, 171, 193n1
    discontent, 3, 10, 42, 44, 48,
        61, 88, 89, 90, 95, 96, 106,
        115, 118, 121, 144, 148, 150,
        152, 153, 155, 180, 186, 189,
        192n3, 197n1
    expressed through performative
        use of Mao symbols, 52
    fear, 29, 33, 57, 60, 62, 65, 73,
        80, 82, 167, 192n3
    feeling, 73, 92, 155, 160
    frustration, 35, 37, 42, 73, 100,
        101, 115
    hopelessness, 42
    indignation, 73, 189
    mood, 155
    outrage, 48, 49, 50, 73, 97, 102
    pain, 73, 149, 155
    resentment, 155, 165
    sadness, 37
    sympathy, 37, 38, 40, 92, 97,
        107, 151, 155, 157
    worry, 66, 73
    See also affect, body
Esherick, Joseph W. and
        Wasserstrom, Jeffrey N.
    on Chinese performative politics,
        18

on "political theater," 20, 48, 94
*See also* theater, stage
expressive
    actions, forms and practices, 3, 9, 12, 15, 16, 52, 53, 54, 67, 124, 149, 161, 168, 182
    activities, scenes and relations, 88
    aspect ignored by Chatterjee, 15
    dimensions of popular politics, 23
    enactment, 31
    expressiveness of Wukan protest, 103
    forms improvised from within state, 15
    means and mechanisms, 30
    *See also* dramatic, attention
event
    and norms of visibility, 51
    art and, 144
    contentious, 70
    embodied, 6, 68
    emotional power produced by dramatic, 10
    image, 35, 96, 97, 182, 192n4
    media, 97
    spectacular, 3, 16, 171
    *See also* emergency

factionalism
    in Occupy Central, 122–123, 126–137, 185
    *See also* leadership, representation, nativism
Foucault, Michel
    on revolt, 1
    on "the will not being governed like that," 11
    *See also* governmentality

government
    and artists, 157
    and body, 19
    and demolition, 38, 43
    and expressive actions, 15
    and image events, 97
    and kneeling down, 37
    and Mao Zedong, 52
    and mourning, 47
    and Occupy Central, 121, 122, 124, 126, 128, 131–134, 137–138, 152, 155
    and popular politics, 168
    and state norms, 93
    and union, 106
    and workers, 59, 60, 71, 73, 74, 75, 77, 80–82, 106–109, 192n8, 193n2
    anti-government sentiment, 115
    as political allies, 77
    attention, 15, 41
    benevolent and responsible, 53
    clean, 98
    compound, buildings and offices (as site of protest), 15, 16, 18, 20, 30, 34, 35, 38, 46, 48, 49, 69, 75, 76, 81, 94–95, 101, 102, 113, 125, 133, 134, 147, 152, 191n4
    central, 10, 40, 41, 74, 89, 92, 104, 107, 115, 185, 186, 188
    citizen-government relations, 58–59
    claims making, 87
    collusion with business, 41, 67, 118, 182, 193
    conflicts of interest among government departments, 59, 90
    concessions, 125, 132, 134
    control of currency value, 65
    corrupt practices of local, 11, 165
    Daqing, 29–30
    decisions, 12, 195n2
    *egao*, 168–178
    emergency response, 40
    Hong Kong, 115, 118, 121, 128, 131–134, 137–138, 155

government *(continued)*
  intervention, 40, 73, 77, 98, 109, 121
  land seizure, 44, 47, 50, 101–102
  local, 29, 30, 35, 35, 37, 38, 39, 43, 44, 46, 47, 49, 50, 53, 59, 60, 67, 69, 72, 73, 89–93, 95, 101, 103, 108, 147, 149, 151, 180, 186, 192n3, 193
  lower-level, 31, 40, 59, 91, 92, 99, 109
  Macau, 164–178, 186
  misbehavior, 90
  mode of response to social conflicts, 92–93, 109
  municipal, 34, 37, 73, 102, 195n14
  negotiation (and dialogue) with, 103, 128, 131, 137
  online attacks on officials, 166–167
  performative politics against, 181
  petition, 20, 41, 76, 77
  political authority of, 2
  political crisis of Chinese, 1
  political process involving, 58
  power abuse, 59, 89
  pressure on, 15, 49, 70, 72, 91, 103, 126, 131, 149
  pro-government forces (Macau), 164, 165–166, 168, 173, 187
  pro-government media in Hong Kong, 114
  propaganda on labor laws, 61
  provincial, 35, 74, 80
  Qidong, 95
  repression, 33, 40, 109
  satirical images aimed at officials, 25
  soft authoritarian, 177
  spaces controlled by, 152, 186
  strategies of government-connected contestation, 88
  tolerance of protest, 10, 121, 138, 183, 188
  tougher rules on local, 44
  town, 34, 73
  transfer of state's decision-making power, 59
  upper-level (and higher-level), 37, 40, 48, 49, 77, 98
  unwillingness to intervene, 82
  waiting game, 132
  *See also* hierarchy
governmentality
  and socioeconomic rights, 14
  definition of, 89
  new forms of, 10, 14
  performative politics and, 12, 13, 14, 161
  popular sovereignty and, 22–23
  state and, 23, 89, 179
  struggles and critique of, 14
  subaltern people as object of, 14
Graeber, David and Hui, Yuk
  on Occupy Central, 117, 124, 139
  *See also* leadership, representation, factionalism

hierarchy
  and intervention, 183
  and political organization in Hong Kong, 116–118
  contradiction between local and central authorities, 91
  leadership, 137
  non-hierarchical collective, 120
  political, 59, 185
  protestors and, 92
  state, 87, 89, 90, 91
  vertical, 122

Wukan protest and Guangdong's administrative, 100, 103
Ho, Hau-Wah Edmund 164–165, 173–174
See also *egao*

identity
  and postcolonialism, 5
  and protest movements, 10
  art and class, 160
  articulation of, 21, 192n6
  boundaries, 88, 90
  expressive practices and, 16
  nativist, 159
  oppositional, 18, 186
  performance, 9, 24
  performative politics and, 181
  politics, 183
  Us/Them distinction, 90, 166
  See also Laclau, nativism
image
  affect and, 155
  and mobilization, 18
  as cultural form, 9
  as resource of cultural innovation, 17, 168
  dissent and, 158
  distribution of, 146
  events, 35, 96, 97, 182, 192n4
  media, 97, 171, 174
  popular democracy and, 18
  publicity and, 30
  spoofed, 12, 153, 168–178, 197n5
  See also visual, *egao*, visibility
Internet
  and culture, 16
  distribution of the sensible, 97, 107
  local misconduct and, 103
  Macau, 25, 163, 166–178, 186
  performative power and, 18
  popular democracy and, 18
  See also media, censorship, cyberpolitics
intervention
  aesthetic practices and, 17
  and media, 95, 101, 107
  and performative politics, 12
  and workers, 73–74, 77, 82, 83, 99, 107, 108, 109
  as triggered by death threat, 40
  as triggered by kneeling down, 37
  as triggered by suicidal protest, 44
  center-local cleavage, 24
  condition of, 22, 98
  democratic, 23
  disruption and, 16, 88
  forcing of, 19
  from above, 90, 99, 101, 104, 109, 183, 184
  government's unwillingness to intervene, 82
  imaginative, 151
  Occupy Central's political, 117
  of Hong Kong government, 121
  of public security, 74
  police, 34, 148, 194n10
  state, 12, 19, 44, 83, 89, 91, 99, 100, 106, 109, 110, 149, 157, 183, 197n1
  strategic opportunities for, 24
  threshold of, 98
  upper-level (and higher-level), 11, 40, 77, 98, 101, 108
  Wukan protest, 100–101
  See also stability, emergency, hierarchy
Isin, Engin F.
  on activist citizen, 32
  on "acts of citizenship," 30, 32
  on citizenship rights, 33

Jasper, James M.
  on anger and indignation, 73
  on cultural artifacts, 152
  on cultural forms, 9
  on figurative forms of performativity, 17
  on live performances, 149
  on micro-social levels, 87
  on music, 155
  on public spaces, 148
  on traditional symbols and rituals, 10
  *See also* culture

Laclau, Ernesto
  on articulation, 21
  on identity, 90, 192n6
  on representation, 25
  *See also* antagonism
law
  and disruptive actions, 69, 188
  and mass demonstration, 101–102
  and unrest, 30
  and workers, 60, 63, 64, 66–67, 74, 91, 92, 107, 193n3, 194n13
  approval of new, 44, 61
  as a means to control struggle, 93
  enforcement, 11, 185
  labor, 61, 91, 92, 107, 193n2
  lawful rights of citizens, 23
  lawyers in Occupy Central, 138
  mediation of, 23
  national security, 167
  opposition lawmakers in Occupy Central, 137
  rule of, 60, 94, 115
  state, 22, 23, 44, 57, 61, 66, 93
  transgression of, 23
  violence against, 44
  Wukan protest, 104–105
  *See also* legal, citizenship

leadership
  Hong Kong social movement, 117
  leaderless movements, 7, 25, 116, 117
  Occupy Central, 116, 117, 121–139
  rejection of leadership in protest movements, 5
  *See also* factionalism, representation
legal
  advisor, 107
  basis of workers' demands, 74
  channels and institutions, 31, 60
  characterizations of citizenship, 53
  citizenship, 31
  coverage of social insurance, 66, 67
  demands presented in legal terms, 19, 61
  depoliticization through legalization, 188
  dimension of citizenship, 31
  facts of equal citizenship, 22
  forms of conflict resolution, 61
  knowledge, 61
  legality as source of legitimacy, 10
  legality of land seizure, 44
  mobilization, 61, 91, 193n3
  norms, 93, 94
  petition as quasi-legal action, 77
  power of collective bargaining, 61
  protection of workers, 61, 108
  regime, 10, 185
  resources, 89, 185
  rights, 14, 19, 30, 31, 57, 72, 77, 93, 104, 184
  space, 108, 185
  *See also* law

Mao, Zedong
    as performative resource, 51–53, 98, 192n11
    See also Maoism, body
Maoism
    and Chinese political culture, 51
    in popular politics, 98
    See also Mao, socialism
Marx, Karl, 179
mass-line tradition 97–99, 184
    See also socialism, intervention
media
    as space of appearance, 95–97
    attention to embodied practices, 1, 20, 30, 34–45, 47–51, 53, 55, 69, 71, 72, 75, 76, 78, 79, 80, 114, 124, 129, 137
    contentious process and, 87
    culture and, 16
    performative politics and, 12, 13, 17, 18, 143, 163, 165–167, 171, 173–178, 186, 187
    state intervention and, 98, 99, 100–108
    visibility and, 88, 147, 150, 153, 158, 161
    See also image, visual
moral
    discourse of justice and fairness, 49
    economy, 9, 33
    leverage, 104
    resource, 98
    sympathy and compassion, 37
Mouffe, Chantal
    on artistic practice, 146
    on Us/Them distinction, 166
    See also identity
music
    and social movement, 152, 155
    and workers, 160
    as cultural form, 9
    as street art, 146
    performances, 121
    See also song, Jasper

nativism 115, 125, 129, 131–132, 134–137, 151, 159
    See also identity, factionalism
norm
    and performative politics, 13, 93
    compliance with state, 69, 77, 185
    defiance of state, 48
    deviance from state, 9
    embodied in Marxism-Leninism-Mao Zedong thought, 98
    of behavior, 16
    of flexible work, 82
    of public appearance and recognition, 184
    of visibility, 51, 70, 76
    party, 98
    performative use of state, 93–95, 97, 195n1
    protestors and state, 23, 184
    reinvention of, 9
    reiteration and redeployment of state, 100, 110, 118
    transgression of hegemonic, 17
    See also legal, obedient

obedient
    act of kneeling down, 36
    act of petitioning, 76
    combination of obedience and disobedience, 22, 93
    labor force, 57, 60
    subject, 13
    to the Communist Party of China (CPC), 91

occupation
    and "temporary affective space," 151, 155
    art of, 151–155, 156, 159, 160
    as disruptive action, 68
    as symbolic action, 10, 20
    as tactic, 2–3
    critique of Occupy Studies, 5–8
    Occupy Central, 113–139
    Occupy Wall Street (OWS), 113, 118, 120, 121, 136
    of factory, 77–78
    performative politics and, 181
    *See also* body, space

party
    anti-party, 8, 90
    as institutional actor, 18
    cadres, 59, 99, 103
    chief of Guangdong, 109
    committee, 36, 41
    Communist, 10, 104, 115
    control of localities, 59
    elites, 110
    line, 48
    multi-party structures, 6, 110
    norms, 94, 98
    party-state, 97
    secretary, 34, 37, 47, 48, 94, 103, 105
    *See also* center
patriotic
    being recognized as, 104, 185
    songs and slogans, 106
    *See also* obedient
people
    absence of, 180
    as political subjects, 17, 93, 182
    as rights-bearing subjects, 9
    Chatterjee on subaltern, 14
    non-acknowledgment of voices of, 12
    Postcolonial Studies and, 4–5

perception
    alternative frames of, 97, 181
    artistic practice and public, 145–146
    distribution of the sensible and, 12, 145
    protest as altering public, 9, 12, 145–146
    Rancière on, 12, 97, 145–146
    *See also* visibility
performative
    act of speech, 45
    articulation, 21, 59
    body, 19–20, 54
    conceptions of popular democracy, 17
    dimension of embodied protest, 7
    mourning, 47
    perspective on citizenship, 31
    perspective on protest, 9
    perspective on rights, 13
    politics, 11–18, 21–24, 30, 53, 69, 76, 82, 87, 88, 89, 93, 95, 97, 98, 100, 109, 110, 143, 144, 146, 151, 161, 163, 179, 181, 182, 183, 184, 186, 187, 188, 189
    subjects, 14
    use of Mao, 52
    use of state rhetoric and norms, 22, 93–95
    *See also* Butler, sensible, visibility, performativity, expressive
performativity
    Butler on, 3, 12
    figurative forms of, 17
    of body, 20, 69
    of embodied agency, 69
    of rights practices, 9
    *See also* performative
petition
    and disruptive action, 95
    and elderly, 38

and nudity, 39
and state norms, 77
as expressive form, 15
as peaceful action, 68, 69, 94
as prescribed form of performative politics, 76
as protest action, 191
channels, 15, 96
collective, 77, 101, 191
government, 20
humble, 76
offices, 41, 76, 180
skip-level, 98
threaten with death, 40–41
workers, 69, 70, 72–73, 76, 77, 80, 81, 195n14
Wukan protest, 100–101
See also appeal, obedient, legal
politics
as possibility of creating visibility, 57
Butler on, 19
by other means, 168
Chatterjee on subaltern, 14
in Postcolonial Studies, 4–5
of the governed, 3
prefigurative, 20
Rancière on, 12, 107, 145–146
See also people
Postcolonial Studies
critique of, 4–5
power
abuse, 59–60, 89, 95, 98, 100–101, 174, 180
art's subversion of, 156
business elite's political, 115
Butler on police, 102
China's global economic, 3, 10
class, 61
cleavage between central and local, 24, 88, 91, 184, 186
configurations in different regions, 183
decentralization, 181
disciplinary, 68
disenfranchisement of access to, 22, 181
*egao* and, 169
HKFS's decision-making, 129
legal, 61
Macau Chief Executive's, 164–165
massive bodily presence as source of, 7, 125
moral, 10, 48
network counter-power, 6
occupation's symbolic, 6
Occupy Central, 133, 136
Occupy Studies' interest in popular, 6
of dispossession, 42
of demonstrations, 55
of expressive practices, 16
of image events, 97
of local government, 46
of village committee, 105
of "walking," 33–34
opportunity and structure of, 110
mobilizing, 18
people as powerless victims of dictatorship, 17
performative, 6, 18, 42, 76, 77, 95, 102
performative politics and relations of, 3, 33
popular, 99
postcolonialism and, 4
regime and agency, 13
resistance and threat to state, 1, 113, 181
spatial organization of, 70
sovereign, 21, 90, 185, 187
state (and regime), 6, 14, 18, 30, 59, 76, 89, 90, 91, 93, 181, 182, 183, 188, 189

power *(continued)*
  symbolic, 185
  theatrical, 182
precarity
  intensification of, 62–67
  *See also* dispossession
pressure
  cost-cutting pressure, 65
  from police, 72
  from state, 109
  from Wukan villagers, 103, 105
  of labor regime, 193n6
  on employer, 70, 71, 72, 73
  on governments (and bureaucracies), 15, 22, 37, 38, 39, 40, 41, 43, 49, 70, 72, 91, 95, 96, 101, 103, 106, 108, 128, 131 138, 149, 187
  on local union, 72
  on wages, 65
  political, 8
  as produced by dissidents, 97
  public, 37, 38
  to maintain stability, 92, 98
  to promote economic growth, 59
  *See also* intervention, emergency
protest
  as a site of cultural performances, 9
  as discursive constructions, 10

Rancière, Jacques
  and performative politics, 12, 182
  dissensus and disagreement, 182, 189
  on aesthetics and politics, 145–146, 156
  on democracy, 106
  on social order and visibility, 12, 70, 97
  on distribution of the sensible, 12, 13, 101, 107
  polemical verification of equality, 57
  *See also* audibility, art, subject, perception
recognition
  border of the unrecognizable, 181
  by authority, 90, 185, 187
  by state, 31, 96, 104
  of grievability, 47
  of social rights, 31
  performative politics and, 12
  recognizable identity, 87
Reed, T.V.
  on aestheticization of protest, 143–144
  on dramatic events, 10
  on poster imagery, 148
  on protest culture, 9, 10
  *See also* culture, art
regime
  and deaths, 49
  and Hong Kong Chief Executive election, 115
  and local governance, 183
  and Mao Zedong, 51–52
  and people's agency, 13
  antagonism toward, 116
  as benevolent and responsible, 53
  as supported by protestors, 93, 183
  challenge to, 185
  change, 92
  citizenship, 57–58, 182
  concern for legitimacy, 15, 89, 91, 108, 186
  contentious interaction, 110
  control political use of bodies, 6–7
  disciplinary, 68
  hegemony, 93l
  interaction with protestors, 6
  labor, 24, 42, 59, 64, 67, 193
  legal, 10, 185

legal and institutional channels, 61–62
legal protection from, 108
legal rights endorsed by, 104
legitimacy (Hong Kong), 115
loyalty, 104
non-regime-threatening tactics, 16, 33, 184
normative, 145
obedience, 186
of popular political activity, 3
of public perception, 145
opportunities and constraints for protestors, 87
patriarchal, 62
political and discursive, 4
prevention of mass movements, 98
production, 82, 192n. 8
protestors' agency derived from, 188
representativeness, 188
repressive, 6
socialist tradition, 97
stability, 180
targeting of local officials, 188
tolerance of protest, 91
undemocratic, 106
Wukan protest, 104
*See also* CPC, party, center

representation
anti-representational politics, 8
as site of struggle, 25, 189
body and, 76
Castells on, 6
CPC, 22
desire for self-representation, 25
divide over, 128–131, 133–134
Hong Kong social movement, 117
lack of, 25, 67, 188
Laclau on, 25

local government, 90
Occupy Central, 25, 117–118, 122, 128–131, 133–134
of Macau Chief Executive, 165
of others, 166
of "work unit," 58
of workers, 64, 67, 109, 193n2, 193n5
of workers' experience, 160–161
"politics without representatives," 7
political, 23, 60, 187, 188
question of political, 7
rejection of, 7, 130
resistance to political, 116, 122
state as source of political, 15, 23, 187–188
*See also* leadership, factionalism

resistance
aestheticization of, 25
against state power, 1, 113
anti-imperialist, 5
art and, 146, 150
body as medium of, 24, 68, 80
creative, 149, 181
cultural, 25, 139
culture as resource for, 139
different styles of, 183
embodied, 7, 58
fluid forms of, 9
gathering as form of, 70
gendered, 7
Hong Kong, 1, 113, 122, 128, 130, 131, 133, 134
labor, 58, 60, 64, 68, 70, 75, 79, 82, 106
masked, 34–36, 192n3
multiple points of, 1, 180
peasant, 101
performance of, 20, 80, 166
space of, 75
to capitalism, 122

resistance *(continued)*
  to dispossession, 4
  to hierarchy and representation, 116
  to neoliberalism, 24
  to precarity, 7
  to student leadership, 128, 130, 131, 133
  Wukan, 101
resource
  allocation of, 180
  available in social realm, 16
  body as, 53, 69, 82
  critical artists seeking, 157, 158
  cultural, 161, 168–169
  culture as, 139
  daily, 120
  economic, 9
  everyday item as, 152
  for performative politics, 13, 97, 181
  for reconfiguring visibility, 147, 152
  government, 89, 98
  institutional, 83, 185
  legal, 185
  Mao as performative, 51–53
  media, 108, 110, 161, 187
  monopoly of, 120
  moral, 98
  Occupy Central, 124, 128, 137, 139, 152, 183, 184
  of demonstrations, 102
  offered by creative practices, 25
  offered by state, 23
  performative, 82
  privatization of natural, 11
  resource-poor people (and citizens), 3, 9, 11, 32, 49, 69, 81
  resourceful events, 48
  resourceful opponents, 79
  sharing, 120, 122, 128
  state's redistribution of, 197n1
  symbolic, 23, 24, 52, 83, 88, 89
  to gain access to rights, 184
  *See also* socialism
rights
  and vulnerable people, 14
  Balibar on, 33
  body and, 19
  consciousness, 9
  Isin on, 32
  performative perspective on, 13, 94
  performative politics and, 30, 181, 184
  radical struggle and, 11
  state and, 23, 30–31, 182, 184, 187, 197n1
  to appear, 55–83
  *See also* citizenship, Zivi, Balibar, legal, law
risk
  and fear, 80
  and local cadres, 92
  body's exposure to, 24, 54, 79
  Chinese Protest Studies, 110
  civil society, 182
  concerns over health, 29
  for the common good, 73
  "leaderless" movements, 7
  non-regime-threatening tactics, 16, 184
  of being arrested, 33
  of disruptive actions, 99
  of dissemination protest materials, 147
  of performative body, 15
  of political action, 2
  of repression, 33, 38, 98, 104, 183, 184
  of rights-claiming
  of performative politics, 22, 54, 70

personal, 104
political, 48, 90, 111, 148, 157, 183
Wukan protest, 103
ritual
and creative practices, 17
and identity, 192n6
and political theater, 20, 48
as performative action, 16
embodied, 24
erecting monument as, 46
for claim-making, 17
funeral, 46, 47, 48
grievances expressed through, 48
kneeling down as, 36, 151
Mao-worshiping, 52
media attention to, 51
mourning, 47–49
performance, 48
ritualized actions, 93
ritualized contest over dead body, 46
state, 48
traditional, 10, 13
See also body

sacrifice
and self-immolation, 44–46
bodily, 7
of workers, 42, 50, 59
See also death, moral
scene
and public attention, 19
citizenship and, 31–32
emotions and protest, 18
media and, 96
public visibility and, 143
rights struggle and, 88
space of appearance and, 15
See also image, visual, dramatic
script
activist-citizens' writing of, 32

Chinese cultural, 76
Occupy Central, 126
of worker protest, 106
protest, 183
provided by socialist tradition, 98
sensible
and political subject, 13
distribution of the, 12, 32, 43, 97, 101, 103, 107, 145–146, 156, 182, 186
performative politics and the, 181
state's control over the, 13
See also Rancière, audibility, perception
socialism
performative politics and, 13, 97–98, 106
See also mass-line tradition
society
Chinese, 34, 36
civil, 14, 18, 51, 164, 182
harmonious, 61
political, 15
state's control over, 91
state-society linkages (and relations), 24, 89, 91, 109, 179
vs. state framework, 11
solidarity 16, 21, 47, 78, 111, 123, 128, 155, 194n8
song 52, 106, 147, 149, 155, 160, 168
See also music
sovereignty
popular, 22–23, 184
See also Chatterjee
space
body and, 7, 19, 20, 80
cyberspace, 163–178
occupation and, 2, 10, 20, 113, 116–117, 121–122, 152, 186
of appearance, 12, 15, 17, 18, 19, 21, 24, 42, 55, 62, 69, 70,

space *(continued)*
    75–79, 81, 83, 95–97, 139, 146, 156, 184, 185, 186, 189
    of encounter, 20, 21, 186
    of political theater, 48
    spatial practices, 19, 20, 186, 75–79
    spatiality of state power, 18
    temporary affective, 151, 155
    walking and, 33
    *See also* Butler, Arendt, media
spontaneity
    factions, 127–128, 130
    Hong Kong social movements, 117
    limitation of, 117
    Occupy Central's cult of, 25, 138
    of *egao*, 168
    privileging of, 139
    tactical use of, 134–136
    *See also* leadership, representation
stability
    disruptive actions and, 69
    employment, 193n4
    maintenance, 91, 92, 93, 98, 115, 188
    regime, 180
    social, 74, 91, 92, 164, 182
    state's obsession with, 46
    violence produced in the name of, 44
    *See also* CPC, center
stage
    and media, 96
    body's invention of, 20
    creation of theatrical, 70, 95
    Esherick and Wasserstrom on theatrical, 18
    factory as, 75
    Occupy Central's main, 130, 131, 133, 134
    *See also* theater

state
    alliance with, 23, 89–93
    and distribution of the sensible, 13, 146, 156
    art and, 149, 156–158
    body and, 19, 29–83
    in Occupy Studies, 6–8
    intervention, 12, 19, 22, 110–109, 110
    legitimacy, 10, 11, 21, 110, 179
    local, 10
    media and, 95–97
    norms, 9, 13, 23, 93–95, 110, 195n1
    Occupy Central and, 113–116, 137–139
    performative politics and, 12, 14–16, 21, 22, 87–88, 179–189, 197n1
    Postcolonial Studies and, 5
    vs. society framework 11
    *See also* hierarchy, government, authorities, certification, authorize
street
    performance, 148–150, 151
    *See also* art, aesthetic
subject
    activist citizen and, 32
    appearance of political, 179–182
    articulation and, 21
    body and, 45
    constitution of political, 9, 17, 32
    performative, 14
    precarious, 11
    Rancière on, 12, 107, 145–146, 182
    rights-bearing, 9
    state norms and, 93–94
    the sensible and, 13, 145
    worker, 68
    *See also* people
subjectivity
    agency and, 13

art and, 146
contestation of, 17
culture and, 139
Foucault on, 1
state and, 187–188
*See also* subject

tactic
acts of claim-making, 40
and political theater, 94
and strategy, 118, 139
and sympathy from officials, 92
collective walk as protest, 106
delaying, 79
disruptive, 95, 98, 101
dramatic shift in protest, 113
*egao* as protest, 168
going naked as protest, 39
leaderless, 25
media, 97, 101, 108
migrant workers', 68
non-regime-threatening, 16, 33, 184
occupation as protest, 2, 7, 20
of 2014 Occupy Central, 137–138
of direct democracy, 128
of Hong Kong protestors, 185
of past movements, 98, 101
psychological, 71
radical, 95, 126
rights-seeking, 94
split over, 116, 130, 132
street demonstration as political, 33
street performance art as protest, 148–150
tactical use of "leaderlessness" and "spontaneity," 134–136
"troublemaking," 94
visibility, 35, 187
wearing masks as protest, 34–36, 192n3

*See also* performative, attention, appearance
theater
political, 18, 20, 21, 48, 94, 185
*See also* Esherick and Wasserstrom, stage
Tilly, Charles and Tarrow, Sidney
on activation of identity boundaries, 87, 90
on certification, 90
on coalition, 97
on collective interaction, 103, 110
on constitution of collective actor, 88
on contention, 70
on interactive political-process approach, 87
political opportunity structure, 195n1
*See also* identity, alliance
transgression
in mainland China, 183
of hegemonic norms, 17
of law, 23, 185
of official rhetoric, 17
performances and, 181, 183
workers, 68, 79

visibility
art and, 143–161
body and, 20, 32–54, 70, 76
citizenship and, 32
disruptive action and, 69
*egao* and, 169
media and, 88, 95–97, 107
performative politics and, 12, 16, 181, 184, 187
space and, 77–79
*See also* appearance, attention, visual, image

visual
    archive, 160
    art, 160
    display as critique of power abuse, 95
    effects, 34, 37, 39, 40, 149
    experiences, 36
    expression of demands, 152
    image, 9, 18, 35, 45
    media, 96
    performances and aesthetics, 143, 150
    spoof, 162, 196n3 (chapter 6)
    symbols and signs, 147, 148
    texts and techniques, 147
    See also *egao*
voice
    and media, 95
    and state, 15
    artist, 158
    expressive forms of, 16
    grievance, 39, 53
    Occupy Central, 133
    of dissent, 25, 54, 158, 177
    of people, 12, 30, 31, 35, 87
    silencing of critical, 166
    subaltern class as voiceless object, 5
    workers, 67, 106, 160–161
    See also audibility

Wang, Hui
    on socialist state's political legacy, 97
    on state-society relation, 179
    See also socialism

Xi, Jinping, 115

Zhao, Dingxin
    on built environment, 75
    on kneeling down, 37
    on protest of 1989 (Tiananmen), 14, 75
    on public space occupation, 20
    See also space
Zivi, Karen
    on rights, 12–13, 184
    on practices of claim-making, 15, 19, 94
    on norms and conventions, 93
    See also rights

www.ingramcontent.com/pod-product-compliance
Lightning Source LLC
Chambersburg PA
CBHW020649230426
43665CB00008B/362